Astrid Lindgren

Astrid Lindgren

The Woman behind Pippi Longstocking

Jens Andersen

Translated by Caroline Waight

Yale

UNIVERSITY PRESS

New Haven and London

DANISH ARTS FOUNDATION

Published with assistance from the Danish Arts Foundation.

Published with assistance from the foundation established in memory of
Philip Hamilton McMillan of the Class of 1894, Yale College.

Photos on pages 165 and 250, Saltkråkan AB. All others, private ownership/Saltkråkan AB.

Yale University Press books may be purchased in quantity for educational, business, or
promotional use. For information, please e-mail sales.press@yale.edu (U.S. office) or
sales@yaleup.co.uk (U.K. office).

Set in Bulmer type by IDS Infotech, Ltd.
Printed in the United States of America.

Library of Congress Control Number: 2017940326
ISBN 978-0-300-22610-2 (hardcover : alk. paper)

A catalogue record for this book is available from the British Library.

This paper meets the requirements of ANSI/NISO Z39.48-1992 (Permanence of Paper).

10 9 8 7 6 5 4 3 2 1

What the meaning of life isn't—that I do know. Scraping together money and possessions and things, living a famous person's life and appearing in the gossip pages of weekly magazines, being so afraid of loneliness and silence that you never get to take a step back and think: what am I doing with my short time on this earth?

Astrid Lindgren, 1983

Contents

TEN

The Battle for Fantasy 260

ELEVEN

I Have Been Dancing in My Solitude 289

Acknowledgments

IT TAKES TWO TO WRITE A BIOGRAPHY: the person writing
it and the person being written about. In fact, there are usually lots of other
people involved in the process too, all of whom shape the final work. This
includes writers of previous books and articles about the biographer's subject, which may prove very useful to a later author. In the list of sources at
the back of this book, you can find references to all of the books, articles,
magazines, and websites about Astrid Lindgren's work to which I am in-
debted, accompanied by an index and an overview of Astrid Lindgren's
works published in Danish.

I owe a huge thank-you to everyone who helped me track down other
types of material: first and foremost to Astrid Lindgren's bibliographer
Lena Törnqvist, a tireless source of advice and information. She taught a
Dane to navigate Astrid Lindgren's archive at the National Library of Sweden, which was entered onto UNESCO's Memory of the World register in
2005. Thanks are also due to Britt Almström, stenographer at the Swedish
Riksdag, who helped me decipher some of Astrid Lindgren's notebooks
written in shorthand. Likewise, I'm deeply grateful for the support I received from Anna Eklundh-Jonsson at the Regional State Archives at Vadstena, Bruno Svindborg, research librarian at the National Library of
Denmark in Copenhagen, and Elin Algreen-Petersen, senior editor for children's and young adults' books at Gyldendal.

When working on a biography, you're always reliant on other people's
goodwill, generosity, and willingness to contribute their specialized knowl-
edge and skills. Thanks are due to Tom Alsing, Barbro and Bertil Alvtegen,
Urban Andersson, Ida Balslev-Olesen, Malin Billing, David Bugge, Ning de
Coninck-Smith, Hélène Dahl, Gallie Eng, Belinda Erichsen, Jens Fellke,
Jacob Forsell, Lena Fries-Gedin, Eva Glistrup, Klaus Gottfredsen, Stefan
Hilding, Jesper Høgenhaven, Sven Reiner Johansen, Anneli Karlsson,

Kerstin Kvint, Jeppe Launbjerg, Kathrine Lilleør, Annika Lindgren, Jørn Lund, Carl Olof Nyman, Nils Nyman, Elsa Trolle Önnerfors, Johan Palmberg, Gunvor Runström, Anja Meier Sandreid, Lisbet Stevens Senderovitz, Margareta Strömstedt, Helle Vogt, and Torben Weinreich.

A special thank-you goes to Saltkråkan AB for its practical and technical support, not least with many of the illustrations in the book, to Kjell-Åke Hansson and the staff at Kulturkvarteret Astrid Lindgrens Näs in Vimmerby, a cultural center dedicated to Astrid Lindgren, and to Jakob Nylin Nilsson at Vimmerby Library. Thank you to the Danish Astrid Lindgren translator Kina Bodenhoff, to Jenny Thor at the Gyldendal Group Agency, and to my editors, Vibeke Majnlund and Johannes Riis.

Finally, I'm grateful to the National Arts Foundation, the Gangsted Foundation, and the Danish-Swedish Arts Foundation for financial support, and to my indefatigable first reader, Jette Glargaard. And last but not least, thanks are due to Karin Nyman—Astrid Lindgren's daughter—who thought writing this book was a good idea. Without her interest, insight, and active cooperation in the form of a long series of conversations and correspondence over the past year and a half, it would not have been possible.

Jens Andersen
Copenhagen, August 2014

Astrid Lindgren

ONE

Fan Letters to the Author

BUSINESS THRIVED AT THE POST OFFICE on the corner of Dalagatan and Odengatan over the course of the 1970s, and it was all due to one elderly woman. She looked like any other old lady you might see on the street, in the park, at the produce market, or at the tearoom in the area of Stockholm known as Vasastan. Every day for many years, a handful of letters was dropped through the slot at this old lady's house, and on her milestone birthdays in 1977, 1987, and 1997, the postman had to ring the bell at 46 Dalagatan to deliver sacksful of parcels and letters postmarked from across the world. Once the many notes had been read and answered, they were carried up to the attic in cardboard boxes that contained not only cheerful cards and colorful children's drawings but also gilt-edged greetings from statesmen and royals, as well as more ordinary letters from people who just wanted an autograph, or were requesting financial help or moral support for some sort of political cause.

The vast majority of letters addressed to Astrid Lindgren over the years, however, were first and foremost expressions of spontaneous enthusiasm and admiration, although their authors often took the opportunity to slip in a question or two. Not all of them were quite so innocent as the one posed by a Swedish kindergarten class, who wanted to know whether horses could really eat ice cream, or Kristina from Jäfälla's question about how Pippi Longstocking's dad in the television series was able to send a message in a bottle while stuck in jail. There was also a huge number of more self-aware, grown-up queries among the piles of mail: a tinsmith from Kalmar by the name of Karlsson requested permission to call his firm Karlsson on the Roof, a forester in Jämtland wondered whether the nature-loving writer might be interested in a few hectares of pine woodland, and a man in prison for murdering his wife asked whether Lindgren would like to write his life story.

More than a few of the seventy-five thousand letters received by the popular, well-known author right up till her death in January 2002, letters that today are held in the Astrid Lindgren archive at Sweden's National Library in Stockholm, were highly personal in nature. When it came to Pippi and Emil's mother, people evidently paid little attention to the boundary between public and private. As she grew older, Astrid Lindgren came to be perceived as Scandinavia's "kloka gumma"—a nearly mythical kind of wise woman or healer, a spiritual adviser to whom you could open your heart and pour out your troubles. One woman, for instance, wrote asking "Astrid" to mediate a bitter dispute with her neighbors, while another inquired how best to cope with her burdensome old mother. A third female letter writer deluged the prosperous children's book author with begging letters: seventy-two in total, each containing new and detailed requests for financial help with such issues as buying new glasses, fixing the car, paying contractor's bills, and settling gambling debts. An Austrian man who had been wanting a new house for years wrote from abroad to ask whether Pippi's mother might give him a large sum of money in dollars to build his dream home, Villa Villekulla. For forty years, one Danish father used to send long Christmas letters, reporting all sorts of family news and enclosing a few of his children's home-baked treats. Meanwhile, the Stockholm suburb of Hässelby was the source of a veritable bombardment of letters proposing marriage: they came from an older man who threw in the towel only when the widowed Mrs. Lindgren's publisher intervened and threatened the importunate suitor with a restraining order.

Fan letters make up most of the archive, illustrating the colossal significance Lindgren's work—whether in print, on film, or on television—has always had. From the moment the landmark Pippi books were published in the 1940s, the stream of letters steadily increased, and around 1960 they became something of a burden for the hardworking author and busy editor. Lindgren wrote her books in the mornings and during holidays, spending her afternoons at the publishing house where she worked and her evenings reading other people's books and manuscripts. It was only in the 1970s, however, once Lindgren had retired from her editing job, that the stream of letters turned into more of an avalanche, and from the early 1980s onward she had to employ secretarial help to organize her extensive correspondence with her fans. Three events were responsible for this development: the publication of *The Brothers Lionheart* (1973), the so-called Pomperipossa case (1976), when Lindgren caused a stir by protesting the amount of tax she had to pay, and her receipt of the Peace Prize of the German Book Trade (1978) during a period of disarmament, when Lindgren, a pacifist, used her acceptance speech to declare that the struggle for lasting world peace began in the nursery—through the way in which future generations were brought up.

Karin Nyman, daughter of Astrid and Sture Lindgren, born in Stockholm in May 1934, was a witness for more than fifty years to the growing cult around her mother's writing and personality. She recounts that men and women of all ages not only wrote but phoned Lindgren, or even knocked on her front door on Dalagatan, often for no other reason than to shake her hand and express their gratitude for all the happiness and comfort they had found in the imaginary world of her books. Many of them were young people from other countries, Nyman explains, who were writing to Astrid to ask for help: "There were unhappy children and young people in Germany who wanted to move to the Sweden they had read about in her books, Noisy Village or Seacrow Island. It created a problem for Astrid, because although she always wanted to sort things out as best she could for people in trouble, there wasn't much she could do for them."

Most often what lay behind those long, desperate letters from teenagers was a dysfunctional homelife, a lack of affection, and an overwhelming emotional distance between them and their parents. In 1974, for instance, one unhappy German teenager wrote to ask for Lindgren's help: inspired by her books, the young girl had taught herself Swedish. She described how her father tyrannized his family and had even brought his lover to live in their home. Astrid found it difficult to forget about that letter, and couldn't help referencing it in one she wrote to a Swedish teenager, who she felt would benefit from hearing about the problems and challenges

facing someone of her own age in another country. The sixty-six-year-old
Lindgren wrote: "Evidently there's no one in the entire country of Germany she can turn to. She doesn't even want to live. She doesn't know what
she wants, so she tries one thing after another, getting tired of them very
quickly. . . . The girl must have some serious psychological problems, I
think, but I can't quite pin it down, and in any case I can't help her. . . . God,
how much misery there is."

Others of the thirty thousand to thirty-five thousand letters in the
archive that came from children and young people—from fifty countries—
inquired about potential sequels to particular books, wondered how people
wrote books in the first place, or asked "Aunt Astrid" to help the letter
writer jump the queue for a theatrical audition or casting call. The dream of
becoming a star in the next Astrid Lindgren film adaptation was a major
theme in one special letter dropped through the front door at Dalagatan in
the spring of 1971. It had been sent from a town in Småland by twelve-year-
old Sara Ljungcrantz, and at the top of the first page, expressively written in
several different kinds of handwriting and with a barrage of exclamation
marks, were the words: "Will you make me H A P P Y ?"

This question proved to be the start of a long exchange of letters
throughout the 1970s between the elderly, world-famous author, on the
verge of entering the twilight of her career, and a rootless and pensive Swedish girl who felt like an outsider in most situations and couldn't figure out
how to be a young adult. At the beginning of their correspondence, which
is reproduced in the book *I'm Putting Your Letters under the Mattress,* it's
clear that Lindgren wanted to help twelve-year-old Sara Ljungcrantz, but
also that the sixty-three-year-old writer needed to get to know the tempera-
mental girl. She hadn't much cared for Sara's first letter: anything but unas-
suming, it announced her wish to be screen-tested, following up with a
diatribe against the child actors in the latest Pippi film and a scathing critique of Björn Berg's illustrations in the new Emil of Lönneberga book. The
girl didn't appear to have low self-esteem, but deep down that's exactly
what she was trying to convey.

Astrid Lindgren's first answer to Sara was therefore brief and rather
chilly. In fact, it was a bit of a dressing-down, and reading it made the girl so

upset that she flushed it down the toilet. The author of some of Sara's favorite books reminded her of the dangers of envying others, taking it a step
further by asking whether Sara realized why she had so few friends, was
usually by herself, and felt so lonely all the time.

It was precisely this idea of loneliness—which in Scandinavian culture is a taboo-laden and negatively charged word, hard to describe even
though we all know the feeling and experience of being alone in many different ways over the course of our lives—that became a connecting thread
throughout the following years' correspondence between the lonely teenager and the lonely writer. By the 1970s, Astrid Lindgren could look back at
a life during which—as a child, young woman, single mother, wife, widow,
and artist—she had thought a lot about being left to herself and thrown onto
her own company. At times she had feared that loneliness, at others longed
for it desperately. And although she always set clear boundaries to limit
what the public knew about the woman behind the author, keeping to her
Småland family motto "Vi sä'r inget utåt" (We don't talk to the outside
world), in her private life Lindgren often spoke with surprising candor
about loneliness when asked. An example of this can be found in an interview with a Swedish newspaper in the 1950s, when the journalist wanted to
know how Lindgren was coping with the sudden loss of her husband in
1952. She answered: "First of all I want to be with my children. Then I want
to be with my friends. And finally I want to be with myself. Just myself. If
they've never learned to be alone, people develop only weak and fragile
defenses against the ways life decides to hurt them. It's almost the most
important thing of all."

Astrid Lindgren's conviction that people should be able to cope with
being alone at any age was also a central theme in her carefully worded advice to Sara, who was having a lot of trouble dealing with family members,
friends, schoolteachers, and psychologists, yet didn't much enjoy her own
company either. After reading Sara's first four or five letters, as Lindgren
gradually began to recognize something of herself in the young girl's feeling
that she was—as she put it—"lonely and forgotten and pissed on," the aging
writer started to lift the veil on her own difficult youth: "Oh, I wish so much
that you could be allowed to be happy and didn't have so many tears on

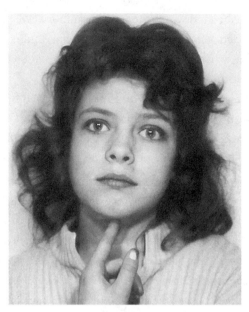

Two teenagers separated by half a century. In her correspondence with Sara Ljungcrantz, top, in the 1970s, Astrid Lindgren saw an echo of herself as a young, awkward girl living in Vimmerby at the beginning of the 1920s.

your cheeks. But it's good that you *can* feel and worry about other people, and think caring thoughts—I feel closer to you because of it. The most difficult periods in a person's life, I think, are their early youth and old age. I remember my youth as dreadfully melancholic and difficult."

Sara hid all of Astrid's letters under the mattress. Her long letters never talked down to their young recipient but focused on the girl's problems and the conflicts in her life, offering solidarity and reflecting the awkward, out-of-place young woman Astrid herself had been in the days when her last name was Ericsson: an intelligent teenager growing up in a remote, rural town in the 1920s, deeply melancholic, rebellious, wistful, and confused about her identity. This extended reprise of her own youth climaxed in the spring of 1972, when Sara dashed off a highly dramatic letter about her brief stay at a psychiatric clinic for young people, where she had been taken after a panic attack and repeated clashes with her family. Never before had Sara felt so "ugly, stupid, silly and lazy," she wrote. Astrid Lindgren responded immediately, beginning her sympathetic letter with the consoling words, "Sara, my Sara," which, like the title of the novel *Mio, My Son* (*Mio, min Mio* in the original Swedish), could be directed to any child sitting alone on a bench in an empty park, both literally and metaphorically: "'Ugly, stupid, silly, lazy' you called yourself in your letter. I can tell with certainty from your letters that you're not stupid and you're not silly, though of course I can't comment on the rest. But when you're thirteen you *always* think you're ugly. At that age I was convinced I was the ugliest girl in the world, and that nobody would *ever* fall in love with me—but as time went on I discovered things weren't as bad as I thought."

The exchange of letters between them peaked when *The Brothers Lionheart* came out in 1973–74, and Astrid Lindgren became intensely busy, partly with interviews and readings both at home and abroad but also because a number of people close to her died. Chief among them was her brother Gunnar, who was only slightly older than she. In their youth he'd been a close confidante, to whom Astrid had poured out her wild, dance-loving heart in letters that were often full of dark humor. Amid her grief over Gunnar's premature death in 1974, it seemed as if all the world wanted to discuss *The Brothers Lionheart* with its author.

Including Sara. Having received a copy of the book through the post, complete with dedication, she threw herself into it before reading a "stupid" review in the newspaper *Dagens Nyheter*, as she wrote consolingly to Astrid. How could anyone not love a book that was so vividly exciting yet so heartwarming and full of solace? Astrid Lindgren had no answer to that. Instead there was something else in Sara's letters over the winter of 1973–74 that she wanted to discuss: the news that the now fifteen-year-old girl had fallen in love with one of her teachers. Life and love had gradually become so closely intertwined for Sara that in a December 1973 letter to Astrid she tried to analyze herself, using a separate sheet of paper: "I had wondered for a long time about the reason why I wasn't really living. I'd got as far in my deliberations as falseness and lost identity. I wanted so much to be myself. But who was I? And I don't think I know a single person who is themselves."

Astrid Lindgren became so fascinated by Sara's letter that on New Year's Eve—when she generally shunned society in favor of enjoying time alone with the sounds of Beethoven and Mozart, a good book, and her usual diary entry, in which she reflected on the past twelve months—she instead answered Sara's letter. Sitting in front of her typewriter during the final hours of the year, she let her thoughts wander back in time, to her youth in Vimmerby, a provincial city: "When I read what you write about yourself, I feel I recognize much of what I brooded about when I was your age." It was the philosophical beginning of Sara's analysis, in particular, which focused on the human unwillingness to show one's true self, that Lindgren wanted to address: "You're absolutely right about that! No person opens herself fully and completely, even though she longs to be able to. But every single one of us is trapped in our loneliness. All people are lonely, although many have so many people around them that they don't understand or realize it. Until one day . . . But you're in love, and that's a wonderful thing to feel."

The other thing that piqued Lindgren's interest about Sara's soul-searching Christmas letter was her description of being in love with a teacher. Lindgren carefully avoided wagging a moralizing or warning finger. Instead, she wrote—and repeated in several subsequent letters—that love was the world's best cure for anxiety and uncertainty: "Love, even if it's 'unhappy,' intensifies one's feeling for life. That's indisputable."

Sara Ljungcrantz and Astrid Lindgren never met face to face, and they were never closer than in the letters of 1972–74. Sara wrote a single letter in 1976, in which she reported on her rereading of Astrid's three books about young Kati from Kaptensgatan (1950–53). The trilogy, about a young girl who visits the United States, Italy, and Paris, had given Sara the travel bug as well as a zest for life, but she also wanted to ask the author whether the main character was modeled on her eighteen- or nineteen-year-old self: "Were you really like Kati when you were young?"

This pertinent question put sixty-eight-year-old Astrid Lindgren in mind of something she had found when she was clearing out some drawers: a few letters and yellowed scraps of paper from the difficult year of 1926, when she'd had to leave home.

> I found a scrap of paper . . . one I wrote when I was about your age, it was in a letter and it read as follows: Life is not so rotten as it seems. But I thought—just like you—that life was rotten to the core. So it may be that the Kati books are a little "lie-ish" if you want them to express what it's like to be *really* young. But Kati was a little more grown-up, of course, she wasn't all that young. All the time I was nineteen or twenty I wanted to kill myself, and I lived with a girl who wanted to even more. . . . But later, bit by bit, I began to adjust, and I thought life was rather pleasant. Now, at my present advanced age, I think it's tremendously difficult to be happy, considering that the world looks as it does, and my comfort is that I'm *not* young any longer. God, how cheerful this is becoming. I suddenly realize. I'm sorry! . . . Goodbye to you, Sara. Life is not so rotten as it seems.

À la garçonne

"FROM FIFTEEN TO TWENTY-FIVE, YOU live about four different lives," declared Astrid Lindgren in a German TV broadcast from the
1960s, which was about the successive stages of a woman's life. With the
same natural charisma that had made the children's book author a star on
Swedish radio at the end of the forties, she described the overwhelming
feeling of being four different women within the space of ten years: "So,
starting with the first one—what was I like when I was fifteen? I was aware I
was grown-up, and I wasn't happy about it."

This insecure, occasionally unhappy, lonely fifteen-year-old, who
found comfort and meaning in the world of books, transformed at the age of
sixteen or seventeen into an extroverted, progressive girl who lived and
breathed the spirit of the age: "I underwent a rapid and colossal change,
turning from one day to the next into a proper jazz gal. This was around the
time jazz had its breakthrough in the roaring twenties, you see. I cut my hair
short, to the utter horror of my parents, who were farmers, and partial to
convention."

It was in 1924 that Astrid Lindgren (née Ericsson)—not yet seventeen—
plunged into a youthful revolution that caused a sensation in Vimmerby. The
town had a movie house, a theater, an evangelical bookshop, and a folk-
dancing troupe called the Smålanders, but as a dance-crazy young woman,
Astrid longed to move to the rhythm of her own era. Summer offered the
chance to dance outdoors, while in winter the Stadshotell hosted "soirees
with dancing" on Saturdays. Evenings usually began with a lengthy concert,
during which the two sexes sat demurely and expectantly in their separate
rows, but from nine o'clock till one in the morning there was dancing to the

latest hits, "featuring special decorations and magical lighting," as the Stadshotell advertised on the front page of the local newspaper *Vimmerby Tidning*
in 1924–25.

Meanwhile, Astrid's best friend, Anne-Marie Ingeström (later Fries),
was still wearing long, feminine dresses that both hid and highlighted her
burgeoning womanly form. A beautiful girl, the daughter of a bank manager,
she was nicknamed Madicken and had grown up in a white villa at the
middle-class end of Prästgårdsallén. She liked to show off her long dark hair,
especially in photographs, where she fully embodied the image of traditional
female sensuality. Astrid, by contrast, had begun to dress in masculine clothing. Long trousers, jackets, and ties had crept into her wardrobe, as well as
hats and caps she drew down tightly over her close-cropped head, which—
as she later observed in an interview—contained little in the way of down-to-
earth, sensible thoughts. Instead, it swarmed with fragmentary quotations
from Nietzsche, Dickens, Schopenhauer, Dostoyevsky, and Edith Södergran, as well as notions gleaned from the movies about how Greta Garbo and
contemporary femmes fatales looked and acted: "There were around 3,500
inhabitants of Vimmerby, and I was the first person in town to cut my hair
short. Sometimes people I met on the street would come over and ask me to
take my hat off and show them my shorn head. It was around the same time
that Victor Margueritte, a French writer, published his book *La Garçonne*, a
very shocking book that became a worldwide success. It seemed every girl
right across the world tried to be like La Garçonne—I did, anyway."

Victor Margueritte's novel, which sold more than a million copies
around the globe in the 1920s, became a cult book for many young women
who dreamt of rebelling against outdated gender roles and Victorian pro-
priety. Monique Lerbier—the main character in the novel—is a walking and
talking thorn in the side of bourgeois society. She cuts her long hair like a
boy's, wears jackets and ties, smokes and drinks in public—usually the preserve of men—dances wildly, and gives birth to a child out of wedlock. She's
a self-confident, self-made woman who chooses freedom above family, opt-
ing for a life she herself colors and shapes.

"La Garçonne" rapidly became an international phenomenon in the
world of fashion, shocking men with its androgynous look. All of a sudden,

major cities across the world were teeming with short-haired women clad in men's clothes or shapeless dresses and cloche hats. The point of this dual-gendered wardrobe was impossible to mistake. The modern young woman of the 1920s didn't want to be like her mother and grandmother. She rejected corsets and long, heavy gowns in favor of a more functional style of dress that allowed her to move more freely. Like the La Garçonne haircut, these clothes were intended to make women resemble the gender with which they were increasingly drawing level.

As a curious, eager reader and a culturally interested young woman who used newspapers, magazines, books, films, and music as a window onto the big wide world, Astrid Ericsson was aware of the fuss these new women's fashions had stirred up outside Småland's borders. In Scandinavian newspapers and weeklies, a number of male columnists saw it as their calling to dissuade women from cutting their hair short. The "shingle bob," as the La Garçonne style was also known, was referred to in explicitly racist terms, including the "Apache cut" and "Hottentot hair," and behind these bogeymen lay fears about women's new role. Would the man of the future lose the standing he had held since time immemorial? Not entirely. The majority of these young La Garçonne–inspired women dreamt of security and family, a husband and children. What was new, however, was that they also wanted to work outside the home, they sought companionship with men, and—not least—they wanted control over their own bodies and sexuality.

How well and how naturally this new, boyish look and the associated lifestyle suited Astrid Ericsson is clear from various photographs taken at Anne-Marie's seventeenth birthday in August 1924, in which four youths—Sonja, Märta, Greta, and Astrid—are gathered around the birthday girl. The four disguised friends playfully arranged themselves in two different tableaus, pretending to be rival suitors kneeling before a fair maiden. Compared to the three other "young men" in the pictures, there is something magnificently coherent about Astrid Ericsson's appearance. She's not playing a role; she's herself: a tomboy. Astrid, who had always played with other children regardless of gender, had never wanted to be anything other than a girl, despite her lack of confidence during her teenage years. As she

On August 28, 1924, Anne-Marie Ingeström, seated, turned seventeen, and her best friends Sonja, Märta, Greta, and Astrid, right, dressed up as young men hovering around the graceful Madicken.

Young Astrid from Näs puts on a fashionable expression, presenting herself as a self-aware, freedom-loving woman in the Edith Södergran mold.

explained in the newspaper *Göteborgs-Posten* in 1983: "Perhaps because we never drew a distinction in our games at home in Näs"—the Vimmerby farm where she grew up—"girls and boys played together equally wildly."

The same "tomboy" aura is strikingly present in other photographs of Astrid Lindgren taken in the 1920s and early 1930s. In them we see a slender woman between twenty and twenty-five, clad in long trousers, and sometimes in a waistcoat and bow tie. A woman smoking cigarettes almost ostentatiously, her challenging posture underscored in many images by a small, subtle, knowing smile. It's as if the young woman in the photographs exists in a zone of untouchability and independence, illustrating some of the strong, self-aware lines from the young Astrid Lindgren's favorite poet, Edith Södergran, in "Vierge moderne," a poem about a modern virgin:

I am no woman. I am neuter.
I am a child, a page and a bold decision,
I am a laughing streak of scarlet sun . . .
I am a net for all voracious fish,
I am a toast to every woman's honor,
I am a step toward accident and undoing,
I am a leap into freedom and the self . . .

Echoes of this can be found in the masculine, dynamic main characters in Astrid Lindgren's books for young girls, *Confidences of Britt-Mari*
(1944), *Kerstin and I* (1945), and especially in the three books about
freedom-hungry Kati. The orphaned twenty-year-old who narrates the
three books travels to America in the first installment, and while in God's
own country she can't help comparing herself and her gender with Colum-
bus and generations of masculine conquerors, becoming indignant at what
she sees. Opposition, outspokenness, and protest when necessary serve as
a natural, indivisible part of Kati's femininity: "Of course, men are a wild
and adventurous and magnificent race! Why are we women never allowed
to discover new parts of the world? It's really rather lousy being a woman."

What Mother Would Say

If Astrid Ericsson's rebellion in Vimmerby in 1924 provoked a certain scandal, it was in no small part because she was the daughter of tenant farmers
living at the rectory. The position gave the Ericsson family distinct prece-
dence over ordinary farmers and townsfolk. Samuel August Ericsson (1875–
1969) was a church warden and respected farmer with a broad knowledge of
agriculture, animals, and people, and he held various local offices over the
years. So did his hardworking, intelligent wife, Hanna Ericsson (1879–1961).
As well as efficiently running a large household at Näs, including four children, grandparents, and an extensive staff of helpers on the fields and farm,
Hanna was involved in Vimmerby's organizations for poor relief, child welfare, and public health. She was also famous in the town and its surroundings for her poultry keeping, regularly winning first prize at markets and

cattle shows. A pious, deeply religious woman, Hanna was the ever-vigilant moral guardian of Astrid Lindgren's childhood home, where the four children had to attend Sunday school, and churchgoing was mandatory.

On the day in 1924 when Astrid had her hair cut like the heroine of Victor Margueritte's novel, she phoned home to Näs hoping Samuel August would pick up, because he, unlike Hanna, would take a milder (albeit scarcely more understanding) view of his daughter's actions. Her father listened, answered in a heavy voice, and added that it probably wouldn't be a good idea for her to come home right away. Yet Astrid Ericsson stood by her decision: making a show of rebellion was, after all, the point. A while later, Astrid agreed to cut the hair of a younger relative who asked her to do so at a family get-together. In an interview on the CD *Astrids röst* (Astrid's voice), the elderly Lindgren describes what happened, explaining that she used the opportunity to begin spreading the spirit of rebellion among her relatives, and that her grandmother Lovisa told the two girls she quite liked Astrid's short hair.

Nonetheless, Astrid Lindgren never forgot the reception she got at her childhood home on the day she came back with her new haircut. You could have heard a pin drop when she walked into the kitchen at Näs and sat down on a chair: "Nobody said a word; they just moved around me in silence." Hanna's reaction on that occasion, along with any comment she might have made, is unknown, but there can be little doubt that she made it clear to Astrid later—once they were alone—what her feelings were. Scenes of rebellion and instances of willful self-expression among the four Ericsson children were rare, and when one of them did get carried away, it was always Hanna who reacted. The disciplinary aspect of child-rearing was not Samuel August's strength. As Astrid Lindgren recounted: "I do remember one time when I opposed my mother. I was very little, three or four years old, when I decided one day that she was stupid and that I was going to leave home, to the outdoor privy. I couldn't have been away long, but when I came back my siblings had been given hard candy. I thought that was so unfair I kicked at my mother in a rage. But then I was taken into the dining room and given a spanking."

That was what childhood in Näs was like for Astrid, Gunnar, Stina, and Ingegerd. None of them doubted their mother's love for them, but

Samuel August and Hanna Ericsson with their four children. From left to right: Ingegerd (born 1916) on her father's lap, Astrid (1907), Stina (1911), and Gunnar (1906), holding his mother's hand.

while Samuel August liked to hug his children, Hanna was reticent and sparing with her affection. It was Hanna, too, who called them to account when they forgot the time after a long summer's evening dancing to accordion music among the fluorescent birches in the park, or losing themselves in thought on benches by the water tower. Afterward they'd hurry back home down Prästgårdsallén, and, as they cautiously opened the door, the big question was what their mother would say.

"She was the one who brought us up. I can't remember Samuel August ever getting involved," wrote Astrid Lindgren in the 1970s, in a beautiful and tender essay about her parents, *Samuel August from Sevedstorp and Hanna from Hult.* In it she wrote about her mother's spiritual side, which lent her, like Samuel August, a gift for language that was inherited by all their children. As Astrid Lindgren commented in an interview with the newspaper *Aftonbladet* in 1967: "Mother wrote poems when she had the time. She wrote them in an album. She was the most intelligent of the two of them, and she was stricter than Father. Father was very, very fond of children."

Both Samuel August and Hanna were agreed on one demand, however, which was not up for discussion: the four children had to help on the farm and in the fields. All year round, often before they left for school in Vimmerby and even on the day of their confirmation, they were expected to dig up beets before washing and getting changed. A parallel to this firm working partnership between children and adults, and to the pedagogical view of work as ennobling, can be found in Astrid's novel *Kerstin and I,* about the twins Kerstin and Barbro. The reader is presented with a couple whose marriage is reminiscent in various ways of the solidarity between Hanna and Samuel August. The hardworking, capable, and ubiquitous mother figure in the book, which was published in the fall of 1945, at the same time as the first Pippi Longstocking title, is described as the family's commander in chief, with a broad overview of its goings-on and an unrelenting eye for practical detail. The father, on the other hand, is an impractical daydreamer whose familial strengths lie in his idolization of his wife and children. As he says of his relationship with his twin daughters: "I'm the kind of unfortunate parent who never strikes his children except in self-defense."

At the beginning of the book, this gentle man among three strong women has just retired from the military, where he was a major, and has persuaded his wife and daughters to abandon life in the big city and settle down in the country on the family farm, Lillhamra, which has been empty for years and thus needs a loving hand. It proves to be a tremendous slog for the whole family, and again and again the mother has to emphasize to her two

Vimmerby, August 1909. Samuel August, Hanna, and their two eldest children, Astrid and Gunnar, on a visit with relatives. As in many later photographs, Astrid has sought out her father's embrace.

tomboy daughters, Kerstin and Barbro, that farm work isn't merely necessary for the community but also builds character. Her pragmatic philosophy of life can be summed up in two basic messages, which the Ericsson children were also taught at Näs during the years between 1910 and 1920: "You have to renounce that which is less necessary to achieve that which is necessary" and "Only those who work and learn to love work can ever be happy."

Astrid Ericsson carried these doctrines about privation and working till you drop into adult life, by which time they were ingrained. Her daughter Karin Nyman relates that in the 1930s and during the war her mother had a knack for the difficult art of getting the most out of the family's modest means, including by working twice as hard, something she continued to do for many years after the war, and indeed throughout most of her life, according to her daughter, in her own remarkably effortless way: "It was my mother's natural tendency to beaver steadily away without stress or fuss; to move easily between different tasks, answering letters and supervising things and doing housework; making beds, clearing the table after breakfast, washing up after dinner, all as automatically as she brushed her teeth, all quickly and efficiently."

The necessity of sacrifice and hard work were such obvious virtues for Astrid Lindgren that she never impressed them on her children in the form of admonishments or commands. On the other hand, Karin Nyman recalls, their mother always found strength in thinking of Hanna's advice to her children when work got to be too much and too dull, and they were looking forward to getting to school: " 'Just set to, just keep at it,' said Hanna, when they were in the middle of some protracted and monotonous task like thinning beets or bundling hay. And as an adult Astrid unconsciously made the gesture she had made as a child when she tightened the bundle—as if taking a run-up to something demanding."

Girls with Pens

In May 1923, fifteen-year-old Astrid Ericsson's school career came to an end. She wasn't sorry, because although she had done well in her studies, choosing in the final Swedish exam to write on a conspicuously virtuous topic—"Klosterfolkets verksamhet under medeltiden," activities of convent inhabitants during the Middle Ages—she often felt like the more tomboyish of the twins in *Kerstin and I:* "I got pins and needles all over my body, and I felt like screaming and flailing around wildly. Best of all I liked running about and keeping busy."

She was hardly the school troublemaker, but she did get the fidgets. You can see it in old photographs of the classroom, where all the children are sitting nice and calm and gazing at the photographer. All except for Astrid, who's standing up and fluttering one arm. She was small and slim, lithe, with braids rather than short hair. As one of the slightly older girls in Vimmerby—Greta Fahlstedt—recalled in the *Vimmerby Tidning* on the occasion of Lindgren's ninetieth birthday in 1997: "She was so lively even in those days. She practically gave off sparks." And she got nothing but excellent grades in her final exams in 1923, when she was leaving lower secondary education. Among her papers in Swedish, German, and English, the Swedish one about busy medieval nuns was especially revealing of the fifteen-year-old writer's well-developed imagination—and sense of humor: "One thing nuns spent a lot of time on was needlework. They embroidered elaborate altar cloths, made lace, sewed clothes and much more. They were unbelievably talented, and I think if nuns had been allowed to marry, which wasn't the case, they would have had magnificent trousseaus."

We know nothing of the parental discussions conducted across the bedroom in 1923-24, as Hanna and Samuel August lay in their separate beds and talked in low voices about their eldest daughter's future—or her clothing—before singing a psalm and blowing out the candle. On the whole there is little in Astrid Lindgren's autobiographical writings about her childhood paradise at Näs that reveals or hints at what Hanna and Samuel August thought and did about their offspring's potentially questionable decisions.

We don't know, for instance, whether Hanna supported her fifteen-going-on-sixteen-year-old daughter's aspirations to become a trainee journalist at the *Vimmerby Tidning* when the opportunity arose. And what was Samuel August's stance on the matter? Had he already come to an agreement with the newspaper's editor in chief? If so, then it can't have been without a degree of concern and opposition from Hanna. Female journalists were a rarity, and the newspaper was a male-dominated world, still far from reflecting the democratic breakthrough in women's rights that Sweden was undergoing around 1920. Still, we can't assume that Hanna—inwardly, at least—didn't support her daughter's wish to develop her talent for writing, to indulge the same urge to inhabit the world of words that she herself had once felt. In *Samuel August from Sevedstorp and Hanna from Hult,* Astrid

Lindgren describes her mother's dreams of using and developing her considerable reading and writing skills as a young, unmarried woman: "She was a gifted girl who was awarded perfect grades in all subjects without exception when she left school. Once she had hoped to become a teacher, but her mother was against it. Did she feel that she would be irretrievably giving something up by getting married?"

Hanna probably felt uneasy, yet at the same time rather proud of her talented daughter's employment at the town's leading newspaper. It was unusual for women, especially women as young as Astrid, to be allowed to publish their writing in such a forum and thereby help shape the flow of news. Since the Modern Breakthrough in the 1870s—a shift in Swedish literary culture from romanticism to naturalism—there had been female journalists in Scandinavia, but not many, and in 1920s Sweden recruitment continued to be slow. This was despite Elin Wägner's novel *The Pen*, published in 1910, which had significantly heightened interest in new, intellectual working environments for women. Quick-witted, spirited Barbro, the main character in Wägner's novel, was intended not just to personify the modern independent woman but also to shed light on a new and vital female type: the opinion maker. Nicknamed "pens," these women brought to the fore a discussion about female voices and roles outside the home. In this sense, Wägner predicted, in *The Pen* as well as in her 1908 debut novel *The Norrtull League,* the coming exodus from the country to the city by young women like Astrid Lindgren. As Wägner wrote: "Just wait until independent women truly begin creating homes for themselves all over Stockholm: There will be so many small powerhouses, and the world will marvel at what we can achieve."

In Sweden in the 1920s it wasn't necessary for journalists to have attended an institution of higher education. The newspaper itself trained its staff, and the basic view among contemporary writers was that you were either born to do the job or you weren't. As in Astrid Ericsson's case, talent (along with good connections) was a springboard to employment as a trainee. The training itself was highly individual, varying from paper to paper, which meant that the probationary period could last from a few months to a few years.

The decision to give Astrid Lindgren a job at the *Vimmerby Tidning* at such a young age was made by the editor in chief and owner of the paper, Reinhold Blomberg (1877–1947). He had become aware of the young girl's remarkable talent for writing several years earlier. Astrid attended Vimmerby Samskola Secondary School with some of Blomberg's children. One day in August or September 1921 the editor in chief received a visit at his office in Storgatan from Mr. Tengström, who taught Swedish, German, and English at the school. The teacher wanted to show him an exceptional essay written by Astrid Ericsson, then just thirteen. Would the paper be interested in printing it? It began with the words: "It's a beautiful August morning. The sun has just risen, and the asters growing in a bed in the middle of the yard are beginning to raise their dew-laden heads. It's so silent, so silent in the yard. There's not a person to be seen. No, wait: Here come two little girls, chatting eagerly to one other."

Although Blomberg was neither a journalist nor an author, he could hear the difference between good and bad storytelling. It was a necessary skill in those days, when newspapers were transforming themselves from old-fashioned party-political publications to modern, general-interest broadsheets that addressed the whole family and were expected to sell on more than just advertisements, announcements, partisan opinion, and moralistic screeds. The readers of the future had to be kept informed and entertained. As a businessman, Blomberg understood that.

"On Our Farm," as Astrid Ericsson's school essay was called, was printed in the *Vimmerby Tidning* on September 7, 1921. The text, which was presented to the readers as "a demonstration by one of our young, exceptionally stylistically gifted people," had everything one might want from an entertaining piece of journalism in a modern paper: a scene set in the first sentence, vivid and memorable characters, and language that fizzes with energy and feeling. Moreover, the essay is about something universal, something adult readers of both sexes and all ages can identify with and miss, something that became one of Astrid Lindgren's authorial hallmarks later in life: children playing freely.

Almost all children's play in rural areas around 1920 took place outdoors, arising from a close relationship between people, animals, and

Four playmates at Näs, armed with a trowel, spade, and barrow. From left: Gunnar, Astrid, the cowman's daughter Edit, who read unforgettable stories to Gunnar and Astrid, and a grandchild of the priest who lived next door.

nature. When the Ericsson children weren't helping in the fields, their childhood was so full of games that—as Astrid often repeated—they almost played themselves to death. As she wrote in a nostalgic passage in the book *Fyra syskon berätter* (Four siblings speak): "Games, yes, which filled our days! What would my childhood have been without them? What, for that matter, would any childhood be if play weren't a part of it?"

The school essay printed in the *Vimmerby Tidning* in 1921 centered around the intense world of play, which was coming to an end for the thirteen-year-old writer. The reader meets two girls who are busily preparing to give a dead rat a solemn funeral. With great seriousness and dignity, the animal and its long, thick tail are wrapped up in a dainty white handker-chief and laid carefully in the ground, before being commended to God: "The little children stood grave and silent, Maja even squeezing out a tear for decency's sake. Then the sun smiled, and the asters bowed whisperingly toward each other. Or maybe it was just the wind bending their heads together."

After the rat is buried, there's no wake or coffee in the living room. Instead, a group of children gather in the twilight to play more games, but for once they can't decide what game to play. Increasingly tired and having had enough for one day, they eventually end up going their separate ways. Yet the piece ends on an upbeat note. Tomorrow will bring a new day with new games: "Good night, scallywags!"

Physics for Journalists

Blomberg forgot neither the essay nor the writer. He may also have been presented with other evidence of young Astrid Ericsson's skill, as his older children occasionally were when Mr. Tengström read out one of her essays in class. Previously unknown and unpublished exercise books from those days testify to the impressive scope of her talent. Five different Swedish essays from 1921, apart from the published "On Our Farm" and the paper on nuns from 1923, reveal a prodigiously expert storyteller, well aware of her linguistic toolkit, of genres and styles, and possessed of a sophisticated command of tone.

"The rest of us wrote so conventionally," remarked ninety-year-old Greta Rundqvist in the *Vimmerby Tidning* in 1997. "Even at school, Astrid's essays were in a class of their own, and were often read aloud by the teacher, who recognized her talent." Whether she was recounting a solitary walk from Vimmerby to Krön, describing Christmas Eve at Näs, telling tall tales about a local traveler to America, or reporting on an exciting experi-ment in physics class, she knew how to make every single text lively and relevant for her reader. A striking example is the essay "An Electrical Experiment" from December 1921, in which fourteen-year-old Astrid, tasked with writing a physics report, chose to approach it journalistically.

Using the narrative devices of a newspaper article and larding the report with direct speech, she manages to interest even unqualified readers in physics:

> "Now, we're going to do an experiment," said Miss H. She fetched six glass bottles with metal rods inside. "What is this?" she asked. Deep silence. "This is an electroscope. I'm going to tell you what they're made of. So, there's a glass bottle with an ebonite stopper. Through the stopper, a metal rod runs down into the bottle. At the top of the metal rod is a shiny ball of foil, and at the end of the rod are two gold leaves. Today we'll be looking at electroscopes," Miss H. concluded her presentation. We were split up into groups, each of which was given an electroscope and an ebonite rod. "What shall we use the ebonite rod for?" we cried. "To charge the electroscope," answered Miss H. "How are we supposed to do that?" "Well, I'll tell you, if I can get a word in edgeways, but the way you're chattering it's nearly impossible. Now, you already know that a thing can become electrically charged if you rub it. So you're going to rub your ebonite rods with a woolen cloth. Afterward you're going to touch it to the foil ball on the electroscope, put your finger on the ball, take it away again, then remove the ebonite rod. Now, look, the gold leaves that used to be close together have spread out. Can anyone tell me why that happens?" "I know," cried one of the girls. "There are two kinds of electricity, negative and positive. The gold leaves have been charged with the same kind, so they push each other away, because two charges with the same sign repel each other, while those with different signs attract each other." "That's absolutely right," said Miss H.

Just over a year after she received her lower-secondary-school exam results in the summer of 1923, Astrid Ericsson was taken on by the *Vimmerby Tidning* as an apprentice journalist. A monthly wage of sixty kronor was the going rate in contemporary Sweden for trainees, who were expected not only to write burial notices, small articles, and reviews, but also to answer the phones, keep records, proofread, and run errands in town.

The *Vimmerby Tidning* appeared twice a week and consisted of eight pages in tabloid format, sprinkled with advertisements and public announcements and featuring a wide and disparate range of news from at home and abroad: from international politics and natural disasters to short paragraphs about yet another unmarried mother somewhere in Sweden being accused of having suffocated or drowned her newborn. In more cheerful corners of the newspaper, readers could find articles about sports, fashion, and household management, as well as the occasional crossword and the ever-popular column "Here and There," which contained brief, sensational news items about crimes, accidents, and peculiar incidents all around the country. These curious tales, drawn from real life, provided excellent fodder for an imaginative, story-loving trainee journalist when the opportunity arose to practice her writing. You could read, for instance, about an elderly man in Hultsfred who, in the spring of 1925, was about to give a speech over his friend's coffin, which had just been lowered into the earth, when he suddenly keeled over dead himself. In an equally sensational funeral story from Mulseryd, a woman who'd been mute for twenty-two years began talking loudly to people in church at her mother's burial service.

A copy of the *Vimmerby Tidning* cost ten öre, and if you wanted an annual subscription you had to hand over four kronor. The daily circulation was stable at around five thousand copies, and although Reinhold Blomberg didn't have a monopoly on news in the town, the competing *Nya Posten* was only half as big and could match neither the quantity of advertising, the supply of informative and entertaining journalism, nor the number of staff and contributors based in small rural communities around Vimmerby.

Since almost all the articles in the paper were unsigned, it's impossible to say exactly what the budding journalist contributed during the more than two years she was employed at the "Vimmerby Rag," as Astrid nicknamed the paper in letters to her older brother Gunnar, an agricultural apprentice in Skåne during those years. It is clear from Reinhold Blomberg's

warm letter of recommendation in August 1926, however, when her employment was abruptly terminated, that she was a talented, alert, and unusually hardworking trainee who contributed to various departments of the
paper over the years. The letter reveals that she carried out all kinds of ad-
ministrative and editorial work, and never failed to pitch in when needed—
always with "good humor and a willingness that has been remarkable," the
editor in chief emphasized.

Gunnar, who had also fancied the journalism route but, as the only
son at Näs, was expected to take over the farm, got a sense of how much
young Astrid dreamt of a future as a "newsperson" in a letter dated March
18, 1925. A radiantly happy little sister informed him that she would soon be
leaving for Stockholm, where she would learn to draw (although she
struggled even to spell the word *croquis,* or life-drawing). It was a skill that
might be useful in her future activities as a journalist, thought Blomberg,
who had gotten Astrid into his brother's newly established art school in
the capital:

> I've got big news for you. I'm going to Stockholm on April 1 and
> enrolling in Henrik Blomberg's art school. It lasts two months.
> You probably think it would've been more appropriate if you'd
> been allowed to do it instead. And I definitely think so too.
> You'd certainly have been much better suited to being a news-
> person than me. But, you know, I nagged and begged until I got
> permission. It'll be fun, I hope. But it's a shame I won't be there
> when you come home in the spring. I'm supposed to learn *cro-
> cis,* or whatever it's called. It'll benefit me as a newsperson, they
> tell me. But probably not straight away at the Vimmerby paper.

Wandering Women

Astrid Lindgren, looking back on her time as a diligent trainee, specifically
mentioned writing a few of the unsigned articles, notices, and columns in
the *Vimmerby Tidning* between spring 1924 and summer 1926. And Blomberg called some of these longer articles "stories" in his recommendation

letter of August 1926, emphasizing them as Astrid Ericsson's particular strength. One of them, printed in the newspaper on October 15, 1924, was about the opening of a new stretch of railway between Vimmerby and Ydrefors. The event had brought together all the bigwigs at the railway company, as well as the mayors, the parish councilors, and most of Småland's journalists: sixty in all, exclusively men, many of whose names were supposed to be rattled off at the beginning of the four-column article. After the first paralyzingly boring column of names, upon which the editor in chief had apparently insisted, the sixteen-year-old reporter was finally allowed to reveal her facility as a storyteller. The mood of the article immediately lifted; suddenly you could hear the train, see the smoke in the distance, and then . . .

> It finally arrived. Flags and garlands on the carriage. After a minute's pause it set off again, while thirteen flags waved a cheerful farewell. In America, as we know, the trains whistle off at such terrifying speed that days and nights flit past like streaks of black and white. This train, however, did not. It puffed off at a thoroughly appropriate speed, so you could enjoy the beautiful Småland countryside. Now and again you reached a little station with a red guardhouse and long, decorative festoons, filled with people staring and waving. And everywhere, of course, the Swedish flag was flying.

Readers were offered another example of Astrid Ericsson's journalistic talents in the summer of 1925. "På luffen" (Traveling) was the title of a spirited, feminist-minded serial in three installments, following six Vimmerby girls on an exhausting summer walking tour through Småland and Östergötland. In accordance with good journalistic practice, the premise was explained to readers at the beginning of the piece, printed in the *Vimmerby Tidning* on July 11, 1925:

> This will be travel reportage, allegedly. It will, without doubt, be a miserable example of it, but we ask for your forbearance—

Five hale and hearty hikers in a row (plus a sixth, the photographer), heading westward. Ahead of them lies a nearly two hundred–mile route along Vättern, an enormous lake, through the towns of Motala and Linköping, and home again to Vimmerby.

pleading our youth. For this article is the product of six young ladies who set off on foot one morning, taking Vimmerby as their starting point. It consists of impressions and episodes from this walking tour, which we wish to share with a large public. So let's look lively! It's probably best to begin at the beginning, which took place on the square when the church bell had just struck nine. We had rucksacks on our backs and sturdy shoes on our feet. We then proceeded to march off down the dusty track and loudly christened ourselves knights of the road.

It was something of an event, widely noticed and discussed in Vimmerby. Six proud daughters of the town, two of whom had just left school,
got ready to set off on the main square one July morning, clad in identical,
practical walking dresses with short arms and high necklines, with girl
scout–like neckerchiefs, cloche hats or students' caps on their heads, rucksacks and blankets on their backs, and sturdy boots on their feet. Elvira,
Anne-Marie, Astrid, Greta, Sonja, and Märta had known one another since
their first year at school, as Greta Rundqvist recounted in 1997 in the
Vimmerby Tidning: "A clique of five, six, seven girls who went everywhere
together until life pulled us apart, and we started studying and working.
But none of us became nurses, which was the future everybody dreamt of in
the 1920s."

The year before, four of the girls had pretended to be men in the photographs taken on Anne-Marie's seventeenth birthday, and in 1925 they still
found it easy to imitate the opposite sex, this time as traveling journeymen
venturing out into the unknown. And venture they did, doing five to twenty
miles per day and nearly two hundred in all. Most of those miles were on
foot, but also, where possible, by train, car, boat, and horse-drawn cart,
sitting on bales of hay and cans of milk. Their route took them from
Vimmerby toward Tranås and Gränna, farther up along the eastern bank
of Vättern, an enormous lake, over the mysterious, wooded mountain of
Omberg, and out across the flat country around the Abbey of St. Bridget at
Vadstena. Then came a boat trip through Motala, via the locks, onward
to the major city of Linköping, and finally due south, back to where they'd
begun.

Walking so many miles on foot required endurance, good comrade-
ship, and solid footwear. In a long letter to Gunnar dated July 26, 1925,
written in the playfully pompous jargon the two used in their correspondence, Astrid summarized the many challenges of the trip into three main
points:

> You've probably been reading our charming travel reportage in
> the Vimmerby rag. In which case you already know most of
> what's happened. I would, however, like to draw your attention

to the following: First—that we managed the aforementioned journey on foot remarkably nicely, despite all the derisive words and remarks when we set off. Second—that we received no blisters worthy of the name apart from on the first day, which induced me to buy a new pair of slightly more comfortable shoes on credit at Tranås. Third—that we didn't drive a car or permit ourselves to be transported by any other vehicle for more than a very modest portion of the journey. *Now* come and tell us we can't hike!

Astrid's well-developed sense of irony revealed itself in the way the series of articles slyly punctured the six girls' mannish project. Indeed, one obvious way of reading the articles is as the younger generation's humorous contribution to the discussion of gender roles, a discussion that still hadn't really reached Vimmerby. With a twinkle in her eye, the correspondent-at-large admitted that even young, strong, feminist women could get dehydrated, develop blisters on their feet, and accept a chivalrously offered ride. In fact, the travelers ended up being driven almost every day. After all, who could say no to such lively, intelligent company?

Once we'd walked about ten kilometers in the blazing sun and had started hallucinating oranges, we saw a car approaching. Quickly we arranged our faces into suitable expressions, until we were the very picture of despair, arms hanging limply down our bodies, feet dragging a few meters behind, and a call of distress from six throats: "Can we get a riiiide?" Best possible result! Offered a lift all the way to Stora Åby. Sweden's most beautiful country road. Rejoicing! . . .

The two hundred–mile journey practically wrote itself, and readers at home in Vimmerby never knew what news the next article might bring—whether the girls would be overnighting at a manor house, a hotel, a hostel, or a hayrick. On the second leg of the journey, having reached Gränna, a small town known for its *polkagris* candy, when they ought to have been tending their blisters in the falling dusk, the girls were drawn into a party with the locals. This was one of the episodes the seventeen-year-old correspondent *didn't* telephone to dictate in its entirety for the serial, which was read by the six girls' mothers as carefully as the *Vimmerby Tidning*'s recurrent stories about the white slave trade. It was only Gunnar who, in a letter dated July 26, 1925, got the whole story about the six vagabonds from Småland at the street party:

> Things didn't get really fun until Gränna. We were put up at the manor house at Vretaholm, a little way outside the town, because Elna had a friend who had a friend who was married to the steward there, and currently Elna's friend was visiting her friend. Are you following? As it happened, there was a local festival going on in the good city of Gränna, and naturally we took part to pep the whole thing up a bit. As you read in the *Vimmerby Tidning*, we gatecrashed, which was uncommonly easy. They didn't dance, they just played singing games. At first we didn't want to join in, but then, "after many invitations" . . . Then the Gränna girls got furious because we were laying claim to the handsomest menfolk. Alas, it's not easy being human, and marriage isn't a ceasefire.

Ellen Key's Bedhead

Two days later, after having spent the night at the ruined castle near Alvastra, the girls decided to walk the final miles down the winding, hilly path to writer Ellen Key's fabled villa, Strand, which lay on the steep slopes down toward Vättern. Perhaps the seventy-five-year-old author of the world-famous book *The Century of the Child* would be at home. She might even invite them in. As the girls approached the big house, its mistress suddenly appeared on a balcony and shouted, "Vad vill flickorna?" *What do the girls want?*

Ellen Key, who in the 1910s had made Strand a nodal point for a range of cultural, female-oriented networks, and whose guestbook contained many thousands of names, felt increasingly irked by unannounced visitors

The knights of the road rest their legs on Göta Kanal between Motala and the lock at Berg, aboard the good ship *Pallas,* which was filled with Swedish and especially German tourists. In the evening they sang each other's national anthems and danced, and one particularly spirited German, wrote the *Vimmerby Tidning*'s correspondent, drank to "my health, your health, all pretty girls' health!"

as she got older. It was therefore something of a scoop that the six Vimmerby girls got the author's permission to take a closer look at the huge and distinctive garden around Strand, laid out in plateaus down toward the lake and planted with wild Swedish flowers, exotic perennials, and bushes. Various fantastically shaped beehives stood at the end of winding paths on terraces with names like "Rousseau's Way," and out on Vättern was a round landing stage with an antique roof and columns, intended to resemble a Sicilian temple of the sun. During the extraordinary visit, Key's big dog suddenly revealed its inhospitable side and bit one of the girls. The house-keeper, Miss Blomsterberg, hurried to help, and naturally the *Vimmerby Tidning*'s correspondent seized the opportunity to scribble most of it down on her pad:

> A terrifying St. Bernard came hurtling out and sank its teeth into one of our twelve legs. (The owner of the aforementioned leg is now wandering proudly round and telling people she was bitten by Ellen Key's dog.) Ellen Key's good heart ran away with her, and to comfort and reward us we were given permission to view the interior of Strand. It was a very special occasion! One would have to search a long time to find a lovelier home.

Six pairs of eyes could scarcely believe what they saw during their tour of the house: light, cheerful colors everywhere and beautiful, simple furniture, collections of books in most rooms, and fantastical architectural and decorative details, great and small, wherever you looked. At the top of all four walls in the entrance hall, for instance, various maxims were painted, including one from the Swedish Enlightenment philosopher and poet Thomas Thorild: "Denna dagen, ett lif" (This day, one life). It's difficult to imagine a better caption for their intense morning and unforgettable en-counter with Strand, Ellen Key, and her dog. Astrid never forgot the words on the wall, but the young trainee never mentioned it in her travel reportage in the paper, nor did she include the rather peculiar moment when the fa-mous writer suddenly asked for help buttoning her petticoat.

Fifty years later, in Margareta Strömstedt's biography of Astrid Lind-gren, the younger author recalled the episode clearly, but looked back on it with very different and much more Key-critical eyes than in 1925. Now, sud-denly, it was not the author but her formidable dog that had made the first move, while Ellen Key herself seemed equally fierce as she stood there in her undergarments, hair all messy, shouting angrily at the girls. Strömstedt wrote: " 'What do you want, girls?' she yelled, shrill and annoyed. The girls explained shyly that they wanted to see Strand, but Ellen Key made no move to let them in. Suddenly the door downstairs flew open and Ellen Key's big dog came dashing out and bit one of the girls in the leg. Huge commotion. The housekeeper let them into the entrance hall to bandage up the girl who'd been bitten. Ellen Key herself came down as she was, half-dressed, holding her petticoats together with one hand. Suddenly she turned to Astrid and said sharply: 'Button my skirts!' Embarrassed and taken aback, Astrid did as she was told."

The truth about the visit to Strand probably lies somewhere between the euphoria of the 1925 articles and the rationalization of the 1977 biography, in which the seventy-year-old Lindgren evidently wanted to express reservations about Ellen Key's personality that she didn't have as a seventeen-year-old. Whatever really happened, the girls were each given a rose before they set off toward Omberg and Borghamn, and in a photo taken of them in Ellen Key's garden even her dog seems sociable, posing nicely at the bottom of the frame.

After the publication of *The Century of the Child* in 1900, Ellen Key became a much bigger and more recognizable name overseas than at home in Sweden. Her landmark book contained chapters with titles like "The Right of the Child to Choose His Parents" and "Soul Murder in the Schools," and was a remarkable mixture of visions, dreams, and debates about upbringing, emphasizing the necessity of love between parents and children. Key believed the way people lived together would alter drastically in the future, and for the better. More than any previous historical era, the new century would focus on humanity's most important resource—its children.

The cooling of Astrid Lindgren's enthusiasm for Ellen Key echoed the skepticism and mistrust of the Swedish feminist movement in the 1970s toward her ideas and worldview. She was considered outdated, too reactionary to be a proper role model, her views too esoteric and full of contradictions. Key had, for example, advocated for women's rights to education, work, financial independence, and the vote, yet she had simultaneously insisted that a woman's most important contribution to society lay in the family and in her role as a mother, a role she ought to maintain as long as she could.

From today's perspective, and without having to determine which Astrid was correct in her assessment of Ellen Key, there is something magnificently symbolic about the meeting at Strand on July 7, 1925, between the aging humanist and the curious young journalist. Lindgren's revolutionary children's book two decades later would launch a career that drew in many respects on the ideas found in *The Century of the Child,* including Key's faith in human creativity, her thoughts about a freer upbringing, and— especially—her rejection of corporal punishment. As Ellen Key put it: "These brutal attacks work on the active sensitive feelings, lacerating and confusing them. They have no educative power on all the innumerable fine processes in the life of the child's soul, on their obscurely related combinations."

Ellen Key died on April, 25 1926, less than a year after the six travelers had dropped by. The *Vimmerby Tidning* published two articles about her death and burial, both featuring photographs and prominently positioned on the paper's back page. The author of the articles was, as usual, not mentioned, but it wasn't a writer accustomed to obituaries. The anonymous obituarist did, however, seem to possess extremely detailed knowledge of the author's house, including the layout of the garden and its surroundings. It was almost as if she were picturing Strand in her memory: "That beautiful path over the evocative plains toward Vättern and up to the ridge, where she so often stood and observed the magnificent landscape that composed the foreground to her own beautiful home."

The *Vimmerby Tidning*'s readers were offered no grand literary-historical assessment of the renowned Swedish author's work and significance: Not so much as a book title or date was even mentioned. Instead, the obituary was crammed with the vivid adjectives typical of the previous summer's series of articles, which had ended with the teasing and—given the writer—prophetic words: "Dear little Vimmerby, it's not that you're a stupid town to come home to, but God preserve us from having to stay here forever."

THREE

The Mysteries of Procreation

WHAT WAS SHAPING UP TO BE AN EXTREMELY promising journalistic career came to an abrupt halt in August 1926, when it could no longer be hidden that the *Vimmerby Tidning*'s trainee was pregnant. It was only a question of time before people started whispering and gossiping, and the grander ladies of the town stuck their noses in the air when they caught sight of Astrid Ericsson on the street. That's just how it was in those days, recalls an elderly Småland woman in the book *The Rebel from Vimmerby* (Rebellen från Vimmerby), in which she also describes the options open to a young country girl who fell pregnant without being married or engaged: "Flee and give birth, or stay and bring shame on your family."

It was neither an old schoolfriend, a local farmhand, nor a traveling salesman who was the father of Astrid's baby, but the *Vimmerby Tidning*'s owner and editor in chief: fifty-year-old Reinhold Blomberg, who had re-married after his first wife's death in 1919 had left him with seven children, several of them close in age to Astrid Ericsson.

Trained as an agricultural engineer, Blomberg had owned and run a large farm on Gotland for many years. In 1912, however, after a major fire, he gave up the life of a farmer and transferred himself and his money to Småland, buying a carpentry business in Södra Vi before changing his mind and purchasing the *Vimmerby Tidning* and its associated printing house in 1913. In the same year Blomberg acquired ownership of a house at Storgatan 30, moving in with his six children and his wife, Elvira, who was pregnant again. Several years later, space was also found in the building for the newspaper's editorial office.

Throughout the 1920s, both Blomberg and his newspaper proved hugely successful. He invested in property, land, a cement works and acres of forest, but the newspaper remained the focus of his business. In a small community like Vimmerby, an editor in chief found himself playing many lucrative roles, and Blomberg turned out to have a knack for all of them. He became a member of the Writer's Club and Newspaper Publishers' Association in Småland and turned his paper into a profitable bulletin board for local-government announcements and advertisements placed by the increasing number of tradespeople in the little market town. He also was politically active, and was selected for the town council several times.

This enterprising, influential man fell in love with his newspaper's seventeen-year-old trainee, becoming infatuated with her in a way Astrid Ericsson had never experienced, but must have heard and read about. She didn't refuse him, and they entered into a romantic relationship which for obvious reasons had to remain secret, and which probably lasted six months—Karin Nyman estimates—before Astrid became pregnant in March 1926. Astrid, who had found it so difficult to fall in love and make the opposite sex fall in love with her, was now being assiduously courted. For her part, Astrid was less smitten than surprised at the overwhelming interest in her "soul and body," as Reinhold phrased it in a letter. Yet there was something unknown and dangerous about the relationship that attracted her, as she explained in 1991 in a lengthy television interview that was later printed in *Stina Dabrowski Meets Seven Women* (Stina Dabrowski möter sju kvinnor): "Girls are so silly. Nobody had ever been seriously in love with me before, and he was. So of course I thought it was rather thrilling."

And transgressive. Not merely because Astrid Ericsson was sexually inexperienced, but also because Reinhold Blomberg was a married man with a divorce case hanging over his head. Then there was the fact that the *Vimmerby Tidning*'s editor in chief wasn't just acquainted with the well-respected Ericssons at Näs but had actually worked closely with them on several occasions. In 1924, for instance, Reinhold Blomberg, Hanna, and Samuel August took charge of organizing Agriculture Day, and the whole town was hurled into frantic activity for three days; and when Samuel August turned fifty the next year, Blomberg made sure to pay him the homage he was due in the newspaper: "It happens from time to time that Mr. Ericsson has an errand to run at our venerable editorial offices, and at those times he usually introduces himself as 'the rectory farmer.' As a farmer he merits both honor and respect, for whatever he touches with his hands within his area of expertise seems to succeed, bringing joy and profit. His farm is a model farm, and few parishes can boast his equal as a breeder of livestock."

Notes for a Biography

The precise circumstances of Astrid's affair with her boss, who at that point was no longer living under the same roof as his wife, Olivia Blomberg, are unclear. Few letters have been preserved from this dramatic year, when Astrid became pregnant in March, moved to Stockholm in September, and gave birth to her son Lars in Copenhagen in December. The identity of her boy's father never became public knowledge during her lifetime, although her own family, a few members of Reinhold Blomberg's extensive clan, and the Vimmerby locals did know who it was. Astrid wanted to keep it secret as long as possible, mainly out of consideration for Lars, who was generally known by the diminutive form Lasse.

"I knew what I wanted and didn't want. I wanted the child but not the child's father." Astrid put it that bluntly in the notes she prepared in 1976–77 for Margareta Strömstedt, who had been working on her biography for several years, interviewing her and accompanying her on trips to her childhood home in Småland. Today some of these notes have been preserved in stenographic form in Astrid Lindgren's archive, and in some of them she seems to be trying to put words in the mouth of her biographer. She also supplied Strömstedt with a brief autobiographical sketch, a rounded and tidily written chapter in itself, which has no title and begins with the words: "When Astrid was eighteen, something happened that precipitated a radical change in her life. She describes it as follows: What happened was that I got pregnant."

Astrid Lindgren's own account of what happened in 1926 has never been published in its entirety, but it was extensively paraphrased and quoted by Strömstedt in her biography *Astrid Lindgren: A Life* (Astrid Lindgren: En levnadsteckning), which appeared shortly before the author's seventieth birthday in 1977. Lindgren's notes formed the basis of the biography's sensational passages about eighteen-year-old Astrid Erics-son's pregnancy, Lasse's birth, and his years living with a foster family in Copenhagen. All of it was utterly new to the public. Thirty years of portraits and interviews had created the impression that Lindgren moved to Stock-holm as a young woman to attend school, and there, after a few years, met Sture Lindgren, whom she married and bore two children, Lasse and Karin.

Yet the truth was otherwise, and after many conversations with the author, Margareta Strömstedt came to believe it was necessary to explore the issue in her biography. The subject herself disagreed, but Strömstedt stuck to her guns. As she explained in an interview with the newspaper *Berlingske Tidende* in 2006, the difference of opinion developed into a fully fledged dispute: "One day we held important negotiations at Rabén and Sjögren, the publisher, with an editor observing. We agreed that Astrid should write about that chapter of her life in her own words—about the trouble that 'shook Vimmerby harder than when Gustav Vasa revoked the city charter,' as she put it, with a lightness that concealed a far deeper pain. A biography of Lindgren had to explore that pain, I thought, as a kind of response to a body of work that was teeming with fatherless boys."

Eventually Astrid Lindgren agreed to reflect back on this period of radical change. Even so, she was sparing with the truth. The story about the unwanted pregnancy was described as a "tale of misfortune," and the fa-ther's identity was left shrouded in darkness. It was a mistake, that was all: "I knew what I wanted and didn't want. I wanted the child but not the child's father."

In fact, the calculation hadn't been that easy. Correspondence between Astrid Ericsson and Reinhold Blomberg in the years 1927–29, as well as the monthly letters Lasse's Copenhagen foster family sent to Astrid over three years, reveals that she was far more conflicted about her relationship with Lasse's father than she would later admit. Reinhold Blomberg, for his part, remained in love with Astrid, and paid for the couple's joint visit to see their little boy in Copenhagen in 1927, where they stayed at a hotel, and for a week-end sojourn in Linköping that same year. Only in March 1928 did she de-finitively break things off, telling him that their paths would henceforth diverge. As early as the summer of 1927, however, when the editor in chief's divorce case had just been settled and Blomberg promptly began renovating and refurnishing the house in Storgatan, she dropped a heavy hint. On a visit to Stockholm he showed Astrid sketches for the home where he hoped they would live with Lasse and his other children, and Astrid refused to give a firm answer; instead she asked for time to think. It could be—she indicated—six months to a year. Little by little, the fifty-year-old Blomberg realized that the battle was lost. Yet he continued doggedly to write lovesick, clichéd letters to his "beloved, beloved enchanting little angel," expressing hope that Astrid would use her break to "dream and feel your beloved's closeness in enchanting dreams of betrothal," as he put it in a letter dated August 23, 1927.

From the beginning of their relationship, Reinhold's affections had been possessive and controlling, to Astrid's dismay. When she moved to Stockholm in September 1926, he reproached her for enrolling in a secretarial course without running the decision by him first, taking it as a sign that Astrid was already thinking of a future without him. He also thought she was going to the theater and the movies too much, and in 1927 he forbade her to go dancing. In the same letter, he even vented his jealousy about her strong bond with her family: "I really know so little about what's happened between you and your parents as regards our relationship. . . . It hurts and offends me that in this case, too, I have to yield priority to people who should rightly take second place when it comes to humanity's greatest and most honorable emotion—love."

Astrid instinctively resisted Reinhold's attempts to control her when they saw each other in Linköping and Stockholm, or when they took those three or four trips together to see their son in 1927–28. Her deliberately superficial letters frustrated the demanding romantic in Vimmerby, who had laid out a plan for their future and refused to be held at arm's length. "You write so briefly about yourself. Don't you understand that I want to know much, much more about you?"

Both Astrid's mother Hanna and the older Astrid Lindgren wondered what she saw in Reinhold, apart from the fact that he was the first man in her life and the father of her child. In the notes the aging author prepared for Margareta Strömstedt in 1976–77, she made no attempt to hide the pleasure she took in the role of seductive temptress. With Reinhold, she felt for the first time the special power a woman can exercise over a man, the kind of power many of the books she read were about:

> Hanna occasionally asked, sorrowfully and with unconcealed astonishment: "How could you?" She felt that if I had to be pregnant, it ought to have been with a different father. And, truthfully, I felt the same. I couldn't give myself or Hanna an answer to the question, "How could you?" But when have young, inexperienced, naïve little dimwits ever been able to answer such a question? How was it put in Sigurd's short story about Lena Gadabout? I read about her when I was very young. She wasn't at all pretty, the author assured us, "but was nonetheless much sought-after on the market of desire," and when I read that I thought, with a certain jealousy, "Oh, if only I could be like that!" And it turns out I could. I just didn't reckon with the result.

It wasn't merely self-awareness and guilt that lay behind Astrid Lindgren's use of the quotation "much sought-after on the market of desire," but also pent-up bitterness: Blomberg, as a much older and more experienced man, would have been fully aware of the risk he and especially she were running by not using contraception. He also knew very well the shame in store for a young woman who gave birth to a child outside of wedlock in 1920s Sweden. Astrid, according to Karin Nyman, placed far too much trust in her boss's reassurances that if they just did this or that, then nothing would happen. Nyman adds that the young Astrid Lindgren, having grown up on a farm in a rural community surrounded by cows and horses, was obviously aware of the mysteries of procreation. How to protect herself against constant reproduction, on the other hand, was a riddle.

Contraception and Puritanism

In our enlightened age, we might wonder why a bright, well-read young woman like Astrid Ericsson knew nothing about contraception. As she later expressed it in an angry letter to the aging Reinhold Blomberg, dated

February 22, 1943, looking back on their affair with bitterness: "I didn't know a scrap about contraceptive methods, so I never realized how dreadfully irresponsibly you behaved toward me."

The reason for her ignorance originated in the puritanism that in the 1920s continued to dominate sexual politics in Sweden, which lagged far behind developments in the rest of Scandinavia. According to Swedish law, selling contraceptive devices was permitted but advertising condoms and diaphragms was not. This law had been prompted by a 1910 speech in which the socialist politician Hinke Bergegren encouraged working women at the Folkets Hus in Stockholm to use contraception: "Better love without children than children without love." The speech was met with bourgeois indignation. Bergegren spent time in jail for his revolutionary campaign, and at lightning speed a law was passed—it remained in effect until the beginning of the 1930s—that forbade any form of advertising or public discussion of contraception, even though you could buy it if you knew where to find it.

Swedish women thus knew very little about how to avoid pregnancy, especially in rural areas, as the journalist Ester Blenda Nordström illuminated in 1914 in her exposé *A Maid among Maids* (En piga bland pigor). A journalist from the big city, Nordström went undercover as a maid on a farm in Södermanland for a month, documenting the sixteen- or seventeen-hour workdays of these low-paid girls and the difficulties they experienced with the sexual demands of men. Like many of her peers, Astrid had devoured the book as a young girl, and in the early summer of 1925 she noted that, according to the *Vimmerby Tidning*, the book was going to be performed as a piece of outdoor theater, which would be toured all around Småland.

Other pioneers fought for Swedish women's rights during those years, including Norwegian-born Elise Ottesen-Jensen, also known as Ottar, who traveled around Sweden advocating for sexual hygiene and protesting the double standard of the contraception law. In her suitcase Ottar carried samples of diaphragms, informational posters, brochures, and her own pamphlet from 1926, *Unwanted Children: A Word to Women* (Ovälkomna barn: Ett ord till kvinnorna). Ottar's campaign, promoting a freer and less fear-bound sexual life for women, continued well into the 1930s, when feminism in Sweden became an integral part of the Social Democratic movement. Her language lived on long after her: "I dream of the day when all children who are born are welcome, where all men and women are equal, and sexuality is an expression of intimacy, tenderness, and pleasure."

Astrid Ericsson paid a high price for her affair with Blomberg. She lost her job and any prospect of a career as a journalist on a larger paper than the *Vimmerby Tidning*. In the late summer of 1926, as the pregnancy became progressively harder to hide, she had to leave her childhood home and the town of her birth for Stockholm, where she had lived for two months in spring 1925 while attending Henrik Blomberg's school of art. In her notes for Margareta Strömstedt fifty years later, Astrid Lindgren described saying goodbye to Vimmerby as a joyous escape: "Never have so many gossiped so much about so little, at least not in Vimmerby. Being the object of the gossip felt almost like being in a snake pit, so I decided to leave the snake pit as soon as possible. It wasn't—as many people thought—that I was thrown out of the house in good-old traditional fashion. Far from it! I threw myself out. Ten wild horses couldn't have held me back."

She rented a room at a boardinghouse and began a course in stenography and typing. One day she read about a Stockholm-based woman, a lawyer, who helped unmarried, pregnant girls in unfortunate circumstances. Astrid tracked down the lawyer, who arranged for her to travel to Copenhagen in November 1926 and give birth at the Rigshospital, the only place in Scandinavia where a woman wasn't required to give her own and the father's name in connection with the birth; other hospitals usually passed on this information to the national register or other authorities.

Strömstedt's 1977 biography explained the necessity of this clandestine arrangement by arguing that eighteen-year-old Astrid knew she didn't want anything more to do with the father of her child. In her notes for the biographer, sixty-nine-year-old Lindgren supplemented this by adding the following: "Something that had a certain significance for me at that time." The cryptic phrase hardly made Strömstedt any the wiser about what had actually happened and why, and the sentence didn't find its way into the biography. Strömstedt did, however, describe the Stockholm lawyer's surprise that Astrid had no one to help her with her problem. She repeatedly inquired about Astrid's isolation: "'Don't you have anybody you can talk to?' 'No,' I answered, staring at her with my most innocent eyes. She couldn't know, of course, how things were: 'We don't talk to the outside world!'"

In fact, Astrid Ericsson wasn't entirely alone in the fall of 1926. Despite having scandalized her family at Näs, she received help from her parents—when they could, and when she let them. What went unsaid in the Strömstedt papers was that, in the months leading up to the birth in Denmark, Astrid was also in regular contact with the child's father. Since her arrival in Stockholm at the end of August, she and Reinhold had been trying to find a private maternity home where Astrid could give birth to the child as discreetly as possible before handing it over to a Swedish foster mother for an indefinite period. Although Blomberg assumed they would soon be married, they had to wait—and Astrid's pregnancy and delivery had to be kept under wraps—because of the pending divorce case. Blomberg was separated, but on paper he was still married to his wife, Olivia, who had no intention of letting him get off lightly—or cheaply.

At the beginning of her stay in Stockholm, Astrid had assumed they would find a private clinic near the capital, but soon she and Reinhold changed their minds, deciding to choose a town in the provinces where the risk of being recognized was lower. It was only at the eleventh hour that she ended up in another place entirely, in another country.

Domestic Disputes

The many acts of this drama can be followed both in and between the lines of the extensive, detailed records of Reinhold and Olivia Blomberg's divorce case, which was heard by the Sevede Häradsrätt, the local district court, in 1926–27. Sessions were held at the town hall in Vimmerby and documented in large leather-bound books that today can be found at the Regional State Archives in Vadstena. The case was rooted in the couple's disagreement about a man's right to dispose of his wife's money. As the

articulate Olivia Blomberg summarized the problem in court: "My husband suffers from an unhealthy desire for my financial assets. In everything,
even down to the smallest detail, my husband has tried to pester and tor-
ment me because of my modest private fortune."

The friction between the two had begun in 1922, two years after their
marriage and the birth of a little girl, who died soon afterward. Their quar-
rels became more frequent, deteriorating into disputes characterized by
loud arguments, shouting, and much banging on closed windows and
locked doors. The confrontation escalated when Blomberg tried to have his
wife, who he believed he could prove was of unsound mind, declared
incapable of managing her affairs, at which point she demanded they separate. In addition to her husband's attempt to forcibly access her money,
Olivia cited also his repeated affairs with the young, foreign women who
helped around the house in Storgatan. Olivia herself had worked in the
house before she became Mrs. Blomberg in 1920.

The court records in the old archives suggest that the *Vimmerby Tidning*'s editor in chief knew nothing about Swedish women's newly acquired
rights, which indeed weren't particularly evident in Swedish society during
the first half of the twenties. He did, however, know plenty about money
and investment opportunities, and always kept a vigilant eye out for potential injections of capital that might help his business grow. Saving up, buying reliable securities, and hoarding silverware in the cupboard weren't in
Blomberg's nature; he loved risk. As a witness testified during one of the
court hearings, "he suffered from a passion for speculation when it came to
business."

Throughout the protracted divorce case, Blomberg remained sur-
prisingly reticent, even subdued. In the records, where the couple's various
gambits and defenses were carefully noted, he comes across as his wife's
rhetorical and tactical inferior. Mr. Blomberg often struggled to parry
Mrs. Blomberg's assertions and to contain the new fronts she was constantly opening up, ably seconded by her talented brother, a lawyer from
Tingsryd in southern Småland.

Blomberg's most convincing counterattack in the long court case,
which unfolded in several stages over the years 1924–27, was the suggestion

that a feminist conspiracy lay behind his wife's legal proceedings. Even the gender imbalance of the witnesses Olivia Blomberg called to testify that she had always "worked in the family's best interests" seemed both to prove him right and to indicate what was at stake: not simply one woman's honor but the rights of her gender in contemporary and future Sweden. That, insisted Blomberg, explained the similarity between certain of Olivia's witnesses and some of the animated women he'd found outside his front door on the very day that somebody snipped holes in his winter wardrobe up in the loft.

In early September 1926, this toxic marriage was again brought before the court, and now—Blomberg was sure—it was coming to an end. Following a two-year separation, the district court was going to make the divorce official and decide how to apportion the vexed couple's financial assets, after which they could leave Vimmerby Town Hall as ex-husband and ex-wife. Over the spring Blomberg had been busy gathering the paperwork needed to settle the divorce, including documents from their priest. By this time Astrid was pregnant, though only a few people in the town knew about it, and this probably explains his haste. If it came out that he was the father of the child in Astrid Ericsson's belly, his wife would have damning evidence that, in the worst-case scenario, could bring about the collapse of Blomberg's business empire, thwarting his plans to marry for a third time.

When the court gathered on September 2, 1926, at Vimmerby Town Hall, Reinhold's fears were realized. A final decision on the case was postponed on the grounds of new and important information that had come to the attention of Olivia Blomberg and her lawyer, which demanded further, thorough, investigation. Reinhold, sensing which way the wind was blowing, protested in court against the delay, but Olivia Blomberg got her way and the next sitting was scheduled for October 28. Five weeks before Astrid's due date.

Two months passed and, when the court gathered again, the divorce case took the worst conceivable turn for Blomberg. Olivia's investigation had borne fruit, and she now served a writ upon her husband for adultery. Since she still didn't have definitive proof, however, she and her brother asked for a further postponement of the case. Again the court granted Olivia her wish, and Blomberg's protests fell on deaf ears. When Reinhold and

Astrid's child was born in early December 1926, the case was still no closer to a resolution.

A Child of Betrothal

From that point on, young Astrid Ericsson—in absentia, without being named and without risk of being called as a witness, since she wasn't yet of age—took a leading role in the divorce case that journalist Jens Fellke, in the *Dagens Nyheter* in 2007, called "a marital dance of death in which all parties involved were doomed to lose."

Were they? Reinhold Blomberg kept living in Vimmerby after the case, still an editor in chief and still a wealthy businessman. He married for the third time in 1928, fathered another four children, and wrote a short book about his family, in which Olivia, Astrid, and Lasse were conspicuous by their absence from his extensive family tree. Olivia Frölund, formerly Blomberg, got both vindication and compensation, albeit of symbolic proportions. And Astrid Ericsson? She gave birth to a *trolovningsbarn*, a child conceived during betrothal rather than wedlock, in December 1926, and eventually escaped marriage to Blomberg.

"Trolovelse" is an old Nordic word for betrothal. According to Swedish law in the 1920s, although a trolovningsbarn was born out of wedlock, the child was due the same rights as one born within marriage, because the parents had been betrothed either before or after conception. If one of the parents chose to break off the engagement, which could be either public or secret, the child remained a trolovningsbarn, with the right to inherit its father's estate and bear his name.

We don't know for sure when Reinhold and Astrid got engaged, but a letter she wrote to him at Easter 1928 suggests that it was two years earlier, around Easter 1926. The betrothal, which of course had to be secret, was incredibly important for Astrid Ericsson, because it secured the rights of her illegitimate child no matter how things ended between her and Reinhold. Who informed the expectant mother of this crucial fact is unknown. It's not impossible that Hanna and Samuel August knew about this part of Swedish marriage law, although they took a while to get over their shock

and grief at the pregnancy. As Astrid Lindgren explained to Stina Dabrowski in 1993: "That my parents were terribly upset was hardly remarkable. You can't ask a couple of farmers who grew up thinking of pregnancy
outside marriage as a calamity to be anything other than upset. . . . They
didn't say much. There wasn't much to say. In any case, I feel they were
honest, and they helped me as much as they could."

It may even have been Blomberg who made Astrid aware of how
important it was that they get engaged and keep it secret. Everything
indicates that the editor in chief was smitten with the journalism trainee,
and intended to propose as soon as he'd escaped the chains of his current
marriage. It's even possible that Blomberg had something to do with the
Vimmerby Tidning's publication of two lengthy articles in the summer
of 1926 on the subject of "Children outside Marriage," in which the legal
circumstances around a trolovningsbarn were thoroughly explored.

The Sevede Häradsrätt record books from 1926–27 document that
Astrid Ericsson was in touch with Reinhold Blomberg throughout the fall
and up till the birth on December 4, 1926, particularly during September
and October, when the couple agreed that Astrid should give birth at the
private clinic Gott Hem in Vättersnäs, near Huskvarna and Jönköping.
At that point the Rigshospital in Copenhagen wasn't in the picture; that
would happen later, when charges of adultery exacerbated the bitterness of
Blomberg's divorce case.

In September, Gott Hem in Vättersnäs had advertised assiduously in
the *Dagens Nyheter* and *Svenska Dagbladet,* and Blomberg saw the name
during his daily perusal of the national papers. It was billed as offering "discreet and understanding hospitality." He immediately sent an anonymous
inquiry to the clinic, requesting a swift response to a post office box that
later turned out to be rented to the *Vimmerby Tidning.* That fact emerged
in March 1927, during the court's scrutiny of the complex and mysterious
events of fall 1926. It was also during that part of the investigation that Olivia
Blomberg hired a graphologist to prove that Reinhold Blomberg had written the anonymous letters to Gott Hem, which featured his distinctively
knotty abbreviations and the expression "ung dam obemärkt" (young lady
unnoticed), code for a pregnant, unmarried woman who wanted to live
"unnoticed"—that is, in an unfamiliar place—in order to have her baby

We don't know for sure what future eighteen-year-old Astrid Ericsson was inwardly imagining in the fall of 1926. She was engaged to Blomberg—secretly, of course— which meant that the child she was expecting would be a trolovningsbarn, with the right to inherit. Blomberg, accused of infidelity, continued to write affectionate letters to his young fiancée, whose answers protested her affection for him; she didn't quite know what else to do. Blomberg, for his part, always felt that Astrid was dreaming of a future with the child but without its father.

there: "Regarding the advertisement, I am inquiring whether an absolutely discreet and understanding stay can be arranged at the beginning of Dec. for a young lady in a certain condition, and whether the delivery can happen in the same place? Please also provide information about costs etc. Your detailed response gratefully expected at the following address: Box 27, Vimmerby. A home for the child not required at the present time."

The answer to Blomberg's inquiry in September 1926 came promptly. Gott Hem's owner, a nurse named Alva Svahn, informed him that there was space available in both November and December. Another letter from Blomberg followed immediately, this time under the pseudonym Axel Gustavsson, telling Ms. Svahn that "Gustavsson" had forwarded her letter to his fiancée in Stockholm, who would provisionally be arriving in Vättersnäs around November 1 and would spend her last month before the birth at the clinic. He thus indicated that he was withdrawing from the correspondence and leaving the rest to his fiancée. No sooner said than done: The first of three letters from Astrid Ericsson, pasted into the record books in March 1927 as evidence in Blomberg's divorce and adultery case, was received by Alva Svahn on October 8:

> I write in reference to your letter addressed to Box 27, Vimmerby. The letter to you was written by my fiancé, who happens to be staying in V-by. My childhood home is in Vimmerby, but I have recently been living in Stockholm, so that the circumstances, as you write, don't become widely known. I intend to arrive around November 1, but I would like to ask for more information. Will you be able to arrange a foster family for the child, at least initially? A really good home is definitely preferred. Then there is another matter. Will the delivery take place under anesthetic? Are there doctors nearby? Are there many other discreet residents at your institution? I would like answers to these questions before I make a decision. I assume the delivery will take place at the beginning of December so that I can be home by Christmas. I am very young, no older than nineteen, and would appreciate help and understanding.

Do You Have a Sewing Machine?

Alva Svahn was one of many hospital-trained women in Scandinavia who ran maternity clinics in the 1920s, part of what has since been called "the foster child industry." Private maternity clinics constituted an important link in the trafficking of infants born outside marriage. Many of them were taken to orphanages, while others went to foster mothers or foster parents, who might be just as loving and self-sacrificing as Lasse's foster mother in Copenhagen, where Astrid and Reinhold's little boy spent the first three years of his life, or just as cold and unfeeling as the foster parents in *Mio, My Son*. Private maternity clinics, orphanages, and foster families earned good money from the misfortune of others during a period of widespread unemployment, and many children did not get the love and attention they were due. Astrid Ericsson was aware of the ongoing debates around such failures of care, which was why she asked specifically what Gott Hem could do for her child after the birth.

Alva Svahn replied by telegram that she would indeed find a loving foster mother, and that the delivery could easily be carried out under anesthetic. In response, Astrid sat down and wrote a new letter, dated October 10, 1926, in which she expressed satisfaction with the various answers and explained the reason that her previous letter had asked about other young women at Gott Hem. It wasn't fear of meeting people at the clinic; on the contrary:

> When you've ended up in the same unfortunate situation, you need to stick together as closely as possible. How long do the other young women you mentioned mean to stay? I also need to find out my parents' opinion on the matter and make my excuses with the other place before I make a definitive decision. However, I think I can assure you now that I will be grateful if I can arrive on Nov. 1. I daren't stay any longer in Sthlm. But there was one more thing—do you have a sewing machine I might be allowed to make use of? I have a lot of things I need sewed. Yours sincerely, Astrid Ericsson.

The answer came without delay. Of course Alva Svahn had a sewing machine, and she would be happy to help Miss Ericsson with her clothing. On October 19 Astrid replied to say that she had firmly decided on Gott Hem. She intended to arrive on October 31 and stay in Vättersnäs until the birth at the beginning of December. The 150 kronor for the stay would be paid promptly by her fiancé. Miss Ericsson also hoped that Ms. Svahn would be able to pick her up at the station in Jönköping, because it was unclear whether her suitcase could be checked in as luggage all the way to Huskvarna.

A nine-month journey looked to be nearing its conclusion, but neither the suitcase nor Astrid Ericsson turned up at the station in Jönköping on October 31. Instead, a telegram arrived, with the message that Miss Ericsson had been delayed. Alva Svahn remembered that very clearly as she stood in the witness box at Vimmerby Town Hall four months later. Something had gone wrong.

Very wrong. Blomberg's divorce, as we have seen, hadn't been settled on October 28. Olivia Blomberg, fighting tirelessly to unmask her adulterous husband, had again gotten the case postponed, this time to December 9. In the meantime Olivia planned to do everything she could to track down decisive proof. The alleged mother of the alleged child couldn't be called as a witness, but somebody had to know—or know somebody who knew— where the child was going to be born . . .

In other words, Reinhold and Astrid were presented with a completely new situation. Under no circumstances could they make the betrothal public before the birth, since Blomberg was still married, which meant that suddenly Gott Hem wasn't suitable: a birth on Swedish soil would generate a birth certificate, a copy of which would be sent to the national register, revealing that the child's last name was Blomberg. More than ever before, it was necessary to keep the birth as far out of Olivia Blomberg's reach as possible, making sure the child was invisible until the court case was over and the scandal had died down.

There was certainly plenty for Astrid and Reinhold to discuss in the days after the disastrous court hearing in Vimmerby on October 28. They had less than five weeks before the due date, and everything was agreed

and arranged with Alva Svahn and Gott Hem. What now? In the first
instance, Astrid chose to remain in Stockholm, sending a telegram to
the clinic in Vättersnäs to inform them that she would be delayed. A
subsequent message—as Alva Svahn later testified in court—announced
that Miss Ericsson would arrive on the evening of November 3 instead.

Astrid used the sudden, unexpected free days in Stockholm to come
up with a new plan for the birth. For the first time during her pregnancy, she
took matters into her own hands and went to see Eva Andén, the lawyer
she had read about, in her office on Lilla Vattugatan in Gamla Stan. On
October 30, 1926, she knocked, entered, and laid most of her cards on the
lawyer's table, describing not just her own unfortunate situation but also
the secret engagement and Reinhold's divorce case, which was increasingly
affecting the birth. She acted as though she had been thrown upon her own
resources.

Eva Andén, the first woman ever to join the Swedish Bar Association,
was known for her legal work with female clients and closely associated
with the feminist magazine *Tidevarvet* (The age) and the advice bureau set
up one year earlier by the magazine's editor: Ada Nilsson, a doctor. In 1924
Andén had written long articles in *Tidevarvet* about the latest amendments
to legislation regarding children "inside marriage" and children "outside
marriage," emphasizing the ways in which pregnant unmarried women
could make provision for their children. What Andén strongly hinted was
that the relatively nonbinding institution of betrothal could be a golden
opportunity for pregnant unmarried women to secure their children's
future without shackling themselves to the father forever.

By Word and Deed

After her conversation with Eva Andén, Astrid was sent for a consultation
with Ada Nilsson at her office at Triewaldsgränd 2, also in Gamla Stan,
where she received a checkup and was advised on medical complications
that might arise. That evening she sat down in her fifth-floor room at the
boarding house in Artillerigatan and wrote an optimistic letter to Reinhold
at home in Vimmerby, reminding him to put his reply in an envelope with

Samuel August's name and address on the back so that they didn't risk the letter falling into the wrong hands and being used as evidence:

> Today I've been to see a female lawyer called Eva Andén. She was so incredibly kind to me and didn't take any money. . . . She thinks I should find really good lodgings in Copenhagen and have the child at a hospital there, I can't remember what it's called, but they have a secret birth register where you don't need to give the name of the mother or father. . . . She was thoroughly decent and thinks one absolutely has to take responsibility for one's child, as far as possible, so she didn't suggest this idea to help us get rid of the child permanently. She does think it would be dreadful for me to be alone in a foreign country, but I'm sure I can cope with that. . . . She told me that under no circumstances should I get on a train before being examined by a doctor, so she sent me to a female doctor called Ada Nilsson. I didn't have any albumin, so that was good. Write and tell me what you think of my suggestion. I'm going to see the lawyer again on Monday. *Send an envelope with Father's address on the back!*

One of the few places in Sweden in 1926 where a young woman expecting a baby outside marriage could get advice and emergency aid, both medical and legal, was at Tidevarvets Rådgivningsbyrå för Föräldrar (*Tidevarvet*'s advice bureau for parents). The bureau adjoined the magazine's editorial offices and Ada Nilsson's consulting rooms, with a view over the lock and Riddarfjärden Bay. With Eva Andén, Elin Wägner, and other women affiliated with the ambitious magazine, Ada Nilsson had opened the bureau in the winter of 1925, on the model of the Norwegian Katti Anker Møller's consultation offices in Oslo and the even earlier birth control clinics in New York and London, which also inspired the author Thit Jensen, who fought for "voluntary motherhood" in Denmark. As Ada Nilsson wrote in *Tidevarvet*, the aim was "to help mothers-to-be in word and deed." Astrid Lindgren repeated the phrase "in word and deed" fifty years later in

Margareta Strömstedt's biography when she discussed the help and advice she got from the women at *Tidevarvet,* which may not have been as serendipitous as Astrid made it sound: "I happened to read in a newspaper about a lawyer called Eva Andén, and it turned out she was committed to supporting women who needed help in word and deed."

Because of Blomberg's ongoing court case, Astrid was advised to have her baby anonymously at the Maternity Hospital in Copenhagen and give the child to a foster mother in the Danish capital until she and Reinhold were able to bring him home to Sweden. Through the Maternity Hospital, which was affiliated to the Rigshospital, the main hospital in the city, Eva Andén was in contact with a capable and loving foster mother in Brønshoj, who specialized in helping expectant Swedish mothers before and after the birth, assisted by her adolescent son. As Astrid, her mind now made up, wrote to Reinhold in a letter dated October 30: "Think carefully about the Danish suggestion. At first I didn't like it at all, but now it seems like a really good one. Ms. Andén thinks I was really silly to find a place through an advertisement. She doesn't seem to have much faith in the midwife—she thinks it would be easy to squeeze quite a lot out of her."

It happened just as Eva Andén feared. Olivia Blomberg and her brother tracked down Gott Hem and squeezed plenty out of Alva Svahn. When the case resumed on March 10, 1927, and for the first time the parties involved requested the proceedings be *in camera,* Alva Svahn was ready to testify against Reinhold Blomberg. Moreover, the nurse wasn't alone in the witness box: the prosecution also presented two witnesses who had recognized Blomberg and Astrid Ericsson among the guests at the Hotel Continental in Nässjö on Saturday and Sunday, November 6–7, when the couple had been staying in the same room.

Alva Svahn recounted Astrid Ericsson's peculiar conduct when she finally turned up in Vättersnäs on November 3 and announced that she had other plans for the birth itself. She couldn't stay at the clinic beyond November 20, she said, because she was going to marry her fiancé, an engineer who was in the process of getting divorced from his wife. Miss Ericsson therefore intended to travel down to meet him in Helsingborg, where his family lived, in order to get married and have the baby. Ms. Svahn added that

Miss Ericsson had suddenly departed for Nässjö on November 6, ostensibly to meet her fiancé, who was traveling, and had returned to Gott Hem only the next day.

At this point the two other witnesses in the courtroom at Vimmerby Town Hall on March 10, 1927, took over. The proprietor of the Hotel Continental, as well as one of the hotel guests, who visited Vimmerby from time to time, had recognized Reinhold Blomberg on the Saturday and Sunday in question in the company of a young, heavily pregnant woman. The proprietor recalled that the couple had signed the register as "Engineer Axel Gustavsson and wife," and the hotel guest had observed the couple's awkward attempts to hide in the restaurant, as well as the ring glinting on the woman's hand.

When Astrid Ericsson left Vättersnäs on November 20 to meet her fiancé in Helsingborg, Alva Svahn related in court, she had warned the mother-to-be against the arduous train journey, suggesting that the couple be married at the maternity clinic instead. Miss Ericsson had thanked her for the offer but adamantly turned it down. As she left, she promised to phone and tell Svahn how the journey went. A month went by before Alva Svahn heard anything; then a telegram to Gott Hem informed her that Astrid Ericsson had given birth to a son at the hospital in Helsingborg.

When the case was finally settled in the summer of 1927, neither Alva Svahn, Olivia Blomberg, nor the court knew where the former *Vimmerby Tidning* journalist had really had her baby, or what it would be called. The Sevede Häradsrätt gave the following verdict: "It must be considered confirmed that at the beginning of the year 1926 Reinhold Blomberg offended against his and his wife's, Olivia Blomberg's, marriage through adultery."

The court granted Olivia Blomberg's application for a divorce, awarding her a large sum of money in damages for pain and suffering, though only a fifth of what she and her brother had requested. Reinhold Blomberg, who thereby avoided monthly alimony to his ex-wife, nonetheless had to dip into his pockets to pay the costs—and they were far from negligible.

FOUR

Hope Avenue

ON NOVEMBER 21, 1926, ONE WEEK after her nineteenth birthday, a heavily pregnant Astrid Ericsson got off the train at Copenhagen's main station after a long journey through southern Sweden and a ferry across Øresund. In the arrivals hall a young man with dark, wavy hair and small, friendly eyes behind thick horn-rimmed glasses was waiting for her. He introduced himself as Carl Stevens and said he was supposed to accompany Miss Ericsson to Håbets Allé—literally Hope Avenue. The address sounded a note of encouragement amid all the fear and uncertainty of what lay before her.

They took one of the capital's yellow streetcars down Nørrebrogade while Carl chatted about the places they glimpsed along the way. Once they passed through this densely built-up area, which was teeming with people, cars, horse-drawn carts, and bikes, Copenhagen suddenly opened up into a more countrified area full of fields, soft hills, and small thatched cottages. With a bit of goodwill it could be said to resemble parts of Småland, if it weren't for the detached three- or four-story buildings in the middle of the landscape, looking at a distance like cairns along the road to an expanding town. Up Bellahøj Hill and along Frederikssundsvej they rode the streetcar, heading for Brønshøj Square. At the penultimate stop, Carl and Astrid got out and walked the rest of the way to Håbets Allé, where redbrick villas lay like a string of beads behind multistory blocks housing businesses that faced Frederikssundsvej.

Carl came to a halt outside number 36. "Villa Stevns" was painted on the façade, and in the back garden, which directly overlooked a flat, open field, were two strollers. One belonged to the family on the ground floor, explained Carl, and the other was the domain of a Swedish boy called Esse, who was being fostered by Carl's mother on the second floor. Both families in the house had the last name Stevens, and Astrid later learned that they were from the Stevns Peninsula south of Copenhagen. It had lent its name to both the family and the house. Astrid never forgot the Villa Stevns, visiting it several times across the course of her long life. The final time—in 1996—she knocked without knowing who lived there, introduced herself, and explained her errand to the surprised but honored owners, who gave the famous author permission to sit alone for a while in the second-floor room where she had once breast-fed her newborn son. From there she could see the apple tree in the back garden, where three-year-old Lasse had played with Esse, almost the same age, and his "big brother" Carl.

Marie Stevens, Carl's mother and Esse and Lasse's foster mother, was one of a group of Copenhagen foster mothers in the 1920s who always had a child or two each in their care and who also arranged accommodation for mothers-to-be during the period before and after the birth. The minimum cost of full-time childcare at Villa Stevns was sixty kronor per month, and it was money well spent: "Auntie Stevens," as Astrid called her, was such a capable and conscientious foster mother that the Award-Giving Society for Foster Mothers (Præmieselskabet for Plejemødre) had honored her in 1923 with fifty kronor and a diploma that today hangs at the Workers' Museum in central Copenhagen. The Award-Giving Society was a philanthropic enterprise that had been working to improve the conditions of children in Danish foster homes since 1861; as such, it was a forerunner of the more systematic social welfare programs for children and single mothers that emerged in Denmark during the interwar years.

During the times of crisis and periods of rising unemployment after the establishment of the Award-Giving Society for Foster Mothers, it wasn't always possible to tell whether love or cynicism lay behind certain foster mothers' involvement with children. Some could afford only bottled milk, potentially deadly for infants, while others, known as "angel-makers," were infamous throughout Scandinavia for letting their foster children die of hunger or thirst, or in some cases using even more brutal methods in order to obtain additional children and additional payments.

Mrs. Stevens, however, boasted such a spotless reputation that her name was known even in Sweden. If you stood all the "Swedish ladies" who had stayed at Villa Stevns over the years side by side on Drottninggatan in Stockholm—wrote a playful Carl to Astrid in 1930—they would reach all the way from Mäster Samuelsgatan to Norrström, two landmarks a half-mile apart. Right up until her death, Mrs. Stevens continued to receive many grateful letters with Swedish postmarks, including some from Astrid Lindgren, who called her "the most splendid woman I have ever met in my life." In 1931 she wrote a Christmas letter to Lasse's foster mother in the mixture of Swedish and Danish she had come to adopt in her letters over previous years, telling her that Lasse still dreamt about Mrs. Stevens and occasionally wanted his Swedish mamma to pretend she was his Danish mother at Håbets Allé in Brønshøj. "I was supposed to speak Danish to him, and then he told me he was going to Näs soon and all sorts of other things he thought would be interesting. Then, of course, he wanted us to get on a train and travel down to see Mother. 'Mother is so sweet,' he always says. Yes, Mrs. Stevens, you remain in his memory as something very bright and good, and he will never forget you."

Oxheads on the Road

For nearly sixty years Astrid Lindgren kept in touch with Carl Stevens, who had picked her up at the main railway station in November 1926. The sixteen-year-old high school student, who had dreamt of reading languages and music at university and who ended up becoming a high school teacher in Hellerup, did more than just escort Astrid—barely older than he—home to Brønshøj. In the period leading up to the birth he took her sightseeing in Copenhagen and entertained her with Chopin's Revolutionary Étude, played on the piano in the drawing room.

When the contractions started, it was Carl who took Astrid to the Rigshospital in a taxi. He held her hand, and to distract her from the pain he came up with the idea to count the bronze oxheads hanging over the doors of every butcher's shop they passed. Finally, on January 10, 1930, it was the calm and reliable Carl who accompanied three-year-old Lasse on the train to Stockholm to see his "Lassemamma," as they consistently and discreetly referred to Astrid within the Copenhagen foster family. Lasse coughed most of the way, fidgeting in the dark compartment, shoving Carl and sounding like a little Copenhagener: "Move it!" That, and much more, recalled the eighty-year-old Astrid Lindgren in a letter to Carl in December 1987, in which she thanked him for his birthday card and sent her love to all Carl's children and grandchildren:

> I simply can't get my head round the idea that you, Carl, are the grandfather of a couple of schoolchildren. I can still see the young high school student playing the piano in the drawing room, taking me for walks and showing me all the sights of Copenhagen. I got so exhausted in my pregnant condition that I fell asleep and slept like a log when we got home. Oh, all the memories I have, oxheads and all sorts of things, and your journey with Lasse, when he said: "Move it!" I also remember the time he was hitting and poking you and then said: "Now we're good friends!"

The delivery was set to take place at a division of the Rigshospital called the Maternity Hospital, located on Julia Maries Vej. Since its foundation in the 1700s, the institution's mission had been to offer unmarried mothers a place to stay and a more humane way out of their dilemma than "clandestine childbirth, as so often happens, many times followed by the murder of the infant," as it was expressed in the centuries-old royal charter. In those days it wasn't uncommon for unmarried women to hide their pregnancies for the whole nine months, giving birth in secret without the help of a midwife. Hoping to keep the shameful affair quiet and avoid the misery of an illegitimate child, a number of these mothers suffocated their newborns soon after birth.

In the 1920s, the Maternity Hospital remained a bulwark against this kind of tragedy. A mother could give birth there under the care of a doctor and in good conditions without having to give her own name or the father's. All deliveries were, however, registered in the Rigshospital's card index, where each "secret mother" was assigned a number. Like the one on Lars

Blomberg's birth certificate, for instance, where "1516 b." was written on the dotted line where his parents' names and occupations would normally go. There was no need for the name of the child's godmother in these abbreviated circumstances either, but one was provided: Marie Stevens.

The boy was born on December 4 around ten o'clock in the morning, and although Astrid had a fever for several days after the birth, she returned relatively quickly to Håbets Allé and Mrs. Stevens, Carl, and Esse. This time she was carrying little Lars Blomberg in her arms, and over the next three weeks no one else was allowed to hold him very long. Those weeks were all the time Astrid was able to spend with her baby before traveling back to Småland on December 23 for Christmas at Näs—an idiotic decision, as the older Astrid Lindgren remarked in an interview with Stina Dabrowski in 1993:

> "I should have stayed and breast-fed him, of course, but I didn't understand how important that was. It was for [Hanna and Samuel August's] sake, so they didn't have any unpleasantness about me not coming home, because then everybody would know."
>
> "But everybody knew anyway, didn't they, that you'd gone away to have a baby?"
>
> "I don't know, they probably did. But officially I was in Stockholm to study."

Later in life, Astrid Lindgren always remembered the intoxicating joy she felt the first time she held little Lasse at her breast, alone and undisturbed. It was the same magical atmosphere she described in the moving ending of the *Kati* trilogy in 1952, where the young heroine praises the miracles of nature and the symbiosis between mother and child, though she realizes it's a joy experienced on borrowed time. Loneliness awaits them both:

> My son is lying in my arms. He has such tiny hands. One of them has closed around my index finger, and I daren't move. He might lose his grip, and I couldn't bear that. A divine miracle, that little hand with five small fingers and five small nails. I knew

children had hands, of course, but I hadn't really understood
that my child would too. Because I'm lying here and looking at
the little rose petal that is my son's hand, and I can't stop mar-
veling. He's lying with his eyes closed, his nose buried in my
chest, he has black, downy hair, and I can hear him breathing.
He is a miracle. . . . He was just crying, my son. Like a pitiful,
bleating little goat kid he sounds when he cries, and I can hardly
bear to listen, my love aches. How defenseless you are, my little
goat kid, my fledgling; how will I be able to protect you? My
arms tighten around you. They have been waiting for you, my
arms, they have always been meant for this, to be a nest for you,
my little fledgling. You are mine, you need me now. At this moment you are mine and mine alone. But soon you will begin to
grow. Each passing day will lead you a little farther away from
me. You will never be as close to me as you are now. Perhaps
someday I shall remember this hour with pain.

Starvation in Stockholm

On the day before Christmas Eve in 1926, Astrid bade farewell to her infant,
Auntie Stevens, and Carl. None of them knew when she would be back. She
traveled first to her family at Näs, then north to Stockholm, returning to her
sparsely furnished boardinghouse room with its wretched steel-framed
bed, which made it "look like a military sick-bay," as Astrid wrote to Hanna
and Samuel August. As a still-untrained office girl, she belonged to a class
of young women who were only a few rungs above the urban proletariat on
the social ladder. She did, at least, have a steel-framed bed to sleep in,
clothes to wear, and—usually—enough food on the table. The latter circum-
stance was due in no small part to the baskets of food dispatched from home
roughly every six weeks, which supplied all sorts of goodies from Hanna's
well-stocked larder at Näs. Astrid thanked her parents for these necessities
promptly in her letters, rarely neglecting to mention that the basket would
soon be empty: "It's a truly exclusive pleasure to cut a decent slice of bread,
smear it with first-class Vimmerby dairy butter and add a slice of Mother's

cheese, then eat it. This pleasure is repeated every morning for as long as there's some left in the basket."

In other letters to Näs, or to her brother Gunnar, who was an agricultural apprentice in Skåne, Astrid described how she and one of her friends would sit on the edge of her bed every evening when they got home, cut off a piece of sausage and a piece of cheese, and bite into "first one then the other by turns. It's wonderful, but it's over quickly." Hanna's food baskets to her daughter in the big city rapidly became famous among Astrid's friends, because they were always crammed with food rather than sheets, duvet covers, or other inedible items: "A package from home eventually became a vital necessity. You think of nothing else, then when it finally arrives you become almost childish in your ecstasy."

Those are the words of someone who has known hunger. And longing. Much had been taken from Astrid Ericsson in her life, and even more disappeared when she kissed Lasse goodbye on December 23 and handed him to Auntie Stevens. The experience cut just as deeply into his foster mother's heart: Marie Stevens had never seen a mother who'd given birth under such circumstances be so delighted by her child as Lassemamma. Many years later—in 1950, when the boy had grown so big he had a son of his own—his old foster mother in Copenhagen wrote to Astrid Lindgren, "You loved your little son from the first moment."

Astrid Ericsson returned home to Vimmerby at Christmas 1926 as a happy and cheerful nineteen-year-old. Yet the pervasive feeling of happiness and euphoria she had experienced in the wake of the successful birth came to be replaced by dejection, and a pain and grief that began to feel chronic the following year, as she regularly complained in her letters to Anne-Marie Fries: "I'm not really satisfied with existence. . . . Sometimes I wonder whether I'm going crazy. . . . I don't really have any idea about anything, because I don't write to a single person, only to home every now and then."

As if nothing had happened, Astrid resumed her classes in January 1927 at the Bar-Lock Institute in Hamngatan, which taught typing, bookkeeping, commercial accounting, stenography, and business correspondence. She socialized with the other young women during lunch breaks and spent the evenings with her friends, Sara, Ingar, Märta, Tekla,

Nineteen-year-old Astrid Ericsson's life as a single woman in the big city wasn't always plagued by sorrow and loss. In a letter to her brother Gunnar dated July 26, 1927, she described Stina's visit and what the two merry sisters had done together: bumper cars at Gröna Lund, an amusement park; dancing at Blanch's Café; coffee at Café Söderberg; Skansen, an open-air museum; the National Gallery; and City Hall.

and Gun. Yet photos from those years often show a sad Astrid Ericsson. As she wrote many years later in her article "Homage to Stockholm" (Hyllning till Stockholm), which was reproduced in the anthology *The Meaning of Life* (Livets mening): "I came here when I was nineteen, and ugh, I thought Stockholm was horrible! I mean, of course it seemed incredibly beautiful and very grand and sophisticated for someone who came from the country-side like I did. But I wasn't part of the city. I didn't belong. I wandered the streets and was completely alone and so jealous of all the people in the crowd who looked like they owned the whole city."

When the older Astrid Lindgren looked back on this first chapter in Stockholm, she called it "my lean bachelor life," and here the word "lean" should be understood physically as well as psychologically. In the nineteen- and twenty-year-old Astrid's letters home to her mother and father at Näs, she maintained the façade of a healthy, breezy, and hardworking young girl, but her depressive moods of 1927–28 are apparent in letters to Anne-Marie and, to a certain extent, those to Gunnar. "Every so often I long absolutely convulsively to be a child again, but then other times I think things are getting better every day I'm closer to the grave," she wrote to her old Vimmerby friend in December 1928. A few weeks earlier, Gunnar had received a pessimistic note from his normally redoubtable sister: "I feel lonely and poor, and lonely, maybe because I am, and poor, because my tangible assets consist of a Danish one-øre coin. I take back the 'maybe.' I'm dreading the coming winter."

She also joked a little about the suicidal thoughts that were on her mind. In one of Astrid's 1929 letters to Anne-Marie, for instance, when everything looked a little brighter, because she had found new lodgings in Atlasgatan with her friend Gun, she referred to herself as a "soon-to-be-ex-candidate for suicide." Yet pessimism and melancholy did not release Astrid from their powerful grip. When Anne-Marie confessed in a January 1929 letter that she was again starting to feel alienated from her boyfriend, Astrid, slipping briefly into German, answered that her friend's problem was both tragic and normal, before outlining her own dark perspective on love and relationships: "It can't be otherwise between two wretched human beings, at least not in this worst of all possible worlds. It's as sure as 2x2=4.

Es ist eine alte Geschichte doch bleibt sie immer neu [It's an old story yet always remains new], and is equally unbearable each time."

In the same letter Astrid inquired whether Anne-Marie had read a book by the French short-story writer Édouard Estaunié called *Solitudes,* which had just been translated into Swedish. If not, she should take a look at the last story in the collection, "Les Jauffrelin," about a man who committed suicide because, after many years of living with her, he'd given up trying to understand what was going on in his wife's head. The story made a deep impression on Astrid, corroborating her dwindling faith in the idea that, through love, men and women could ward off the loneliness to which single people were helplessly bound: "There's probably no creature born of woman who is anything other than lonely. Suddenly a person comes rushing up to you and says, 'We're kindred souls, we understand each other.' And inside you hear a voice saying with painful clarity, 'Like Hell we do.' I mean, *your* voice might express itself a little more politely. Recently I've been bowled over by people who feel so connected, so connected to me. And I feel more alone than ever. There's certainly a part of me that's stubbornly, unbearably, bitterly lonely and probably will always be that way."

Such sadness, pessimism, and fleeting thoughts of suicide came especially to the fore on long Sundays, when Astrid was alone in the deserted city. Ceaseless thoughts of Lasse drove her out onto the streets from the early morning onward, and everything that could ordinarily be repressed or drowned with as many work-related tasks as possible bubbled up from her subconscious. Profound longing and nihilism gnawed at her guts, like the hunger she felt when money was tight and the basket of food from Småland had long since been emptied. She often sought out an isolated bench that stood beneath a large bush outside Engelbrekt Church. Salvation, when Astrid sat alone and abandoned on the bench, came not from the church but from Knut Hamsun's novel *Hunger* (Sult), which was Astrid's bible during those years, as she recalled in the newspaper *Expressen* in November 1974:

> Everything blurred into one intense feeling of joy at the book,
> and solidarity with the young Hamsun and everyone else who
> walked around hungry in the cities of the world. Like I did. I

mean, all right, I wasn't starving quite as bitterly as Hamsun in Kristiania [now Oslo], who actually chewed a lump of wood. Here in Stockholm it was just that I almost never felt really full. But that was enough to identify with that crazy young person in Kristiania—and to think he could write such a gripping and frantically amusing book about hunger.

There was something recognizable and reassuring about Hamsun's depiction of the individual's struggle against loneliness, and something downright bracing about the novel's physically palpable description of its impoverished, shabby main character: His clothes became more and more ragged, and even his smallest personal effects had to be pawned, yet he kept his sense of dignity and humor. Despite everything, Astrid wasn't alone in her solitude in Stockholm. There was Hamsun's main character, and there were hundreds of unhappy young office girls who had been robbed of their youth by unwanted pregnancy and who now wandered the city, searching for the meaning of life. As Astrid wrote to Anne-Marie on October 3, 1928: "Yes, life is a cursed and meaningless uproar! Sometimes I think it's like staring into an abyss, but other times I comfort myself by thinking, 'life is not as rotten as it seems.'"

Touch-Typing

Efficient, energetic, and socially competent, twenty-year-old Miss Ericsson was able to blend seamlessly into any office environment. She could touch-type, her fingers moving over the keyboard without looking at the letters, and she was reasonably good at stenography and unafraid of correspondence in English and German—all qualifications that would later serve her well as an author, editor, and prolific letter writer within her family and circle of friends.

Astrid Ericsson's first job, obtained in 1927, involved picking up the phone and saying, "Svenska Bokhandelscentralen, Radio Department!" then listening and apologizing. It was a complaints line for dissatisfied customers who couldn't get their new radios—the hottest gadget of the age—to work. Her prospective boss at the office on Kungsbroplan made it clear during the interview that he wasn't eager to employ nineteen-year-olds, since all the previous ones had abandoned their posts, but Astrid Ericsson employed a skill she had always been immensely good at: selling herself. She turned up the charm, humor, and energy, convincing her interviewer that she was reliable despite her youth. "My salary was 150 kronor per month. You don't get fat off that. Nor can you take many trips to Copenhagen, which was what I most hankered to do. Sometimes, however, I did manage to save and borrow and pawn enough to scrape together the cost of a ticket."

Astrid Ericsson's old passport, full of blue and red stamps from the Danish customs authorities during the years 1926–30, tells its own Scandinavian commuter's story. It documents Lars Blomberg's mother traveling the long route from Stockholm to Copenhagen and back twelve or fifteen times. Often she would take the night train on Friday evening, buying the cheapest return ticket for fifty kronor, thus having to sleep sitting up all night. That way she could reach Copenhagen's main station by the next morning, hop on a streetcar to Brønshøj, and be opening the gate at Villa Stevns before noon. It gave her twenty-four intense hours with Lasse before she had to leave Copenhagen early on Sunday evening in order to reach Stockholm in time for work on Monday morning. These weekend visits were so intense, Astrid Lindgren recalled in her notes for Margareta Strömstedt in 1976–77, "that afterward Lasse slept almost round the clock for a whole week."

Twenty-four or twenty-five hours at the beginning of every second and, later, every third or fifth month for three years doesn't sound like much, but these scattered weekend trips were like precious droplets in a sea of longing. Astrid couldn't be a mother to Lasse during those years, but her visits to Copenhagen, and especially the longer ones over Easter and the summer vacation, helped shape the image of "mamma" in the boy's memory, which Auntie Stevens and Carl did their best to encourage; they were scrupulous when it came to emphasizing that he remember her in their monthly letters to Lassemamma, in which they also reported Lasse's physical and psychological development. These letters, which Astrid kept at her home in Dalagatan all her life, thoroughly updated her on Lasse's current state of health, his linguistic and motor development, and the events of his day-to-day life, which involved a lot of playtime with Esse. Astrid welcomed every detail, swiftly passing on the news in letters to others—Gunnar, for example, who in July 1927 received the following summary of life at Håbets Allé: "Auntie Stevens writes that Lasse is 'extremely humorous,' he can emphasize his words so amusingly: 'Hm, I see,' he says, and 'tremendously important,' all things Carl says from school, and which Lasse knows how to weave in at the right place and time."

During those first three years, when Astrid was cut off from daily contact with Lasse and she met and heard about other young mothers in Stockholm who'd been separated from their children, she developed a critical perspective on the relationship between children and adults that eventually came to form the basis of her approach to writing. One woman who was especially influential in opening Astrid's eyes to the emotional harm being done to children was her roommate Gun Erikson, whom Astrid had met at the clinic, Gott Hem, in November 1926, as Karin Nyman recalls. The two women lived together for a year and a half, first in a much-too-expensive room on Bragevägen and later in a little apartment with a kitchen and bathroom in a new block on Atlasgatan. They also shared lodgings there in 1929, Astrid having found employment at the Royal Automobile Club, but soon had to move again when Gun lost her job that same year.

Gun's little daughter, Britt, had been born at Gott Hem, then taken to an orphanage in Småland, and the more Astrid learned about the place—all while listening to Gun's poor excuses for not going down and spending time with her child—the firmer her decision became: One day she went down to Småland herself to see Gun's little girl, who was the same age as Lasse. She was shocked by the conditions at the orphanage, witnessing firsthand the callous methods they used to teach the children. The little bag of hard candy Astrid had brought for the girl was immediately confiscated by the director and shared among other children nearby. Some got a piece of candy, but others had to settle for watching the lucky ones, and several reacted by bursting helplessly into tears. When Astrid got a chance to sit alone with Britt, the girl cried in a monotone, unhappily and without saying a word, clutching her tightly. As she later wrote to Auntie Stevens in Copenhagen and explained to Margareta Strömstedt many years afterward, it was "just as if she wanted to say: I'm very scared of being here, but I'm even more scared of telling anybody why I'm scared."

During her years of separation from Lasse, Astrid Ericsson learned that the parents of small children should remain as close to their youngsters as possible, because those first years were crucially significant in terms of shaping a human life. She saw and heard the evidence around her, both in Stockholm and at Håbets Allé in Copenhagen. Yet she never turned a blind eye to her own mistakes and inadequacies when it came to Lasse; on the contrary. Many of Astrid's letters to family and friends in the years 1927–31 contain a loving and thoughtful mother's snapshots of Lasse's behavioral and reaction patterns in vulnerable situations, where he was forcibly re-moved from his familiar environment and placed in a new one. Without any excuses or dismissive explanations, the young mother described the heart-breaking moments when the boy's fear and anxiety became evident. Astrid Ericsson had also harmed her child, despite how fond she was of him, de-spite always trying to do her best for him—insofar as was possible—and she made no attempt to pretend otherwise.

Lasse's Troubles

Astrid got a closer look at a deeply unhappy Lars Blomberg at the end of 1929, when she had to rush across to Copenhagen. Auntie Stevens had been taken into hospital with acute heart trouble, and was obliged to give up fostering for a while. The year had otherwise brought Astrid plenty of things to be happy about: a new apartment, a permanent job, a raise, and a boss at the Royal Automobile Club who had informed Miss Ericsson—as Astrid wrote to her family at Näs—that she had a "glittering future" ahead of her. Miss Ericsson and her boss had also begun to see each other outside of work, although the budding romantic relationship wasn't without its issues, partly because of Lasse and partly because Sture Lindgren was in the process of leaving his wife and child. Astrid had started wondering to herself, and in letters to Anne-Marie, whether she and Lasse could be reunited in Stockholm, living as a family with the kindly, literature-mad Sture, who gave her a selection of Edith Södergran's wistful poems on her name day, November 27, 1929.

Sture Lindgren, Astrid's boss at the Royal Automobile Club, developed a romantic interest in young Astrid Ericsson in the winter of 1928–29. He was nine years older and married with a daughter, but was in the process of getting divorced. In November 1929, Sture moved into a little apartment at Vulcanusgatan 12, where he and Astrid got a larger apartment on the top floor after their marriage in the spring of 1931.

At Easter earlier that year, Astrid had been in Copenhagen to visit Lasse. Her relationship with Reinhold Blomberg had improved, and the atmosphere between them had normalized somewhat after their harsh and bitter confrontation in the spring of 1928, when Astrid once and for all had refused to marry Reinhold and move home to Vimmerby as the editor's new wife and the mother of his seven children (not including Lasse). Two long letters Marie Stevens sent to "little Lassemamma" on March 28 and June 2, 1928, indicate that for more than a year after Lasse's birth Astrid still hadn't excluded the possibility that she might one day marry the boy's father, but that under no circumstances would she live in Vimmerby, and certainly not as the mother of Reinhold's many children. Mrs. Stevens expressed to Astrid her admiration for the young single mother's decision:

> We had a letter and money from Lasse's pappa yesterday, and it was very sorrowful, such a shame for all three that it should end like this, because deep down I would have liked to see them reunited for little Lasse's sake. And I'm sure life won't be easy for you—not that I don't believe you've done what you think is best for Lasse. But Lassepappa isn't young, and that sort of blow goes straight to the heart, and I think he was very fond of you and the boy. It would probably be a difficult task to be his wife in Vimmerby, though you might just find the strength, and yet I admire you for turning him down. So many young people want to be provided for, then end up separating again.

After Astrid broke off their relationship in the spring of 1928, Blomberg had threatened to halve his payments to Mrs. Stevens and take Lasse back to Vimmerby himself on July 1. Mrs. Stevens didn't think Lassepappa could do that without Lassemamma's consent, but she knew how tight money was for Lassemamma, so to reassure the agitated mother, she offered to look after Lasse free of charge for a year, should the situation between his parents deteriorate still further. Blomberg, who could be a harsh man, nonetheless had a change of heart over the summer, and by November he was married again—"to a German," as Mrs. Stevens wrote indignantly. The editor's new wife bore him another four children in addition to the eight he already had.

By 1929 the Lasse situation was once more as good as could be expected, given the circumstances. Astrid's Eastertime visit to see her son, who was then two and a half and whom she hadn't seen for nearly six months, was paid for by Reinhold Blomberg, and in a letter to Astrid while she was staying at Håbets Allé he asked her to forgive his behavior the year before. Getting rather sentimental, he recalled the good old days, when they'd both talked about becoming husband and wife. Astrid replied to him on Easter Monday, the day before she was due to leave her son, who had spoken Danish to her every day. In her letter, shot through with all sorts of Danish words and phrases, she thanked Reinhold warmly for the trip, regaled him with funny anecdotes about their lovely, talented son, and counseled him to stop brooding on what was past, exhorting him instead to live in the now:

> You say the whole of Easter is going to be a feast of reflection. No, you've got to stop that. It only makes matters worse. You mustn't grieve over what's lost but make the best of now. . . . You don't need to ask my forgiveness for anything. It's not your fault or mine that we couldn't make it work together. . . . Alas, it's snowing, and somehow wonderfully mournful and soft. You had a painting over your bed in the old days, a depiction of a fall landscape. The mood of that painting is the same as the one that surrounds me today.

It had always been heartbreaking to part from Lasse, thought Astrid, but never as difficult as it was now. More than ever before, he represented the vital force and source of meaning she lacked in her life in Stockholm. Small but proud, the boy had been trotting confidently through the streets of Copenhagen by Astrid's side, holding her hand, when he suddenly remarked: "Mamma and Lasse are walking!" And when she hugged the boy so hard he could barely breathe or, grinning, threatened to gobble him

Summer 1929. Two-year-old Lasse pretends to ride a horse at the Stevens family's allotment on the other side of Frederiksundsvej, near Håbets Allé.

up with her next mouthful, he gazed serenely up at her and said: "Are you trying to be cheeky?"

Over the summer of 1929, both Astrid and Reinhold visited Copenhagen—separately—to see Lasse. Blomberg's trip was a single day, and proved an emotionally charged occasion. Afterward Mrs. Stevens wrote to Astrid and described the flying visit, of which there had been many over the years. As he did in the letters enclosing his monthly payments, he asked after Astrid, and this time he was also unusually pleased to see his boy, observed Auntie Stevens: "'You're so much like your mother,' he said, sitting with little Lasse in his arms and crying. I felt sorry for him."

Astrid traveled in July 1929 to Copenhagen, where she enjoyed the good weather and spent most of her days in the garden behind Villa Stevns, watching Lasse do somersaults, climb trees, and balance on the roof of the privy. Never before had he talked so much or said such odd things in Danish. One moment he was asking Astrid whether she was five years old, and the next he was shouting to the seventeen-year-old milkman leaving the milk bottles outside the front door, "Say hello to the wife and kids!" Lasse's proud mother recounted all of this in her letters home to Sture in Stockholm, also conveying the alarming news that she had been taken to the Rigshospital and put under observation for diphtheria: "And I should be home by this evening. But when I go home to Näs I'll stay there a week anyway. I haven't been home over the summer for three years. So I suppose I'm allowed? But poor Mother will be scared out of her wits. . . . I daren't send a kiss because that's how you get diphtheria, so instead I send lots of greetings."

Astrid didn't have diphtheria, but she kept getting pains in her neck and chest due to an enlarged thyroid gland, and in December 1929 she had to have surgery. During her convalescence, which coincided with the Christmas holiday at Näs, she received a letter with upsetting news from Håbets Allé. Auntie Stevens had been taken to hospital with heart trouble, and Carl had been obliged to rush Lasse and Esse to other foster families in the vicinity. It didn't sound good. In late December, Astrid traveled down to Copenhagen to see Marie Stevens. By then she had been discharged, but had been advised that she had neither the health nor the energy required to run a business as a foster mother.

Lasse's foster mother had already made a few inquiries, and was convinced the boy should be removed as soon as possible from his temporary foster family in Husum and placed somewhere else until the next steps were decided. The options were clear: he could live with Lassemamma in Stockholm, with Lassemamma's parents in Vimmerby, or with Marie Stevens, once she felt better. These were the three possibilities Astrid was presented with in Mrs. Stevens's letter, which concluded with the words: "But dear little Lassemamma, if I die soon, which it doesn't seem for the moment like I will, take your little lad home so you can care for him yourself. Don't ever let him be a lonely child in Denmark, because then I'd feel as though my life had been lived in vain."

Mrs. Stevens was still very much alive when Astrid appeared on December 28, and they went to Husum to fetch Lasse together. The three-year-old's face lit up at the sight of his foster mother, and he pulled and tugged at Mrs. Stevens while Astrid stood and watched. He wanted them to go home to Håbets Allé as soon as possible. They stayed there only a few hours, however, before continuing on to Mrs. Stevens's sister, who ran a boardinghouse for single older people on H.C. Ørsteds Vej. There Lassemamma and Lasse would be able to stay the night.

As Astrid Lindgren wrote in her autobiographical notes for Margareta Strömstedt in 1976–77, it was "the most difficult night of my life." Mrs. Stevens's sister wasn't eager to make up a bed for the mother and child, but since one of the elderly ladies at the boardinghouse had just left, it could be managed. The atmosphere was uneasy, and Lasse sensed that his idyllic days at Håbets Allé were numbered:

> When we got there, and Lasse understood instinctively that nothing was or would be like he thought, he lay on his stomach on a chair and cried without a sound. Utterly without a sound, as if he realized it wouldn't do any good, that they'll do what they want with me anyway! Those tears are crying within me even now, and probably will do for the rest of my days. Maybe it's because of those tears that I always take the child's side so strongly in any and all circumstances, and I get so beside myself when petty, self-important pencil pushers muck children around, moving them from place to place—because it's so easy for children to adapt, they think! It *isn't* easy for them to adapt, although it can look like that. They just resign themselves to superior forces.

Astrid Lindgren also recalled that difficult night in a letter to Carl Stevens on February 22, 1978. In that big, dark, strange apartment on the fourth floor of a block in central Copenhagen, she remarked, it was as though Lasse's life had reached rock bottom. So had Astrid's. There weren't enough beds to go around, so two armchairs were pushed together in the living room for the boy, and when he saw where he was supposed to sleep, he said in Danish, "That's not a bed, that's just two chairs!" A bed was made up for his mother in the elderly lady's room, which overlooked the street. "I lay awake brooding in my desperation about what to do with Lasse, and I realized I had to take him back with me to Stockholm, even though I didn't have a home for him. The next morning, when Lasse saw me, he said in such surprise, 'Oh, look, there's mamma!' He'd been so convinced I'd left him, I think."

As she lay pondering the future, the streetcars thundered down H.C. Ørsteds Vej. Hours passed, and eventually it felt as if they were driving straight through Astrid's head. More and more, faster and faster. When morning came she was still awake, but she had made a decision. No matter what it cost, Lasse was coming home to Sweden. It was going to be cramped in the room at St. Eriksplan 5, where she had moved after living with Gun in Atlasgatan. Astrid didn't know yet whether her landlady, who was usually at home during the day, could be persuaded to look after Lasse while Astrid was at work. In a hasty letter to Sture in Stockholm, dated January 4, 1930, she called the previous few days "a promenade through hell" and quickly brought him up to speed:

> Arriving in Stockholm Tuesday morning on the early train. Come and fetch me! If I don't make it as expected, then wait. The nine o'clock train gets in immediately afterward. Lasse is arriving in Stockholm a few days later. My more detailed plans, which are very sensible, I can't get into now: Please could you go to the child welfare office and find out how much they consider an appropriate monthly payment for a three-year-old child. Then please be so kind as to send a letter to me immediately, so that I receive it on Monday at the following address: Örstedsvej 70, 3rd floor c/o Kröyer. I'm so longing to come home to you and be cradled.

In February 1929, Astrid described her relationship with Sture in a letter to Anne-Marie Fries: "The boss, married, thirty, has discovered what an incredibly enchanting person I really am, and this manifests itself in the looniest remarks, which—if they're not put a stop to in time—might have serious consequences for me, including potential unemployment. That's another alte Geschichte [old story], of course, which I should have been able to foresee with a bit of mental gymnastics. Alas, I wish I were an angel standing among small angels!"

Home to Sweden

On January 10, 1930, Carl Stevens and Lasse boarded the train to Stockholm. Mrs. Stevens had written to let Astrid know in advance that Carl would probably stay a day or two, see a bit of the Swedish capital, and maybe take a trip to Uppsala to visit another Swedish mother who had once lived at Håbets Allé with her young child. She told Astrid about everything that was packed in the suitcases and bags, and finished with the words: "I'm sending my love to you and little Lasse. Take care, perhaps we'll see each other again, and thank you for the time I had with him. Lasse's godmother!"

The long train journey went well, although Lasse had a chesty cough and tried to kick his "big brother" out of the bunk at regular intervals. Carl, who had an interest in art, spent a few enjoyable days with Astrid and "the amiable Mr. Lindgren." He bought books by Strindberg, went to museums, and admired the architecture in Atlas, the area of Stockholm where Sture lived alone in a small apartment. As soon as he got home, he thanked Lassemamma for a few glorious days in Stockholm. They never saw each other again, Carl and Astrid, but they continued to write to each other until his death in 1988, often reminiscing about the old days and the time they'd spent together. A February 1978 letter from Astrid, for instance, recalled the difficult and challenging period after Carl brought Lasse to Stockholm: "Lasse had whooping cough and obviously wasn't very happy. I stood outside the door and listened to him, hearing him mutter to himself: 'Mother and Esse and Carl are sleeping now!' Can you understand that I'm crying again as I write this?' "

It wasn't just whooping cough that was a problem, but also the fact that Astrid was suddenly taking care of the boy all by herself. In Copenhagen she had always had a capable, experienced "mother" close at hand, but now the responsibility was hers and hers alone. Still, the twenty-two-year-old had learned a lot by watching and listening during her brief stays at Håbets Allé, and she also had her intuition and common sense to rely on. The latter approach was recommended in the preface to the Swedish pediatrician Arthur Fürstenberg's book *A Course in Caring for Children* (En kurs i barnavård), which Astrid kept on her bookshelf: "My advice to young mothers is, to cut a long story short, the following: study childcare in practice and theory sooner rather than later, think about what you're doing, and don't rely uncritically on everything you hear from friends and relatives, no matter how old and experienced they are. It's your child you're looking after, and you're the one responsible for how you fulfill your duties!"

This was sometimes easier said than done. Astrid was frequently cast into doubt. At Auntie Stevens's, for example, Lasse and Esse had always worn warm underclothes at night, so naturally Lasse did the same in Stockholm. For a while his mother would lie awake most of the night, ready to tuck the duvet firmly back around her son when he woke up—hot and sweaty—and tried to kick off the suffocating duvet, telling him drowsily,

Mother and son in Vasa Park, April 1930. Behind them is St. Eriksplan, the square where Astrid and Lasse had been sharing a small room at no. 5 for four months.

"You have to put this over you so you don't catch cold!" One morning, as Astrid sat in her underclothes and had her morning wash, Lasse gazed at her thoughtfully before abruptly saying, "Is mamma the only one allowed to catch cold?"

In March 1930, it became clear that mother and son couldn't continue living together like this. Lasse coughed constantly, and Astrid barely got a wink of sleep before she had to get up and go to work. Rescue came from Småland: Hanna and Samuel August—prompted by Astrid's sisters—offered to let Lasse live at Näs for as long as necessary. Astrid accordingly took a few weeks' vacation in April and traveled down to Vimmerby with Lasse. The boy was now about to enter the fourth home of his short life, where he would have to adapt to yet another family. The move did not prove frictionless. As Astrid Lindgren explained to Margareta Strömstedt in 1967–77: "It was a little Danish-speaking grandchild who arrived at Näs in May 1930. Hanna stood at the gate to meet us, but when she went to hug Lasse he clung to me in a panic and said: 'You mustn't leave me!' Because he thought, of course, that something bad was going to happen to him again."

After a few days' skepticism and caution, Lasse calmed down and began to feel safe, and on April 21 an optimistic Astrid wrote to Sture: "Lasse thrives when he's allowed to go where he pleases. The whole house waits on him hand and foot, the whole farm for that matter, and everyone is competing for his favor."

Mother and son spent a few wonderful weeks together at Näs, where Lasse was taken to all the fantastical places of his mother's childhood and played all the games she had played with Gunnar, Stina, and Ingegerd. She showed him the elm tree in the rectory garden where Uncle Gunnar had once put a hen's egg in an owl's nest. The owls soon hatched a chicken, which Uncle Gunnar sold to Grandma Hanna. Astrid also taught Lasse to make dens and tunnels in the hay in the barn, introducing him to all sorts of animals—small and sweet, big and threatening—including stallions, bulls, and a sow, which Lasse immediately christened Bamsen (Teddy Bear). On other days, mother and son would go on long walks, balancing on stone walls and lying on their backs in the grass to see what shapes the clouds took in the sky, before they both fell asleep and were woken by an insect or a drop of rain. In a letter to Sture dated April 29, 1930, Astrid marveled at how rapidly a young child was able to acclimatize to the countryside: "It's animal cruelty to keep children in the city, even in small cities. A child should be brought up among hens and pigs and the flowers of the field. It's spring here, especially in the evening. It's the same blue spring air that awoke my longing for 'the wonderful' in my tender youth."

The farm, fields and meadows, and animals and people at Näs rapidly became a paradise for four-year-old Lasse, who had only known busy urban life among people in small houses and small spaces. In Småland he could move freely and ramble wherever he chose.

When it rained, Lasse learned some of the old indoor games at Näs. There was the gloriously noisy game of tag played across three or four rooms, in which you shouted "Sicken blås" (what a crash) if you bumped into someone else as you ran. Then there was "Inte stöta golvet" (the equivalent of hot lava), where you had to climb over the furniture to avoid touching the floor.

Those few weeks were lived intensely, and mother and son spent almost every waking hour in each other's company. Yet it didn't take much, realized Astrid, for Lasse's fear of abandonment to resurface, and he missed Auntie Stevens badly. One day, when they were going to a large family birthday celebration, he looked at Astrid with big, frightened eyes and said, "Will I stay there forever?" Another day, at home in Näs, there was a sudden knock on the kitchen door while they were sitting at the table. In came one of the Ericsson aunts, who resembled Lasse's Copenhagen foster mother in stature and appearance. "That's Mother!" shouted Lasse, and immediately wanted to go home with her. Astrid had to play along, a lump in her throat, and only when they reached the aunt's house did Lasse work out that something wasn't right. Astrid stood and held out her hand: "I asked him if he wanted to come home to Näs. And he did. But in the street he stopped short and threw up—the poor child!"

Astrid recounted all of this in a long letter to Carl Stevens in February 1978, in which she also mentioned other examples of how a child might react who was in danger of losing a parental figure or suddenly had to adapt to a new one. As far as her son was concerned, concluded the older Astrid Lindgren in her letter to Carl, "It took a very, very long time for Lasse to feel reasonably safe." She expressed deep gratitude for everything Carl's mother had done for her little boy during the first three years of his life, and what she had meant to him: "It certainly wasn't her fault that things were difficult for Lasse. She was quite simply his mother, and as long as I live I'll be grateful for what she did for him."

In the 1978 letter to Carl, she also commented that Mrs. Stevens probably missed Lasse just as much as he missed her in the years after he left Håbets Allé. Such was indeed the case, as Carl could testify. The family knew how much Marie had struggled with the many losses in her life. She missed not only her daughter, who had died at the age of one, and her husband, who had died in 1921, but many of her foster children, with whom she formed close bonds. One by one, they were taken home by their mothers, or by representatives of the families adopting them. The only one who remained at Villa Stevns year after year was Esse, Lasse's playmate, who didn't leave Copenhagen until he turned eighteen and who was convinced for most of his tenure at Håbets Allé that Mrs. Stevens was his real mother and Carl his real big brother.

A Letter to Esse's Mother

Esse's real name was John Erik, and, like Lasse, he was born at the Maternity Hospital in Copenhagen. His mother—a young, unmarried teacher from Norrland—had traveled to Denmark to give birth anonymously. The woman came from a deeply religious family, and they would neither accept nor understand her bringing home an "illegitimate" child. This is presumably why Esse's mother sat down in the summer of 1931 and wrote a letter to Astrid, whose last name was now Lindgren, and who was living with Sture and Lasse in a two-room apartment with a kitchen and bathroom on Vulcanusgatan in Atlas, Stockholm. Bearing in mind their well-appointed household and secure circumstances, Esse's mother, who had met Lassemamma at Håbets Allé, ventured to ask whether she and her husband might consider adopting Esse.

The offer was kindly but firmly refused in a six-page letter dated August 26, 1931, which Esse's mother allowed Marie Stevens to read. She took a copy and kept it for posterity, because she thought it was one of the cleverest and loveliest things she had ever read about the nature of children and adults' way of dealing with them.

Astrid's letter was a long and earnest attempt to make Esse's mother see reason and persuade her to take responsibility for her child, no matter the opinions or actions of her family or the locals in her small town. Twenty-three-year-old Lassemamma drew on her own feelings of guilt and desperation, describing several of the eye-opening experiences she'd had as a young mother separated from her child, among other young, more or less unhappy mothers separated from theirs. Most remarkable about the letter, thought Mrs. Stevens, was that Astrid saw the problem first and foremost from the child's point of view: "I don't think you really understand what an incredible stressor it is for a young child to be torn up by the roots and replanted like that. I didn't realize either before I took Lasse home. From the outside it can look painless, and the child apparently adapts to his new circumstances rapidly and cheerfully, but every once in a while short episodes occur that reveal the boundless fear and uncertainty beneath."

Astrid Lindgren warned Esse's mother against shunting her child around too much; it would, she said, "damage him for the rest of his life." Instead, she should screw up all the courage and willpower she could muster and take Esse home to the town of her birth, showing him off with pride. At this point Astrid told the story of her own long battle in Vimmerby, which had been waged on two fronts: in the town, where the scandal and gossip were monumental, and at Näs, where Hanna and Samuel August had taken several years to accept the way things stood—and to accept little Lasse:

> I grew up in an ultrarespectable home. My parents are very religious. There has never been a spot on the honor of anyone in our family, nor among any of our relatives. I can still remember, from the time before Lasse was born, my mother's horror and indignation at young women who had so-called illegitimate children. And then I had one. I thought it would kill my parents. Yet I still took Lasse back with me. First to Stockholm, because I hadn't got my parents' permission to bring him home. As soon as I had it, I went to Vimmerby with Lasse.

It seems, then, that the boy hadn't been welcome at Näs during those first few years. This explains why Astrid never mentioned her trips to Copenhagen in her letters to Hanna and Samuel August in 1927–29, never breathed a word about their grandchild's state of health or development, and never enclosed any of the photographs Carl Stevens took of Lasse and Esse outside Villa Stevns to send to Lassemamma in Stockholm and

The bond between Lasse and his grandmother and grandfather, who in 1926–29 had struggled to accept their eldest daughter's new circumstances, became a strong and happy one when he moved to Näs in the spring of 1930. He would remain there until fall 1931.

Lassepappa in Vimmerby. Even while his parents were engaged, Lars Blomberg was a taboo subject in the correspondence between Astrid and her parents during the years 1927–29. Naturally this changed radically in 1930, when Näs became Lasse's new home, and for more than a year both Hanna and Samuel August took care of the boy as if he were their own little latecomer.

It had been infinitely liberating, Astrid wrote in the letter to Esse's mother, to confront the inhabitants of Vimmerby while holding Lasse's hand. Among them was Reinhold Blomberg, who had remarried and had several small children. It felt tremendously satisfying for Astrid to walk around the shops that first day, staring down hypocrisy and intolerance with Lasse, who loudly referred to her as Mamma. No one in the little town had forgotten the editor's divorce case, or Astrid Ericsson's sudden disappearance in 1926:

You should have seen how people stared when I showed up
with Lasse. We walked openly around the town together when I
had an errand to run, and he called me Mamma loud and clear,
so there was no doubt as to who he was. You mustn't think that
all the staring and whispering remotely upset me. We were
hugely confident, both Lasse and I. And it didn't take long before people stopped gawping and whispering, and little by little
I was met with something that actually looked a lot like respect.
For you see, the best way to make people stop talking is to show
them that their suspicions are correct. . . . Mark my words:
There's no shame in having a child. It's a joy and an honor, and
deep down everyone knows that perfectly well.

Of course, that was easy enough for a newly married housewife living
in a modern apartment in Stockholm to say. Still, the words came from the
heart. We don't know what Esse's mother thought of the letter, but the boy
never went to Norrland, remaining instead with his foster mother at Håbets
Allé until he was eighteen, when he moved to Sweden. There he got back in
touch with Lasse and the Lindgren family, as Karin Nyman recalls.

For sixteen months, Lasse lived with his grandmother and grandfather in Småland, and if his mother is to be believed—and her account is
supported by Lars Lindgren's own recollections later in life—his "Noisy
Village-esque" existence at Näs was almost as happy as his mother's had
been. He lived in close and reassuring contact with a big family of siblings,
parents, grandparents, boys, and girls. Lasse often went into Vimmerby
with his grandmother and grandfather, or Aunt Stina, Aunt Ingegerd, or
Uncle Gunnar, and while in town he was occasionally seen by his father,
who thought little Lasse resembled the young girl he'd once been so in love
with. Astrid and Reinhold were still on speaking terms; indeed, their connection was so close that in 1930–31 they exchanged friendly letters in which
she teased him for having fathered almost nothing but boys. She also mentioned this to Auntie Stevens in a Christmas letter dated December 16, 1931:
"Lasse's father in Vimmerby has had another boy; I don't think I told you
that before. I wrote to him (we still write from time to time, which our

Astrid Ericsson and Sture Lindgren got married at Näs on April 4, 1931, shortly after Sture's divorce was finalized. In a letter to Astrid a few weeks earlier, he enclosed a short item from the legal column of the newspaper *Sydsvenska Dagbladet,* which announced that the Royal Skåne County Court had, as Sture put it, "given them a wedding present." What he meant was that he had been excused from paying thirty kronor a month to his ex-wife in alimony, which was the amount she had demanded.

respective spouses are aware of) that he ought to have some girls for a change. Lasse and his new father are better friends than I ever dared hope. Lasse loves and admires my husband, who for his part is rather proud of Lasse and thinks he's a splendid boy."

Astrid Lindgren began the new decade on an optimistic note, marrying Sture on April 4, 1931. The wedding took place not in Vimmerby Church but at Hanna and Samuel August's house at Näs, where the parish priest was their closest neighbor. There was no big party and no big wedding photograph, but Astrid kept the happy couple from the top of the wedding cake in a desk drawer for the rest of her life. A few days after the event, when she explained to Lasse that he now had two fathers, one in Vimmerby and one in Stockholm—adding that they were two of the finest he could wish for and were both very fond of him—Lasse gazed up at his mother and said in Swedish: "I've got three. Carl is my pappa too."

Your Children Are Not Your Children

ON THE FIFTH FLOOR AT VULCANUSGATAN 12, Astrid and Sture tried to keep a handle on their household expenditure with *The Housewife's Practical Account Book* (Husmoderns praktiska kassabok). This was a small brown pamphlet with a front cover in the functional style of the day and an old-fashioned back cover with the words: "Seven rules to be kept by people who don't understand thriftiness." Inside there was plenty of space for numbers and columns organizing household expenses, but other kinds of documentation also found their way onto the pages, including unruly children's drawings in crayon and diary-like entries by the grown-ups, side by side with plucky attempts to keep accounts.

There was plenty to keep an inexperienced young housewife busy, and plenty to spend money on. Under "Miscellaneous" in 1931–32 one can find entries such as: mending shoes (1.35); polishing knives (1.75); vacuum cleaner (20.00); sailboat for Lasse (1.35); J. P. Jacobsen's complete works (10.00); needlework box (4.50); tickets to *Uncle Tom's Cabin* (2.35); and "Stupidity" (8.50), whatever that might mean. There was also a clipping, in English, from the *Dagens Nyheter* tucked between two pages:

> Your children are not your children.
> They are the sons and daughters of Life's longing for itself.
> They come through you but not from you,
> And though they are with you yet they belong not to you.
> You may give them your love but not your thoughts,
> For they have their own thoughts.
> You may house their bodies but not their souls,

For their souls dwell in the house of to-morrow, which you
    cannot visit, not even in your dreams.
You may strive to be like them, but seek not to make them
    like you.
For life goes not backward nor tarries with yesterday.

These prophetic-sounding lines, from the Lebanese poet Kahlil
Gibran's 1923 book *The Prophet,* had prompted Astrid to reach for the
scissors. She couldn't agree more. Children were only borrowed, so you
had to give them all the love and respect you were capable of mustering,
every single day. In her efforts to be a good mother, she had begun to jot
down observations about Lasse, using the back pages of the account book
to record when her son was behaving strangely, saying funny things, or asking one of the questions that often developed into something resembling
dialogue in a Marx Brothers movie:

Lars: Is Grandma your mother?

Mamma: Yes!

Lars: And you're my mother?

Mamma: Yes!

Lars: Tell me, is Grandma my boy?

The four-year-old boy got his own room overlooking the back garden
when he went to live with his mother and new father after his long, happy
stay at Näs, while Sture and Astrid slept in the living room overlooking Vulcanusgatan. Marrying her boss meant that Astrid had to give up her job at
the Royal Automobile Club, but with all the care and attention Lasse needed
it was natural that his mother should stay home as much as possible.

    In early September 1931 Lasse was brought to Stockholm by Hanna
and Samuel August, who had hair-raising stories to tell about Lasse's second summer in Småland. One day the lad had toppled off a high wagonload
and gotten a concussion, then another day he'd nearly been run over by
a car on the road. Yet Hanna also had more cheerful stories about her

grandchild, who came out with so many quips that everyone at Näs agreed he took after his mother. One day he'd been out in the privy for a very long time. "Come on, Lasse!" shouted Hanna, to which the boy replied: "Aw, Grandma, I was just about to go and you've messed up the pressure!"

Lasse had grown over the summer—intellectually, too—and was scarcely a child any longer, Astrid felt. He spoke almost like an adult, considering his age, and this was one of the reasons why she decided to record her son's development on the blank pages at the back of *The Housewife's Practical Account Book.* Her notes soon turned into a fleeting series of moments and episodes strung together like a necklace, significantly shorter than the stories a certain Alma Svensson wrote many years later in blue exercise books at Lönneberga. They were the kind of childhood scenes that could so easily vanish into the fog of memory; Astrid called them Larsiana in the account book. She began her notes with the words: "I know how much fun it would have been to have a bit more material from my childhood. That's the reason I'm writing down some of Lasse's little oddities from memory."

Fall 1931 offered many opportunities to reach for her pen and paper, but most weren't the heartening kind. Lasse's first visit to kindergarten, for example, was not a success. He embroidered a mushroom on a piece of cardboard, but he wasn't remotely interested in sitting with the other children and learning a nursery rhyme by heart. His reaction when they got home was intense, but Astrid felt it was healthy: "Last night Lasse wanted to be alone when he got undressed. When I went in to see how he was doing, he said, 'It's so nice to be alone!' Previously he'd said to me that he thought it was nice to sit together in his room and only turn on the pink lamp, but 'it's actually even nicer to be alone and switch the light on.' I'm glad he needs alone time. He's beginning to grow up."

Sometimes weeks and months went by between Astrid's notes, which encompassed everything from her son's morning routine and visits to the dentist to his language skills, motor function, habits, and daydreams. When he grew up, Astrid learned, Lasse was going to build a perpetual-motion machine, or perhaps they would conquer the North Pole: "Mamma, we're going to do so many exciting things together. I just hope we have time!"

It was a new, reborn Lasse who went to live with Astrid and Sture on Vulcanusgatan in the fall of 1931, after nearly a year and a half at Näs. He now had to adapt once more to new circumstances, a new family, and new playmates.

On August 8, 1933, Astrid Lindgren was working as the Royal Automobile Club's racing secretary when it held its annual Summer Grand Prix for Automobiles, a twenty-mile loop near Norra Vram in Skåne. Europe's best racing drivers and car manufacturers, including Maserati, Ford, and Mercedes, took part, but it was the Italian marquis Antonio Brivio in his Alfa Romeo who won, with an average speed of nearly eighty miles per hour.

More to the point, would they have the money? The household accounts paint an all-too-clear picture: the Lindgren family had to scrimp and
save throughout the 1930s, although thrift didn't come naturally to Sture. It
would be years before he was named director of the Swedish Motorists' Association (Motormännens Riksförbund, "M"), and his salary as a department head didn't cover the Lindgrens' basic expenses, especially not after
Karin was born in 1934. This meant that Astrid had to take on freelance
work and office temping jobs while a nanny looked after the children at
home. One piece of regular, well-paid work was the Royal Automobile
Club's annual travel guide and road atlas, and on several occasions she also
functioned as the racing secretary at the club's popular grand prix. On June
20, 1933, the organization's official magazine, *Svensk Motortidning,* ran a
lengthy article entitled "Vacations for Motorists," written by Astrid Lindgren. It was an excerpt from that year's travel guide, which suggested three
alternative routes through the Scandinavian countryside. The style was col-
loquial, good humored, and bursting with images and movement: "Ok, so
you've finally got some time off and you're looking to explore the father-
land? Excellent. Over the course of a few weeks' vacation you should be
able to see plenty. Mind if I suggest a pleasant little ten- or eleven-day drive
through Sweden and Norway? All right then, here goes. First we head down
to the automobile club and find ourselves a permit to take the car across the
border."

For her exuberant article, the writer had chosen a round trip that went
from Stockholm to Dalarna, then northwest to Trondheim, due south to
Oslo, and back to the Swedish capital via Värmland. She predicted that
most busy motorists would probably whiz past Gustaf Fröding's birthplace
in Karlstad, although it would be worth taking their time: "If, like me, you're
fond of poor old unfashionable Fröding, we can take a peek at his childhood home along the way. But if you're a fan of asphalt poetry and machine
culture and the magic of speed and all the other stuff that's tip and top and
slick nowadays, then I'll just say 'whoa' in Kristinehamn and 'hello baby' in
Örebro, and I won't have time to say 'take a pit stop here,' because we're
already in Västerås."

Futuristic Santa

In 1933 the name Astrid Lindgren also appeared in the newspaper *Stockholms-Tidningen* and the magazine *Landsbygdens jul* (Christmas in the countryside). It was her politically active brother Gunnar—who knew the editor of the new magazine through the youth wing of the Farmers' Union, the S.L.U.—who had put in a good word for his little sister. Astrid needed the money, and she needed to write about something other than cars and the Swedish road network. One day a letter dropped through the mailbox from Mr. Dahnberg, the editor, who was prepared to pay thirty-five kronor for a short story by "the well-known writer Astrid Lindgren." This exaggeration came courtesy of Gunnar's playful sense of humor, but it also reminded Astrid of her former teacher Mr. Tengström, who had once talked up "Vimmerby's Selma Lagerlöf" so much that she'd sworn she would never become a writer. Astrid kept her word for many years, and an auto-biographical text from 1955, preserved among the author's papers at the National Library of Sweden, reveals that she was proud of having resisted for so long: "While the children were little I stayed at home, took care of my duties around the house, played with my children and told them masses of fairy-tales and stories. Occasionally, when I was really short of money, I wrote down a silly little tale or two that I sold to a magazine, but on the whole I kept my promise not to become a writer."

This unexpected opportunity arose during a decade that saw a boom in magazine culture. It was just before radio became the dominant family-oriented medium, and there was still a large market for more or less trivial literature, which could be read aloud on holidays and commercial celebra-tions like Mothers Day in May. Children's literature of the type found in publications like *Landsbygdens jul* was particularly despised by the literary establishment, even though a considerable number of prominent Swedish authors contributed to such publications at the beginning and end of their careers. In 1945 children's literary critic Eva von Zweigbergk called the stories that appeared in such annual magazines "opportunistic fairy-tales," arguing that all these works of dubious literary merit were drowning out the genuine article: "It's lucky that in every generation there have been storytellers with their own voice, voices one wants to listen to and won't forget amid the dreadful output characteristic of the modern age. Weeklies, Sunday supplements, and cheap Christmas magazines are streaming toward children with hastily scribbled stories about trolls and princesses."

Zweigbergk's harsh critique was immortalized in *Children and Books* (Barn och böcker) in 1945, which may explain why Astrid Lindgren later disavowed her fairy-tales and stories in *Landsbygdens jul* (and, after 1939, in the magazine *Mother's Praise* [Mors hyllning]), dismissing them as "youthful sins" and "idiotic tales." Clearly she wasn't proud of them, and it has since become a dogma of Astrid Lindgren research that these fifteen or so short pieces of children's prose shouldn't be considered as anything other than curiosities—pieces revealing artistic weaknesses that Lindgren had put behind her by the time *Pippi Longstocking* appeared in 1945, the same year Eva von Zweigbergk published *Children and Books* with her fellow critic Greta Bolin. Zweigbergk and Bolin lauded good, artistically valuable literature for children of various age groups while pointing the finger at authors who wrote assembly-line stories: "It's probably just as easy to write such fairy-tales as it is to knock out romantic short stories for weekly magazines, just with more irresponsibility hidden behind the ostensibly good intention of entertaining the young. For the child's mind is more impressionable than the adult's."

Today these preliminary attempts are available to read in Astrid Lindgren's archive at the National Library, as well as in the anthology *Santa's Wonderful Radio of Pictures* (Jultomtens underbara bildradio), and a more nuanced perspective suggests itself. True, the stories do contain many clichés, and in certain cases are just as moralizing as Zweigbergk and Bolin accused the interwar "opportunistic fairy-tales" of being. Yet there are also some overlooked gems, including "Maja Gets a Fiancé" (Maja får en fästman, 1937), "Also a Mothers Day Gift" (Också en Morsdagsgåva, 1940), and "Thing-Seeker" (Sakletare, 1941). These three texts—more short stories than fairy-tales and appealing almost as much to adults as children—are clear evidence that Astrid Lindgren was progressing as a writer at the end of the 1930s. She was rapidly finding the distinctive perspective and voice that would write her name into the history of children's literature, on a par with such classic authors as Hans Christian Andersen, Lewis Carroll, J. M.

The happy family in Stockholm, 1933. In a letter to his brother-in-law in 1931, when Gunnar was about to marry Gullan, Sture wrote: "I have the unconquerable urge to tell you that marriage is the greatest gift nature can squander on two people who suit each other—in the long term, too."

Barrie, and Elsa Beskow: authors who, like Lindgren, depicted children in their natural state, independent of the adult world.

In young Astrid Lindgren's fiction from the 1930s and early 1940s, the author inevitably comes across as uncertain and unpracticed, searching for a style and tone, yet unafraid to aim high or be unconventional. Take her debut story, for instance, "Santa's Wonderful Radio of Pictures," which first appeared in the *Stockholms-Tidningen*'s Christmas supplement in 1933 and was reprinted in *Landsbygdens jul* in 1938.

The reader is introduced to a Lasse-like seven-year-old, the inquisitive and plucky Lars from Backagården. One day Lars ventures into a cave, where he finds one of the planet's most fabled father figures sitting in an ordinary armchair with a pair of headphones on his head. Santa is online, as we'd say these days, plugged into a hi-tech radio with a screen, which is linked up to surveillance cameras in every Swedish household. "You see," as Father Christmas says to Lars, "even Santa has to keep up with the times."

It was indeed a new age in Sweden, an age in which northern Europe had been struck by unemployment and widespread agricultural and industrial crises in the wake of the Wall Street crash of 1929. Yet in Sweden—at least among the younger generation—there was a palpable and increasing sense of faith in the future. Some people have suggested that this optimism was due to the Stockholm Exhibition in 1930, which showcased a new age and new mindset through its emphasis on functional design, promising new apartments in bigger cities, more cars, and radios and movies for the common man. Others have explained it with the rise of the Social Democrats to power in 1932. Four years earlier, Per Albin Hansson had presented his vision of *Folkhemmet*, the People's Home, when he spoke about future welfare for all and emphasized that there were neither "favorites nor stepchildren, the privileged nor the vulnerable, in a good home." It set in motion progress away from poverty toward the welfare state, which would come to have a huge nationwide impact on the notion of what it meant to be Swedish.

Sharp-witted and imaginative readers of the Christmas story in the *Stockholms-Tidningen*'s 1933 supplement might even have wondered whether the futuristic Santa represented the newly powerful Social Democrats, who had formed a government one year earlier, promising shared social resources as well as equal rights and opportunities for citizens. Was it, perhaps, the prime minister himself, Per Albin Hansson, whom the unknown female writer had dressed up in headphones and a big beard for her humorous Christmas story? It's a rather far-fetched interpretation, admittedly, yet her depiction of old St. Nicholas was certainly highly sophisticated, playing with the frightening thought that Santa can spy on individual citizens from their earliest childhood, stepping in as their moral guardian: "Because Kalle has been naughty every single day, he's not getting any Christmas presents."

Sermonizing

If there's one thing that characterizes Astrid Lindgren's work, it's the absence of Sunday school stories, or what she called sermonizing. In her initial years writing for *Landsbygdens jul,* she clearly struggled to free herself from the old-fashioned style of didactic writing she had grown up with as a child among the storytellers on the farm, but at the apartment in Vulcanusgatan, sermonizing and Sunday school stories were rare. And she would launch into stories at any time or place, remembers Karin Nyman. "It wasn't like she would settle down to tell a story. The story always arose out of something else. Except at bedtime, when she *had* to entertain Lasse or me by reading stories. She made up her own or retold other people's."

Elves and trolls were everywhere in the Lindgren family. Magical creatures that emerged from the Småland-made nooks in Astrid's memory, or from the Scandinavian folk tales and picture books by Elsa Beskow and John Bauer that Astrid, Sture, and the children studied diligently in the 1930s. Karin Nyman recounts that her father was supposed to go into town one day to buy a new suit of clothes but instead came home with an illustrated two-volume edition of Hans Christian Andersen's fairy-tales in Danish, which took a place on Astrid Lindgren's bookcase alongside other family classics: "We read Elsa Beskow's picture books, of course. All of them, I'm sure, and above all Hans Christian Andersen, which our mother read or retold for us, especially 'Little Claus and Big Claus,' though I remember 'The Tinderbox' best myself. And we got Winnie the Pooh, Doctor

Proud grandparents at Christmas and New Year 1934 at Näs. Karin is on her grand-mother Hanna's lap, Lasse in the middle, and Gunvor, daughter of Gunnar and Gullan, in her grandfather's arms.

Dolittle, *The Wonderful Adventures of Nils,* Mark Twain, Swedish folk tales, *One Thousand and One Nights,* the satirical adventures of Falstaff, fakir, and the magazine *Bland tomtar och troll* [Among pixies and trolls] regularly. When Astrid told stories, she only ever did it on impulse. If she was thinking of them in moralistic or didactic terms, then that went right over my head."

Just as the stories Lasse and Karin's mother came up with weren't intended to be educational, her ideas when it came to child-rearing weren't rigid or formulaic. Astrid's teaching was neither old-fashioned nor modern, says Karin Nyman, but imbued with the common sense she and her three siblings at Näs had been brought up with: "The upbringing I got when I was young was quite conventional, I suppose. My father never got involved. I was mostly a 'well-behaved' child, and Astrid was the one who scolded us when necessary. Most likely her ideas about raising children were the same as the ones she had experienced as a child—total parental authority, but without unnecessary meddling in the child's life and without any hectoring. I was expected to curtsey to adults, say my bedtime prayers and 'obey.' But I got exaggerated praise for most of what I did, teaching myself to write at the age of five, writing short stories and that sort of thing."

On the few occasions Astrid Lindgren did moralize to her children, she found that they saw through it. In literary terms, she discovered that didactic elements in stories and fairy-tales weren't merely superfluous but that they underestimated children's ability to think for themselves. This experience would become a cornerstone of Astrid Lindgren's work. That both Lasse and Karin helped shape this foundation is documented in their mother's many small observations about her children at various ages and stages of development, which were either noted in the account book or immortalized in diary entries and letters to friends and acquaintances. Later in life, Astrid Lindgren was able to recall off the top of her head some of the moments when Lasse or Karin realized she was sermonizing. In a Swedish newspaper in the mid-1950s, for instance, Astrid described the wish lists she always wrote for Lasse and Karin when they were young, so that they knew what gifts their mother wanted: "Once, when the children were little, I concluded the list with a sanctimonious wish for 'two well-behaved children.' But my son justly remarked, 'Will there be space for all four of us?' So I struck that one out."

Another example Astrid noted in the account book was from Christmas 1930—Lasse's first in Sweden—which was celebrated at Näs. As usual, lutfisk was served at the Ericsson family table, and as usual Astrid's stomach turned at the sight of the jellylike fish, though evidently her son's didn't: "Lasse ate lutfisk, which I've never been able to bring myself to do. I praised him and said that Santa would definitely say he was a good boy. Lasse's question in response: 'Okay, then what's he going to say to you?'"

Such spontaneous, morally disarming remarks were a large part of why the didactic tone in Astrid Lindgren's first works of fiction quietly disappeared. There were clumsy messages in stories like "Johan's Christmas Eve Adventure" (Johans äventyr på julafton) from 1933, where children were informed that you can get into trouble if you're naughty and mean to others. And there were moral lessons in "Hocus Pocus" (Filiokus) from 1934 and "Pumpernickel and His Brothers" (Pumpernickel och hans bröder) from 1935, which were about what happens to children if they're disobedient and lazy. By 1936, however, something had happened to Astrid Lindgren's writing: that year, she sent two distinctly different stories to *Landsbygdens jul,* "The Big Rat Ball" (Den stora råttbalan) and "Christmas Eve in Lilltorpet" (Julafton i Lilltorpet), each of which addressed readers on two separate levels.

"The Big Rat Ball" takes place in the fall. Mice and rats, returning indoors, organize a party that will never end. The story is an allegorical, satirical depiction of the social mechanisms that become apparent during celebrations, and was thus a tale more for adults than for children—something underscored by the author's use of long compound Swedish words for terms like "rat society," "gentlewoman," "charming," and "railway town." "Christmas Eve in Lilltorpet," on the other hand, was aimed at the younger readers of *Landsbygdens jul.* This deeply melancholy fairy-tale is about Death, who comes, instead of Santa Claus, to visit an impoverished rural household. A single mother of six is ill, and the doctor can't get through in the snowstorm. Ten-year-old Sven, desperate enough to try and fetch help, also has to give up the battle with the forces of nature, and as he sits crying, hungry and numb with cold in Lilltorpet with his four younger siblings, his big sister Anna-Märta keeps watch over their mother's deathbed:

> She's sitting on a chair at the head of the bed, a melancholy little figure in a blue dress she's long since grown too big for. Her index finger traces the woodwork on the bedstead pensively while she waits. It's cold in the room, where the fire is rarely lit. Anna-Märta is shivering a little. For the last time, her mother Katarina wakes up from her torpor. She looks at her daughter and stretches out a groping hand. With her last ounce of strength, she forces out a few words: "Anna-Märta . . . I'm

dying . . . look after the little ones." Anna-Märta nods mutely. Then suddenly all is still.

The narrator pulls out all the stops in this sentimental, social-realist story. For the first time in these early Astrid Lindgren tales, one senses a narrator who is mature and omnipotent yet shows interest in and solidarity with children, and who in certain passages is both empathetic and intellectually perceptive: "Anna-Märta recognizes the silence; it was the same when her father died." There is no moral to the story, and no blame laid on anyone or anything. None of her readers are made to feel guilty. They are, however, invited to feel sympathy for a child grown up much too fast and much too brutally, and who receives the narrator's full attention to the very end: "Evening came. All of them went to sleep except Anna-Märta, who still had plenty to do. At last she too was finished, and crept into the wooden bench beside her little brother. Now it loosens, the lump that's been stuck in her throat all day long. Anna-Märta cries, hushed and still, so as not to wake her siblings. Anna-Märta is just thirteen. Perhaps she's a heroine anyway. But she doesn't understand that. Outside it's still snowing."

What Does an Engagement Cost

A year later, with the story "Maja Gets a Fiancé," printed in *Landsbygdens jul,* Astrid Lindgren inhabited her main character fully, observing the world through the eyes of a five-year-old. His name is Jerker, and—like his two older siblings—he thinks the family's maid, Maja, is the loveliest surrogate mother in the world. Not only can she cook and look after children, she tells fairy-tales and radiates a warmth and intimacy the children's mother can't compete with. The latter is more interested in her social standing, and one day, when the grandest ladies in town are visiting, carrying on a lively, carping conversation over coffee and cakes, Jerker overhears them say that Maja is so ugly she'll never get a fiancé.

Jerker knows the word "ugly" and his mind boggles, because in his eyes Maja is beautiful. The other word the grand ladies keep repeating—"fiancé"—Jerker doesn't know. The boy thinks it over and realizes that he

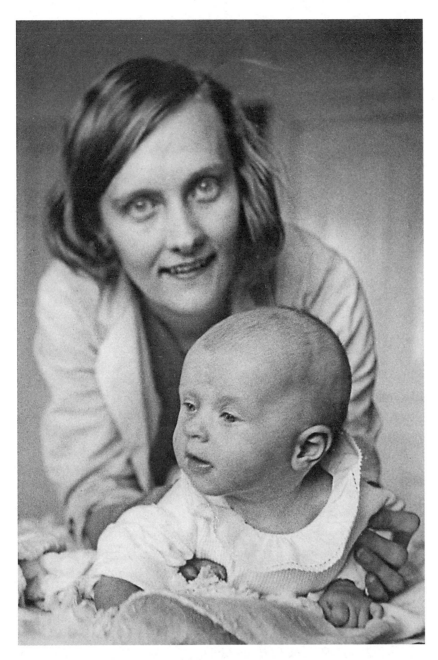

Karin was born at 12:50 a.m. on May 21, 1934, weighing ten pounds, nine ounces. In the days leading up to the birth Astrid had been feeling run down, suffering from a cold, exhaustion, and a "heavy stomach," as she put it in her private notes about the birth.

needs to get Maja a fiancé, cost what it will. So he empties his piggy bank and heads down to the local shopkeeper, who is new in town. On the way Jerker thinks: "There's no knowing how much a fiancé might cost, but for five öre I should be able to get a really nice one." The young shopkeeper listens with interest as Jerker explains his errand, the five-öre piece clenched in his fist, and Jerker is pleased. He isn't used to grown-ups listening to him: "He still wasn't laughing, Jerker realized with satisfaction. It often happened that grown-ups acted serious at first, then suddenly, when you least expected it, started laughing at you."

The shopkeeper asks casually why Jerker wants to buy a fiancé. Who is it for? The boy can't help but pour his heart out to the sympathetic grown-up. The shopkeeper listens with even more interest, and says that Jerker can easily get a fiancé for five öre, but that he can't carry one home himself. For that he needs a grown man, so the kindly shopkeeper volunteers to drop by that evening: " 'Oh, but I'll be asleep then,' objected Jerker. 'There's no other way. I can't leave here any sooner, you see.' 'Then it's a deal,' decided Jerker. Then he went home, very pleased with himself. The matter was settled. Maja was going to get a fiancé, just like all the other young ladies."

This charming tale from 1937, in which children's and adults' different perspectives on the world collide but eventually accommodate each other, is the first example of Astrid Lindgren's ability to enter the mind of a child and interpret reality with a child's logic. Her stories for children soon became increasingly ambitious. From 1939 on, some of them were also printed in *Mors hyllning*, which was published annually before Mothers Day. Fairy-tales and fables about pixies, trolls, and talking animals had to cede ground in the late 1930s to more contemporary, realistic stories drawn from the everyday lives of children, informed by the author's familiarity with what motivated and concerned them.

These efforts were virtually identical to the program for a new kind of children's literature laid out by Alva Myrdal in 1939, in the preface to the Swedish edition of Lucy Sprague Mitchell's classic *Here and Now Story Book*. Myrdal, on a trip to the United States in the 1920s, found Mitchell's book, a collection of experimental fairy-tales for children aged two to seven.

The Swedish politician, who had a particular interest in the family, wrote books about the welfare of children and adults in urban environments in the 1930s, as well as about toys and the education of small children. In her preface, she remarked that contemporary writers for children needed to be more in tune with both children and the modern urban life into which more and more of them were being born. New, contemporary children's literature must engage with the child's own tangible reality and vibrant internal world: "Children's literature is changing. People are beginning to look for 'real' fairy-tales: fairy-tales that are suited to children as they really are. Adult power is diminishing. . . . More than anything else, then, contemporary storytelling must bring urban environments and modern working life into the fantastical world of the child."

What was new about thirty-year-old Astrid Lindgren's stories in *Landsbygdens jul* and *Mors hyllning* in the years 1937–42 was not merely that she wrote about concrete, recognizable children in a concrete, recognizable world. It was the *way* she did it: not from on high, as in earlier children's literature, but from the inside out. From a perspective that made it clear the adult narrator had emotionally and intellectually entered the imaginative world of childhood—on the child's terms—to depict the needs, motivations, and intentions behind children's thoughts and actions.

Behaviorism on the Bookshelf

We might ask ourselves how much inspiration Astrid Lindgren drew from the field of child psychology, which took a quantum leap during the interwar period, producing dozens of new theories and methodologies that were widely translated, presented, and discussed in 1930s Sweden. Researchers and prominent figures in the field, including A. S. Neill, Alfred Adler, and Bertrand Russell, visited Sweden and gave lectures and interviews that were widely discussed, especially in the culturally radical press. There is no doubt that Astrid kept abreast of such debates about child-rearing through the *Dagens Nyheter*, so it's a little surprising to find almost none of the many child psychology and pedagogical works published in Swedish in the 1930s among the author's four thousand–volume collection of books. According to the lists in the archive at the National Library, she owned no works from that period by Neill, Russell, Jean Piaget, Maria Montessori, Charlotte Bühler, Hildegard Hetzer, John Dewey, Adler, Friedrich Fröbel, Sigmund Freud, or, for that matter, Alva Myrdal. The only two titles are D. A. Thom's *Normal Youth and Its Everyday Problems* (1932) and John B. Watson's *Psychological Care of Infant and Child* (1928), which challenged its readers on the title page with the words: "Dedicated to the first mother who brings up a happy child."

Both Thom and Watson belonged to the school of psychology called "behaviorism," founded by John B. Watson in 1913. Behaviorism reached Europe in the twenties, when Watson's books were translated into a number of European languages and published throughout Scandinavia. As a movement, behaviorism rejected the existence of all psychological phenomena that couldn't be observed externally, and Watson—who was thus in opposition to the Freudian school—claimed that psychology should concern itself solely with the observable behavior of human beings: their physical reactions, movements, and actions.

Watson's hands-on, down-to-earth psychology earned him many followers among interwar parents of young children, who were curious to know more about the mysterious nature behind their children's patterns of behavior. His books proved especially sensational because Professor Watson was a talented salesman, familiar with public psychology and aware that provocative messages sell: "*No one today knows enough to raise a child. The world would be considerably better off if we were to stop having children for twenty years (except those reared for experimental purposes) and were then to start again with enough facts to do the job with some degree of skill and accuracy. Parenthood, instead of being an instinctive art, is a science.*"

The scientific facts alluded to were Watson's famous and eventually infamous behaviorist studies of an infant's instinctive reactions to fire, a rat, a rabbit, and a dog, as well as to the sound of heavy percussion behind its back. The experiments were intended to prove, for instance, that "fear" wasn't inherited but was conditioned through environmental influences. This notion was far from self-evident in the 1920s, before child psychology had undergone its scientific breakthrough.

The Lindgren family going swimming at Nordkap (North Cape), which was the local name for the large, soft cliffs on Furusund's northeastern point, overlooking the Baltic.

There is reason to believe that, as the mother of a small boy who had been pulled up by his fragile roots several times, the twenty-four- or twenty-five-year-old Astrid Lindgren took an immediate interest in Watson's studies of fear and its causes. What triggered panic in a child, and how could a parent teach him or her to control such emotions? Watson claimed this was possible, just as one could teach a child to read, write, and play with blocks.

Her encounter with Watson's behaviorist theories in the early 1930s did not, however, make Astrid Lindgren approach raising Lasse and Karin any differently, or any more methodically. She seems to have skimmed *Psychological Care of Infant and Child* with interest, but also with a healthy dose of skepticism and critical distance. The young mother took what she could use, chiefly the idea that parents should carefully observe their child's behavior from birth onward, and ignored Watson's less helpful advice— particularly the professor's warning against kissing and hugging one's child too much, lest it encourage chronic mushiness: "Never hug and kiss them, never let them sit in your lap. If you must, kiss them once on the forehead when they say goodnight."

As far as demonstrative affection went, Astrid Lindgren couldn't have been farther from Watson's behaviorism. Plenty of family photographs from the 1930s and 1940s show a mother who couldn't hide her love for her two children, poised at any moment to kiss and hug them. As Karin Nyman recalls: "Our mother cuddled us a lot. She often said she loved us, frequently in Smålandic. She had an expression, probably a quotation, I don't know where she got it from: 'Come here so I can squeeze the suet out of you,' meaning very hard. And she said that a lot!"

My Chubby Little Daughter

For several years, in letters to Reinhold, Anne-Marie, Gunnar, and Sture, Astrid had been putting into practice Professor Watson's basic advice— stay observant, and always keep notes on how your child's life is being "conditioned"—and she maintained this focus on their development throughout the thirties and forties. Not simply in the accounts book, but also in her diary entries and in letters, now primarily addressed to Stina, Ingegerd, and her sister-in-law Gullan, who had married Gunnar in 1931. After the wedding she had sent Gullan a congratulatory note in the facetious, ironic tone the four siblings excelled at all their lives:

Dear little Gullan! My warmest congratulations! They say sisters-in-law are the absolute worst, but I hope we won't come to feel that way. I still know so little about you, little sister-in-law, but I hope you'll let us get to know one other better when I come home for Christmas. You end up with such a horrible number of "hope"s when you write a letter like this one, but in any case I hope that Gunnar doesn't hit you until you bleed, doesn't run off with anyone else or behave like a brutal ox in some other fashion. But he is my beloved little brother, after all, so for your part you mustn't dare make him anything other than happy. But I'm sure you will be happy, even without my plea. My husband seconds my congratulations. Till we meet again, then! Your devoted Astrid.

Gullan and Astrid didn't just get married within the same year; they gave birth almost simultaneously in the early summer of 1934, and both had girls—Karin and Gunvor—who eventually became just as close as their mothers. Astrid and Gullan remained good friends until the latter's death in 1984, and in the obituary Astrid sent to the *Vimmerby Tidning* she emphasized that Gullan had always remained her own woman, even though she never drew attention to herself. She had been a pillar of strength for the whole family throughout half a century. The bond between the two had always been strong, says Karin Nyman: "In their later years, when they were both widows, they maintained a close relationship on the telephone, telling each other what they were going to make for dinner. Gullan confided unreservedly in her loved ones, and I can imagine that Astrid told her more about her private life than she did most people. They didn't chat so much about their daily lives, I think, but about people. Astrid was strongly attached to Gullan, and missed her when she died."

Around the time of her own and Gullan's delivery in summer 1934, Astrid began to keep a kind of logbook of Karin's development during the first year of her life, which her daughter could read when she was older. Astrid sent Gullan an extract in her New Year's letters: "If you're not already doing it, I think you should keep this sort of daily record of your child, because it's really quite a fun thing to have." Astrid's began in May 1934:

Summer at Näs in the mid-1930s. In the middle of the picture, from top to bottom: Stina, Gunnar, Astrid (in the white hat), Karin crawling, Samuel August with Gunvor in his arms, and Ingegerd at the bottom.

May 20. Woke at two in the morning with symptoms. To the maternity ward at six. Severe contractions all day. Hellish agony from seven a.m.

May 21. Gave birth to my chubby little daughter at ten to one at night. 4,730 g.

May 22. Karin looks like Sture.

23. Producing milk. Karin is sweet and quiet. Lars has got his long-awaited front tooth.

24. Lars has a fever, oh dear, oh dear, oh dear. If only I were home. Karin had colic and screamed like she was possessed, I cried a bit from exhaustion.

25. I had a slight fever. Karin sweet and quiet. Lars healthy again.

27. Karin screamed incessantly the whole of Mothers Day.

28. Karin quiet and sweet. Fever increased.

29. Rain fell, and I cried in the morning. Higher temperature. Worried about Karin.

30. Despair. Running out of milk, and Karin supplemented with cow's milk. Screaming as if possessed.

31. The end of a difficult May. The last day was a bit better. Karin much calmer, my temp. lower.

June 2. Karin screamed.

June 3. Cried in morn. Karin not putting on weight. Now she's to be fed every three hours.

4. Allowed to get up for the first time.

5. Karin screams and throws up.

6. Gunnar and Gullan have had a girl. Karin screams, screams. And throws up.

After her delivery on May 21 at Södra BB, a maternity hospital in Stockholm, Astrid wrote a letter to her sister-in-law in Småland. Gullan was a first-time mother, and would have needed a bit of encouragement from someone who'd believed—for the second time in her life—that she might die: "Dear Gullan, don't be scared. I'm sure you'll be fine. If, like me, you think you're going to die, I can reassure you that nearly everybody thinks that, but dying really isn't that easy."

Gullan gave birth on June 5, 1934, and survived. In the months that followed, the sisters-in-law continued their correspondence, which was mainly about the girls' weight, their experiences breast-feeding, different kinds of vegetable purée, rubber pants, dietary supplements, and various cures for rickets. And in her little logbook, Astrid paid close attention to Karin's day-to-day development. In February 1935, the girl turned eight months, and thankfully could do more than scream and spit up:

2. Karin said "mamma-pappa" this morning. Had her first egg.

3. Karin has tummy ache. Screamed and wouldn't sleep.

4. Karin crawled a long way backward. (And the world's still standing?)

Underneath the Grown-Ups' Table

Her observations about children, whether her own or their playmates, cousins, or random children on the street or at the park, really started finding their way into Astrid Lindgren's fiction only at the end of the 1930s, and they helped shape her narrative perspective. This development can be traced from "Christmas Eve in Lilltorpet" to "Maja Gets a Fiancé" in 1936–37, and is clearly apparent in "Also a Mothers Day Gift" and "Thing-Seeker," both of which were printed in *Mors hyllning* in 1940–41. In these two short stories, Astrid Lindgren found her own space as a writer: underneath the grown-ups' table, with the children who hadn't started school yet.

"Also a Mothers Day Gift" is about two sisters who want to give their mother a newborn kitten on Mothers Day. First they have to wait for the cat to give birth, then they have to find its litter. Without any authorial interjections, the reader follows two ordinary children on a day like any other in a place that could be anywhere in 1930s Sweden. The story begins in a "place to be alone," like the one Lasse asked his mother not to enter after their unsuccessful visit to kindergarten in spring 1931. One day in 1937, three-year-old Karin had also built a similar space under the kitchen table in

Lasse and Karin at the photographer's in the late 1930s.

Vulcanusgatan, with the help of some old clothing and assorted odds and ends. Eventually Astrid peered under the table and said: "No, I don't like you when you do that!" And Karin replied after a little pause: "Mamma, I don't like myself either! This is just silly! But maybe I had some silly blood in my tummy!"

In "Also a Mothers Day Gift," Lillstumpan and her big sister Anna-Stina set up their den underneath a large folding table in the kitchen, screened from the grown-ups, who are busy in the outside world, beyond the borders of the tablecloth. Only Snurran, the cat, is allowed to stay with the sisters, who have their own sovereign perspective on the world outside: "There were Mother's feet in black flat shoes—they were always so busy— and the servant Maja's, which seemed to dance around; there were Father's feet in big boots and sometimes old Grandfather's feet, which tottered gingerly across the floor in thick felt slippers. The grown-ups' conversation and laughter didn't disturb the whispered small-talk underneath the table. They had the den all to themselves."

A year later, in 1941, Astrid Lindgren ventured even further into the magical world of childhood in the short story "Thing-Seeker," which is about the treasure trove of experiences a four-year-old can gather on a single afternoon of free, uninterrupted play. In the opening scene, Kajsa is sitting on a little red stool in the kitchen while her mother stands next to her, kneading dough at the table. The narrator zooms in on the interaction between mother and child. Kajsa's flights of fancy are neither halted nor guided by an adult hand, and the scene at the kitchen table is a study in the close, respectful relationship between children and grown-ups that so much of Astrid Lindgren's work builds on—and seeks. Kajsa tells her mother that she's soon going to set off on a journey to look for treasure. Her mother listens, asking careful and sympathetic questions about the four-year-old's big plans, and Kajsa is so grateful for her mother's interest and confidence that she dedicates one of her important future finds to her on the spur of the moment. Nothing less than a gemstone will do: " 'Just a little gold nugget is all I want for myself,' said Kajsa. 'Or maybe a diamond.' 'Yes, maybe,' said her mother, putting the final tray of buns in the oven. Kajsa smoothed her little red apron over her stomach and walked over to the door on her chubby little legs. 'Farewell, I'm going now, diddley-dum and diddley-dai!' 'Farewell, my love,' said her mother, 'but don't go too far.' 'No,' said Kajsa, turning around at the door. 'Only a thousand kilometers.' "

After the four-year-old says goodbye to her mother, her powers of imagination drive the narrative on her thing-finding journey. The essence of play is revealed as its extravagance: play is never rational or measured but is based on sheer enthusiasm. The child acts of her own accord, sovereign, without intervention from the adult world. First Kajsa feeds the hens, and next she finds a dead bird with a yellow beak and lovely dark-blue wings, then a snail's shell full of beautiful sounds, and then an old coffee dripper she can use to find gold dust. Every object in this imaginative tour de force gives rise to a new phase in the game, sketching out a new direction. From the porch steps to the

henhouse, then to the old spruce tree, the heap of stones, and the pond, over
the fence and into the woods, down to the junkyard with all the trash from
town and out onto the large dirt road, where there are some pretty flowers to
be picked . . . but then tiredness sets in, and Kajsa is convinced she's lost.
Before long, however, Andersson from Lövhult comes clattering along in his
milk cart and asks one of the grown-up questions children find so strange:
" 'Well I never! Is that Kajsa?' 'Who else would it be?' said Kajsa, stretching
up her arms toward him. 'Help me up, I want to go home to Mamma.' "

Park Aunties

The basic pedagogical approach in Astrid Lindgren's short stories for
Landsbygdens jul and *Mors hyllning* around 1940—and in "Måns Starts
School" from 1942, which explored the theme of bullying roughly thirty
years before the term entered the Scandinavian classroom—had been cob-
bled together from various different sources: partly from the author's own
childhood experiences, and from everything she had read and heard as a
young mother, and partly from what she learned in the 1930s from her daily
interactions with children and parents.

Vasa Park and its "park aunties" came to play an important role in this
regard. That was Astrid's term for the mothers around her age, especially Alli
Viridén and Elsa Gullander, whom she got to know in 1934–35, when they
would go for walks with their strollers and sit on the benches around the playground in Vasa Park. Her first meeting with Alli Viridén, Astrid Lindgren later
recalled, gave little indication that they would become friends. Alli's little girl,
named Margareta but never called anything but Matte, seemed unusually pre-
cocious, and Astrid asked one day how old she was. Her mother's answer was
so guarded that Astrid promised herself she would never approach her again.
But a few days afterward they began talking and took a stroll around the park
with their strollers, chatting about children, family, and society.

Gradually these walks around the park became a tradition, continuing—
eventually without the strollers—for nearly sixty years. By that point their
daughters had long since grown up, of course, and had children of their
own, but Alli and Astrid, who both lived near the rolling park with its rock

Mother and daughter in 1935, ready to go for a walk in Vasa Park with other mothers of small children in the local area. Twenty years later, in a letter to her mother and father in Småland, Astrid Lindgren wrote: "In a moment my park aunties, Alli, Elsa Gullander, and Karin Bené, are coming to lunch here, and later we're going to the theater to see *Don Juan*."

formations and dense, ancient trees, kept arranging to meet there, among new generations of parents and children. Such trips had their own predetermined choreography, recalls Karin Nyman. Astrid, coming from Dalagatan, approached the park from the east, while Alli approached from the west, through St. Eriksplan and Atlas; they always met in the middle, where the wide gravel paths crossed, between the old candelabra-shaped linden trees and the playground.

For Astrid Lindgren, whether she was taking a walk, sitting on a bench, or watching from a window in her apartment, Vasa Park also functioned as a psychological laboratory, where she could observe human behavior and personality types, as well as children's games and parents' interactions with their sons and daughters. Even on her first few strolls through the park in 1930–31, Astrid was surprised and upset by what she saw. As she told Margareta Strömstedt in 1976–77: "It was when Lasse was little, and I took him for a walk in Vasa Park, that it really struck me how much children were browbeaten and trampled on by grown-ups. I realized that we rarely listened to them, we 'brought them up' by scolding them and even hitting them. I felt outraged on children's behalf, and the feeling was reinforced when my children started school and I encountered the demands and authoritarianism there."

The progressive view of child-rearing Astrid Lindgren advocated as an author and cultural commentator, which had become evident in her fiction by the late 1930s, took a sharp turn on December 7, 1939. At the bottom of page 13 in the *Dagens Nyheter,* squeezed between large advertisements for stockings, aspirin, and vermouth, was an opinion piece entitled "The Youth Revolt."

The article was ostensibly written by a rebellious teenager. In fact, it drew on a presentation thirteen-year-old Lars Lindgren had given in his secondary school classroom, which his mother had helped him write. Astrid was so taken with the subject matter—"On the Art of Being a Child"—that she reworked Lasse's text and sent it in to the *Dagens Nyheter.* The piece was heavily edited by the op-ed team: half the original text was cut, and the rest was sharpened and presented under the catchier title "The Youth Revolt." An extra line was added near the beginning ("This is a revolutionary speaking"), and *Huckleberry Finn* was swapped out for the author Edgar T.

Summer 1938: the Ericsson clan, gathered on the steps of the house at Näs. Around the two parents, from left to right, are Ingegerd's husband, Ingvar; Ingegerd; Stina and (hidden) her husband, Hans Hergin; Gullan (with little Barbro in her arms); Astrid; and Gunnar. On the bottom step are Karin, Lasse, and Gunvor.

Lawrence in order to better suit the age bracket of the writer. Whether Astrid Lindgren was involved in these changes is unknown, but Ulla Lundqvist's account of the episode in *The Child of the Century* (Århundradets barn), where one can read the article in its original form, offers no indication of that. Nonetheless, the final version packed a punch:

The Youth Revolt

It's not easy being a child, I read recently in a newspaper, and I was utterly astonished, because it's not every day one reads something in the papers that's genuinely true. This is a revolutionary speaking.

It's not easy being a child, no! It's difficult, very difficult. So what does it mean—being a child? It means you have to go to bed, get dressed, eat, brush your teeth, and blow your nose when it suits adults, not when it suits you. It means you have to eat rye bread when you'd rather have white bread, that you have to run down to the store to get a token for the gas without batting an eye, just as you've settled down with Edgar T. Lawrence. It means, moreover, that you've got to listen to the most personal comments from any adult about your appearance, state of health, clothing, and prospects without a word of complaint.

I have often wondered what would happen if we started treating adults in the same manner.

Adults have a tiresome fondness for comparisons. They love talking about their own childhoods. From what I understand, in the whole of human history there has never existed a more intelligent and well-brought-up generation of children than our mothers' and fathers'. . . . A.L. / L IV.

These were the words of a mother writing in the guise of a young, antiauthoritarian high school student on behalf of oppressed children and young people everywhere. The signature "A.L. / L IV" represented a fictional Astrid Lindgren, a student on the Latinlinjen (an educational track that focused on the humanities) in the fourth year. And while the *Dagens Nyheter* editors had amped up the revolutionary angle, making the text blunter and more pugnacious, the article's satirical dissection of parental double standards and exercises of power reveals that Astrid Lindgren was approaching a crossroads. She had to make a choice: continue writing journalistic pieces that were seldom printed, or stake everything on her literary talent?

Astrid's Monkey Tricks

As adults, both Lasse and Karin confirmed that Astrid Lindgren was an atypical mother, equally willing to help her son write a school presentation as to join in with her children's games and leisure pursuits. She was rarely slow to let her own inner child out to play, whether in cozy little indoor games and activities at home in Vulcanusgatan, where the family drew pictures and told stories, or during more physically demanding outdoor activities like sledding, swinging, climbing, running, hopping, jumping, skiing, or skating, either in Vasa Park or nearby Karlsberg Palace Park.

Astrid revealed herself to be a shrewd participant—she knew that an adult's primary contribution to children's games was simply giving them the opportunity to play. Lasse and Karin were never directed when and how to do so. As Astrid put it in an interview in *Vecko Journalen* in spring 1949, "Leave young people in peace, but be within reach if they need you." She raised her children and played with them according to that rule, says Karin Nyman: "I don't think there were ever any situations where Astrid told us children, 'Now we're going to play.' Or where I asked her to. I do remember always wanting to be with her; somehow it was always so eventful and never boring."

Astrid Lindgren reflected on her style of parental authority in a radio broadcast in December 1978. Pippi's mother emphasized that "every child needs norms," explaining her educational technique when it came to Lasse and Karin with the words, "I took their side against myself." It was precisely this dual role—being at once parent and child—that she had taken in the indignant op-ed in the *Dagens Nyheter* in 1939, and she never got so old that she lost that rare skill.

Lithe and slender, Astrid Lindgren could activate her "game-playing" gene at the flick of a switch. Her inner child was always ready to play, except when she was writing, when she had to settle for giving her imagination free rein. When Lindgren was in Motala in 1977 to celebrate the local radio station's birthday, she clambered up one of the tempting radio towers as agilely as a squirrel, much to the delight of the photographer. The same thing happened when the seventy-year-old author, accompanied by her friend Elsa Olenius—ten years older, equally fond of games and every bit as media-savvy—scaled a pine tree, loudly announcing to all the photographers on the ground that there was nothing in the Law of Moses against old biddies climbing trees. At an even more advanced age, when she was no longer physically capable of scrambling up radio towers and pine trees, she instead wrote a newspaper article about her fondness for climbing, which was printed in the Astrid Lindgren Society newsletter in September 2013:

> I believe—just like Darwin—that human beings are descended from monkeys. At least, I am. Why else would I have spent my whole childhood and early youth assiduously climbing up trees and onto roofs and other places best suited for those prepared to risk their necks? One such suitable place, for instance, was the school gym: a peculiar set of pipes ran all the way along the hall, six meters above the ground. That was where I climbed— coming out the other side in one piece, astonishingly. My school friends followed my monkey tricks with mingled fear and delight. . . . Oh yes, I'm absolutely certain I'm descended from monkeys. But nowadays I'm not so aware of it.

As a young mother, however, she was very much aware of this tendency, and there were many occasions when she thought and acted like a child, risking scoldings from nearby adults. From a streetcar conductor in the 1930s, for instance, when Astrid—not setting the best of examples— dashed after it at high speed and leapt aboard, losing a shoe in the process and having to get off at the next stop to hobble back for it.

Other children's mothers and fathers were rarely as spontaneous and childlike, so naturally her behavior attracted attention. One person who never forgot Lasse and Karin's mother was Göran Stäckig, Lasse's faithful playmate and best friend for more than ten years. Göran particularly remembers the icy winter Sundays they spent skating in Vasa Park, when Astrid, after hours of watching the boys' valiant attempts to keep their balance and stay warm, bought food and scalding hot drinks for the small, freezing skaters. In 1986, when an adult Göran—by then living in the United States— heard that Lasse had died, he immediately wrote to "Aunt Lindgren," reminiscing about the boyhood he and her son had shared in the 1930s and emphasizing that, although there were many Astrids in Sweden, there was only one Aunt Lindgren: "You taught me and Lasse to skate. I don't know how you got hold of Lasse's skates, because they had no points—they were beautifully rounded like a pig's tail. You pulled us around on the rink again and again. And you bought us warm pastries that smelled wonderful."

He'd spent many unforgettable hours with Lasse and his playful mother. One day, when Göran arrived at their fifth-floor apartment in Vulcanusgatan, Astrid and her son had stretched some woolen blankets between the two chairs they were sitting on. With wide, friendly smiles, they asked whether Göran wanted to sit in the middle. Assuming it was a bench, he sat down confidently between them—and found himself engulfed in blankets and laughter.

Lasse and Göran's domain spanned the whole of Atlas, the area of Stockholm between the "mountains" of Vasa Park and the "wild waters" of Barnhusviken. They also made the daily trek to and from school at Adolf Fredriks Folkskola, and later—in high school—to Norra Latin, although Lasse's mother worried at the end of every school year that he might be held back. He'd always been a daydreamer, struggling to concentrate in school and sloppy with his homework, so Astrid was always relieved when the two boys began the next year together after a long summer vacation. When she got the chance, she would stand them back-to-back to measure how much they had grown. She did so in August 1939, for instance, but even before the summer—on May 22—she had felt the urge to reach for her account book and write a long entry about the children. After all, they were only on loan:

> My little Lars is getting to be not-so-little anymore. He's in his second year of high school, and he'll be finished in a few days. He and Göran joined the Scouts this spring, and he's got a sleeping bag. He's doing a little better in school than in his first year, and we hope he'll be allowed to move up. He's my beloved child, although I know we fight and row a lot when he and Karin play too many tricks. Yesterday, on Karin's birthday, the whole

family went to the "mountain" [Karlsberg Palace Park], where I hadn't been for ages. And Lars and I used to go there so often with Göran. Sometimes it frightens me when I realize I'm not getting as much out of their childhood as I'd like—not teaching them what I should, generally not taking part in their lives as I ought.

SIX

Mothers of All Lands, Unite!

WHILE THE GERMAN WAR MACHINE WAS trundling toward the
Soviet Union in the spring of 1941, one of the strangest and most wonderful
characters in world literature was stirring into life. She was born in a country at one remove from the war, though the Swedes were uncomfortably
aware of being surrounded by countries that were either occupied by Germans or at war with Russians. It was in these uneasy circumstances that the
peculiarly named Pippi Longstocking first appeared, in a series of stories
invented by a mother who was following the political situation so keenly it
seemed like she was on her way to the front herself.

Pippi's roots in the horrors of the Second World War, and in Astrid
Lindgren's abhorrence of violence, demagoguery, and totalitarian ideolo-
gies, are documented in the autobiographical work she spent two decades
writing and compiling from newspaper clippings. At first she called it her
War Diary, but it burst through those limits in 1945 and morphed into a
postwar diary and Cold War diary, spanning nearly three thousand pages
across nineteen small notebooks. The finishing touches were added in 1961,
when she wrote the last entry and pasted in the last clipping. Her mother
died that year, and Astrid's first grandchild was born, ensuring the continu-
ation of the female line for a future that looked neither bright nor peaceful,
and which sorely needed more strong women. It was as though world
history were going in circles, remarked fifty-two-year-old Astrid Lindgren
on New Year's Day in 1960: "The balance of terror between east and
west continues. In the last few days we've been shaken by an anti-Semitic
neo-Nazi attack in Germany, with the vandalization of the synagogue in
Cologne, etc."

With their broad scope and collagelike assemblage of yellowed newspaper clippings, flanked by handwritten comments on the latest political
news and events in the author's family during the 1940s and 1950s, Astrid
Lindgren's war diaries constitute a unique autobiographical work. From
the outset, the diaries were conceived as an attempt to document the war
and the long shadows it cast over the life of an ordinary family. As Astrid
told Margareta Strömstedt in 1976–77, "I started writing the diaries to organize my memories, and get an overall picture of what was happening in the
world and how it affected us." On September 1, 1939, the day before Children's Day was due to be celebrated in Stockholm, she picked up her pen:

> Alas, war broke out today. Nobody wanted to believe it.
> Yesterday afternoon, Elsa Gullander and I were in Vasa Park
> while the children ran and played around us, and we were com-
> fortably lambasting Hitler and agreeing it probably wouldn't
> come to war—and then today! The Germans bombed several
> Polish cities this morning and are forcing their way into Poland
> from all sides. I've avoided any kind of hoarding for as long as
> possible, but today I bought some cocoa, some tea, some soap,
> and several other things. A ghastly depression has fallen across
> everything and everyone. The radio reports the news at regular
> intervals all day long. Lots of people have been called up.
> They've banned private cars on the roads. God help our poor,
> mad planet!

As for millions of other people, the Second World War proved a
life-altering experience for Astrid Lindgren, changing her perspective on
the world, on life, and on other human beings. In a later interview, she explained that the rage and indignation she felt toward Hitler, Stalin, Mussolini, Nazism, Communism, and fascism had been her "first real political
involvement."

The impulse to understand the causes and effects of the war, and to *do*
something, to protest and inveigh, can be felt throughout the diary, sitting
cheek by jowl with descriptions of peaceful Lindgren family holidays,

birthdays, and vacations. One almost surreal example of the dual reality
lived by many Swedes took place in midsummer 1941, when the Lindgren
family vacationed on the island of Furusund in the Stockholm archipelago.
Sture rowed the family's small boat, Astrid swam and foraged for berries
and mushrooms, and Karin's cousin Gunvor from Småland came to visit.
All seemed idyllic, and in the evenings—accompanied by the distant rum-
ble of clashes between Finnish and Russian troops in the Sea of Åland—
Astrid read the history books she had brought to learn more about world
events. On June 28, she updated her diary:

> Here I ought to paste in Hitler's speech upon the outbreak of
> war, but that will have to come later. I'm sitting in my bed and
> gazing out across the drizzly sea after an uneasy night fighting
> off mosquitos, with guns thundering in the distance. . . .
> National Socialism and Bolshevism are like two great reptiles
> fighting. It's unpleasant having to take sides with either one of
> them, but right now all I can do is hope the Soviets get a good
> thrashing after everything they've seized during this war and all
> the harm they've done to Finland. In England and America
> they've got to side with Bolshevism—that's got to be even more
> difficult, and "the man in the street" probably has trouble un-
> derstanding it. Queen Wilhelmina of Holland said on the radio
> that she was prepared to support Russia, but with the caveat
> that she was still against the principles of Bolshevism. The larg-
> est forces in world history are facing each other on the Eastern
> Front. It's dreadful to think about. Are we on the verge of
> Armageddon? I've been reading about world history here in
> Furusund, and it makes for rather unpleasant reading—war and
> war and war and suffering for humanity. And they *never* learn
> anything, just keep drenching the earth in blood, sweat,
> and tears.

In Revelations, Armageddon is the site of the final confrontation between God and Satan. Throughout Astrid Lindgren's war diaries there are

religious references to the world's impending doom, for example on
November 30, 1939, when Stalin's troops invaded Finland: "Eli, Eli, lama
sabachthani!" (My God, my God, why have you forsaken me?). Or
February 9, 1940, when the first evidence of the barbaric cruelty behind
Communism and Nazism surfaced:

> What a world, what an existence! Reading the newspapers is a
> bleak business. Women and children hounded by bombs and
> machine-gun fire in Finland, seas full of mines and U-boats,
> neutral sailors being killed, or at best being rescued just in time
> on some miserable raft after days of suffering, the tragedy of the
> Polish people unfolding behind closed doors (nobody's sup-
> posed to know what's happening, but it's still in the papers),
> special compartments on the streetcars for "the German master
> race," Poles mustn't go outside after eight o'clock at night, and
> so on. The Germans are talking about their "harsh but fair
> treatment" of the Poles—and you know what that means. It
> leads to such hatred! In the end the world will be so full of
> hatred that we'll all suffocate. I believe this is God's judgment
> being visited upon us. And on top of that we've had a harsher
> winter than any in living memory. . . . I've bought myself a fur
> coat—although I'm sure Armageddon will be here before I've
> had time to wear it out.

A Dirty Job

If Astrid Lindgren was particularly affected by the war on all its fronts, it
was because she was closer to its horrors than most Swedes. Through the
criminologist Harry Söderman, for whom Astrid had worked at the end of
the 1930s at the Institute of Criminology and who was heavily instrumental
in implementing nationwide mail censorship after war broke out, she gained
employment in 1940 as an "inspector" for Swedish intelligence. This was a
secret job based at the censorship department of the Central Post Office.
Until Germany surrendered in May 1945, Astrid Lindgren read tens of

thousands of letters to and from other countries, and was thus extremely well informed about what war does to the soul and to human relationships. A week after she started the job in 1940, she wrote in her war diary: "On the fifteenth of this month I started my secret 'defense work,' which is so secret I don't even dare write about it here. I've been doing it for a week, and it's now crystal clear to me that there is currently no country in Europe so untouched by the war as this one, despite the rationing, increased unemployment, and significant rise in prices. In terms of how people elsewhere perceive us, we've got it pretty good here."

At the General Security Service's mail-inspection center, letters and parcels were scrutinized twenty-four hours a day with the aid of Harry Söderman's criminological equipment, consisting of flasks, pipettes, steam jets, ultraviolet light, chemicals, and sharp steel tools. Between 1939 and 1945, an estimated fifty million items of mail sent between Swedish citizens and their relatives, acquaintances, and business partners overseas were opened and read by several thousand "inspectors," who were scattered across fifty secret mail censorship offices between Kiruna and Karlshamn.

"My dirty job," Astrid Lindgren called her confidential work, which was assigned only to skilled readers and highly reliable employees. Everyone in this invisible army of letter readers, including unemployed academics, teachers, clerks, students, and people from the neutral Swedish military, had signed a document promising to reveal nothing about the nature of the "post office job," which kept censors busy day and night. Astrid Lindgren kept that promise—almost. She let slip only a few words about it in her letters, but in her diary she was able to get all those unbearable secrets off her chest. Occasionally Astrid would copy a particularly gripping letter and paste it into her diary, while other times she would simply empty her memory into it, for instance on March 27, 1941:

> Today I had an extremely distressing Jewish letter, a document of our age in itself. A Jewish person recently arrived in Sweden was writing to a member of the same race in Finland, describing the deportation of Jews from Vienna to Poland. I think it was 1,000 Jews a day who were being forcibly transferred to Poland

in the most wretched conditions. They get a sort of request through the post, then the person has to leave with only a very modest sum of money and a bit of luggage. Conditions before and during transportation and after their arrival in Poland were so bad the letter writer didn't want to describe them. His own brother was among the unlucky ones. Evidently it's Hitler's intention to turn Poland into one big ghetto, where the poor Jews die of hunger and squalor. There's no opportunity for them to wash, for instance. Those poor, wretched people! Hasn't it occurred to the God of Israel to intervene? How *can* Hitler think you can treat fellow human beings like that?

There were gloomy missives from the Baltic states, written in fear of Stalin's soldiers, and passionate love letters between Swedish women and German men who were now in uniform. All these glimpses into what was going on—and into the meaninglessness of life—made the censors at the Central Post Office feel as if they'd been initiated into a secret club, all-knowing but powerless, living with the guilty awareness of their own privileged lot. As Astrid Lindgren wrote in October 1940:

It's also very strange to read letters from people who talk about women and children they know *personally* being killed in bombing raids. While you're just reading about it in the papers it's as though you can stop yourself believing it, but when you read in a letter that "both Jacques's children died during the occupation of Luxembourg" or something similar, it suddenly becomes terrifyingly real. Poor humanity; when I read their letters I'm shaken by how much sickness and affliction, grief, unemployment, shortage of money, and despair there is on this sorry lump of earth. But the Lindgren family's doing great! Today I went to the movies with my well-fed children and saw *Young Tom Edison.* We live in our warm, cozy home; yesterday we ate lobster and liver pâté for dinner, today ox tongue and red cabbage; hard-boiled eggs and goose liver on the table at lunch

(Sture's the loony one). But of course it's only on Saturdays and
Sundays that such gluttony can be permitted, and even then I'm
tormented by my conscience when I think of the French and
their 200g of butter a month.

In her war diary, Astrid also considered what it meant to be Swedish.
Skimming hundreds of letters per week at the Central Post Office was like
eavesdropping at countless doors, walls, and drainpipes, giving Astrid an
overview of what Swedes from every social stratum thought about food
hoarding, military support in Finland, Jewish aid, and the state-approved
transportation of German troops by train in northern Sweden. Such moral
dilemmas burdened the consciences of many Swedes, making them wonder
about the neutral course their nation had chosen. Whose side would
Sweden take, Astrid asked herself in her diary on February 9, 1941, if the
smaller war in Finland suddenly got dragged into the larger one and they
had to pick?

> "The Germans are getting less and less big-headed in Stock-
> holm," said one letter I read yesterday. And the fact is, I think,
> that they're not quite as high and mighty as before. At the same
> time we're perhaps getting a fraction more sure of ourselves—
> thanks to our fabulously well-equipped military, which may be
> nothing compared to those of the major powers but which still
> adds weight to the scale. "Angels and Fritzes are both courting
> Sweden's favor," another letter said. Yes, and I only hope we're
> left in peace—amen!

Small-Scale History

Astrid's account of the Lindgren family's ups and downs over the years—
history on a small scale—was as important as her documentation of the bigger historical picture. At first it was mostly about the ups, and about
overcoming the challenges of rationing. Occasionally her trivial reports of
family life were grotesquely juxtaposed with terrible eyewitness accounts

from newspaper clippings or the letters Astrid had to assess at her job. In fall 1941, the Lindgren family had just acquired a four-room apartment in Dalagatan, where Astrid would live until her death. The occasion felt especially joyous, thrown into relief against the usual dejection and sense of unease about the state of the world. Yet there were new trials on the home front, where those with a degree of foresight had long since started preserving large quantities of eggs in sodium silicate. On October 1, 1941, Astrid made an entry in her diary—the first three words in English:

> Things have happened since I last wrote. On September 17 the Swedish navy suffered a terrible catastrophe at Hårsfjärden. For reasons still unknown, the destroyer *Göteborg* exploded and sank, dragging the destroyers *Klas Horn* and *Klas Uggla* down with it. Burning oil spread across the surface of the water, where the poor crew were trying to save themselves. 33 men died (luckily most of them were on leave). According to "our letters," it was a dreadful sight to behold. Arms, legs, and torn-off heads were scattered everywhere, rescue teams were going around with sticks, fishing shreds of flesh and guts down from the trees. . . . On the home front, I can now report that we're running low on eggs. I'm glad I preserved 20 kilos, because we only get 7 eggs per month per person. The Finns have taken Petrozavodsk, the newspapers say, and the Murmansk Railway is completely closed. But nothing decisive will happen in Russia until the winter. And we've moved from Vulcanusgatan 12 to Dalagatan 46, despite the war and the shortages. I can't help being pleased with our beautiful apartment, even though I'm constantly aware that we don't deserve how lucky we are here, when so many others don't even have a roof over their heads. I lost my diary from 1940 in the move. We've got a big, beautiful front room, the children have a room each, and we have a bedroom too. We've bought a whole load of new furniture and made it really nice; I hope it doesn't all get bombed one day.

A Swedish nuclear family in the year 1941, living almost offensively well off Sture's
salary as head of department (he was soon to be promoted to senior manager), the
income from Astrid's "dirty job," the reliable food parcels from Småland, and Sweden's persistent neutrality, as Astrid acknowledged and often gave thanks for in her
war diaries.

In her war diary, Astrid continued to jot down observations about
Lasse and Karin, recording various details—great and especially small—to
do with the children's physical and psychological well-being and development, as well as about their schooling and illnesses. She also kept account
of what gifts they received and from whom on birthdays and at Christmas.
It was as though their mother were forcing herself to focus on what was near

at hand so that she didn't get swallowed up by events far away. For most of the war diary's three thousand pages, these two perspectives, world history and family history, were in constant flux, and gradually a third one developed out of the second, centering around the diarist herself. It registered Astrid's anxieties about the future of the world, her personal dreams and desires, and an increasing concern about Sture and her marriage. Until 1944 Astrid Lindgren largely kept herself aloof from her descriptions of family life, her Småland modesty making itself felt. Even in a diary, it was important to watch one's words.

Before 1944, her passion and commitment were most evident in her frequently emotional comments about the war and her analyses of the combatants. In places the diary almost became a psychological study of power, as she tried again and again to penetrate the iron masks of Hitler, Stalin, and Mussolini, three representatives of evil incarnate. Evil touches most people at some point during their lives, and this force would later appear in Astrid Lindgren's work under such mythological names as Kato, Tengil, and Katla.

As Astrid explores the nature of evil in her diary, her clippings and notes come across in many places as a protest, an outcry originating from a mutinous woman's heart, speaking on behalf of all mothers. Similarly, a short story from this period, "Jorma and Lisbet," can be read as a mother's call for peace, and should be understood in light of the seven thousand Finnish children fostered with Swedish families during the Winter War of 1940. The effects of this large-scale humanitarian action were felt in the Lindgren family orbit one day in March 1940. Gunnar, who had many Finnish connections, suddenly appeared on their doorstep with a little boy who'd been flown in from Turku the night before. The sight of the unhappy, frightened child, fighting back tears, who disappeared again with Gunnar almost as quickly as they had arrived, inspired Astrid to write "Jorma and Lisbet," which was printed in *Santa's Wonderful Radio of Pictures*. A story for both children and adults, it carries an unambiguous political message: "She thinks of the unknown mother in Finland, who had to send her child away to a foreign country. She thinks of all Earth's mothers. Has it ever been as hard to be a mother as now? And isn't that what all of humanity is crying

The war diary, New Year's Eve, 1939–40: "As the New Year begins, it is with trembling that we look to the future. Will Sweden stay out or join in? Lots of volunteers are going to Finland. And if we do join in, Skåne will most likely become an English-German conflict zone. So they say."

out for—love, a mother's love? Mothers of all lands—she thinks—unite! Send love across the whole world, so Earth's children do not perish."

Pippi in Shorthand

The phenomenon known as Pippi Longstocking first appeared in the spring of 1941, but we have to skip forward three years to find her mentioned by name in the war diary. On March 20, 1944, Astrid Lindgren wrote: "On the home front, Karin's had the measles, a nasty case, and she's still not allowed out of bed. I'm keeping myself well amused with Pippi Longstocking."

We hear nothing more about Pippi until two weeks later, by which time Karin's mother is the bedridden one. During a snowstorm, Astrid slipped on the icy path in Vasa Park and twisted her ankle. The pain was so bad she couldn't stand by herself, so two men had to carry her through the park, across Dalagatan and up to her second-floor apartment. The doctor assured her that evening that nothing was broken, but told her to rest and take good care of the badly sprained ankle for the next four weeks. On April 4, 1944—a few days after Astrid and Sture had danced long into the night at a fortieth-birthday party—she noted in her diary:

> Today I've been married thirteen years. The blushing bride is currently confined to her bed, which gets decidedly dull after any length of time. I enjoy it in the mornings, when I get tea and white bread with smoked salmon served in bed, and I get my bed made and everything tidied around me, but I loathe it at night, when I have a hot compress on my foot and it itches and itches, and Sture is sleeping when I can't. I read Somerset Maugham's *Of Human Bondage* and write about Pippi Long-stocking. Doesn't look like there'll be peace in Finland. There's a children's program just coming on the radio, so I can't write any more for now.

During the daytime, however, when Sture was at work and Lasse and Karin at school, Astrid enjoyed the sudden, unexpected "vacation." She buried herself even more deeply in the *Dagens Nyheter,* following the latest news about the Warsaw ghetto. She read *The Land without a Quisling* (originally titled *Kraj bez quislinga*) by the Polish author Tadeusz Nowacki, who described the true situation in Poland under German occupation. In her war diary she remarked that it was now clear the vast majority of people in the Warsaw ghetto had died from causes other than hunger: "I don't think the Germans are even bothering to deny that Jews are being exterminated." It was during those days that Astrid decided to write a book of stories about

On the use of shorthand in her process of fiction writing, Astrid Lindgren said: "I write and rewrite, tearing out pages and throwing them away and writing on new ones until I've got every single sentence precisely as I want it."

Pippi Longstocking, which would be Karin's tenth birthday present on May 21, 1944. Karin loved writing short books herself, and, like her mother, she toyed with the idea of becoming an author.

Writing down the oral Pippi stories in April 1944, Astrid used neither ordinary cursive nor a typewriter; instead she used shorthand, employing the Melin method she had learned at the Bar-Lock Institute in Stockholm in 1926–27 and had since practiced at various companies, among lawyers, lecturers, and office managers. Using highly distinctive signs that were often developed further by the individual stenographer, it was possible to capture thoughts and ideas in flight, writing down chains of sentences at lightning speed. The only tools needed for shorthand were a pen and pad, which meant that it could be done lying down. The method soon proved emi- nently practical for a bedridden amateur author, and so conducive to scrib- bling down everything she had in her head that Astrid Lindgren continued to write her rough drafts in shorthand for the rest of her career. Often while in bed. As she noted in the war diary on December 13, 1947—by which time the Melin method had become part of her working routine and she had filled her first seven or eight notepads with shorthand—"I'm lying down and writing a few lines of Pippi III." And when a journalist from the *Stockholms-Tidningen* asked in 1952 whether Astrid Lindgren had a favor- ite outfit, she answered: "Yes, that would be pajamas. By now probably the whole of Sweden knows I'm so lazy I lie in bed to write."

In the index of Astrid Lindgren's papers at the National Library in Stockholm, there are few entries for handwritten manuscripts of the old- fashioned kind, on loose paper, full of crossings-out and corrections. In- stead one finds an infinitely long series of neatly typed pages, virtually unaltered. Elsewhere in the archive there is a corresponding number of stenographic pads—660 of them—containing the real drafts of Astrid Lind- gren's books throughout fifty years, and they will forever be unreadable to anyone but a professional, expert stenographer. Even he or she would have trouble interpreting all the extra flourishes in the symbols Astrid Lindgren the secretary had mastered, and behind which Astrid Lindgren the artist hid the first Pippi manuscript in April 1944. This manuscript was not iden- tical with the version of *Pippi Longstocking* published in 1945, and it was not until 2007 that the book appeared in its original form, under the title *Original Pippi* (Ur-Pippi).

Karin Nyman remembers that the eleven chapters in *Original Pippi,* her tenth birthday present from her mother, were written down in one of the spiral-bound stenographic pads Astrid Lindgren always had lying around the house. By that point they were living in Dalagatan, and Astrid

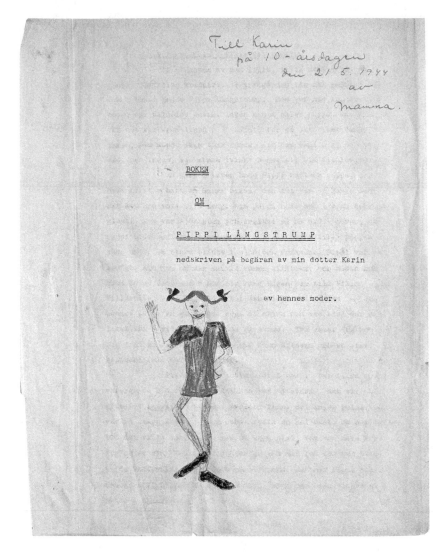

The manuscript for *Original Pippi,* spring 1944.

didn't yet have her own study. In 1944 the room next to the living room, which had a view of Vasa Park, belonged to Lasse. Later, this was where she would sit and make fair copies of her shorthand drafts or answer her thousands of fan letters, but for the time being Astrid sat in the big living room overlooking Dalagatan, at the dining table by the bookcase. There she would clatter away on her old Halda typewriter, which was eventually replaced with a more manageable Facit, but never with anything electric. Her mother used to put carbon paper between two sheets, recalls Karin, sticking them behind the cylinder and typing at incredible speed: "Typing out a fair copy took only a few hours. She went at the pace of a practiced secretary, and all the final corrections had already been made to the shorthand manuscript."

Artist, Secretary, and Businesswoman

The clean manuscript of the literary work we now call *Original Pippi* was finished at the end of April 1944, and it testified to the thirty-six-year-old author's three fundamental, still developing guises: the artist, the secretary, and the businesswoman. While still on her sickbed she'd had the bright idea of sending a copy of Karin's birthday present to Bonniers Förlag, a major publishing company, mailing the manuscript on April 27. A few weeks later, the handmade book, 8¼ by 10¾ inches format, featuring on the cover the author's hand-drawn illustration of a thin, spindly-legged Pippi, was ready to be presented to Karin. Writing in her war diary on May 21, 1944, Astrid remembered to list all the birthday gifts and well-wishers, but only after expressing her concerns that "neutral" Sweden was apparently beginning to trade with Adolf Hitler:

> Today Karin turned ten, her fifth birthday celebrated during wartime. . . . In this country we're at peace, thank God, although things got dicey in the spring. The Allies were most displeased, and probably still are, because we're exporting ball bearings to Germany. . . . To return to Karin's birthday, we celebrated in the usual way. She got the *Folkskolans läsebok* [primary school reader] in three parts, a Peter No-Tail book, plus the manuscript for Pippi Longstocking in a nice black binder. She also got a blue swimsuit, white slip-ons with wooden soles, fabric for a blouse, books from Viridén and Gullander, as well as money from Grandpa plus both Grandmas.

Pippi's public debut was still some way off, but the little girl with su-
perhuman strength was already an institution within the Lindgren family.
Moreover, Astrid's stories about her didn't find an audience just in Karin;
they were also a hit with her friends Matte and Elsa-Lena, and with her
Småland cousins Gunvor, Barbro, and Eivor, who loved hearing Aunt
Astrid update them on Pippi's escapades when the Lindgren, Ericsson, and
Lindström families got together in Stockholm, Furusund, or Näs. It all
began, however, at home by Karin's bedside: "My mother began telling me
about Pippi Longstocking in the late winter of 1941, when I was sick with
something pneumonia-like and had to lie in bed for ages, because in those
days children were on no account allowed out of bed if they had the least
hint of a fever, nor for several days after it had gone. So I demanded extra
entertainment to relieve my boredom. She had to read aloud or tell stories—
ideally improvised ones."

From the first, it was Pippi's boundless energy that bewitched
her young listeners. It was shocking yet infinitely liberating, wrote Karin
Nyman in the preface to *Original Pippi,* to hear about a young girl doing
something as daring as jumping from pew to pew in a church while loudly
calling the pulpit a nest box. She was thinking of a scene from one of
the first Pippi stories, though it never became anything more than an oral
narrative. In one of the Astrid Lindgren Society's newsletters from 2011,
Gunvor Runström recounted the unforgettable moment when Aunt Astrid
launched into a story about the anything-but-pious Pippi before an audience of Vimmerby children that included not just Gunvor and Karin but
also eight or ten children from the three farming families living in the Ericssons' old red house at Näs:

> I remember one time I was afraid that Grandpa—Samuel Au-
> gust, a churchwarden—would come in and listen. Astrid very
> vividly described Pippi attending a service at Vimmerby
> Church, hopping around on the pews then catching sight of the
> priest in the pulpit and saying in astonishment, "There's a
> funny old bird in that nest box—what is it?" The very first Pippi
> spoke with a Småland accent, and we thought it was hilarious!

But also a bit alarming that somebody should dare make fun of
something so solemn as a priest in Vimmerby Church!

Original Pippi's Roots

It's often been said that Pippi Longstocking would never have become the
Pippi we know today if it hadn't been for the debates about childhood education in Sweden in the 1930s, a decade when countless new psychological
and pedagogical theories were introduced. This is true enough, but the
inspiration for the character of Pippi didn't just come from A. S. Neill's
philosophy of freedom and Bertrand Russell's theories about children's
will to power. It also came from fairy-tales, from myths and legends in literary history and interwar popular culture, from literary classics like E. T. A.
Hoffmann's *The Strange Child* (Das fremde Kind) and Lewis Carroll's *Alice
in Wonderland,* Jean Webster's *Daddy-Long-Legs* and L. M. Montgomery's
Anne of Green Gables. Additional influences came from 1930s films and
comics, which were full of preternaturally strong characters like Tarzan and
Superman.

Superman first set foot on Swedish soil in the early 1940s, initially as
part of a comic called *The Titan from Krypton* (Titanen från Krypton),
which came to be better known as *The Man of Steel* (Stålmannen). A pacifist
with superpowers, he makes an unexpected appearance in the shorthand
manuscript for *Original Pippi.* Among the pages of mysterious stenographic
symbols preserving the first written stories about the world's strongest girl,
an unusually muscular and disconcerting version of the superhero crops
up as a pencil drawing, which Karin Nyman will neither confirm nor deny is
her mother's. What is he doing there? We don't know, but Astrid Lindgren
acknowledged Superman as a partial inspiration for Pippi in an interview
with the *Svenska Dagbladet* in December 1967: "Pippi was a stroke of
inspiration, not a carefully considered character from the start. Although,
yes, she was a little Superman right from the word go—strong, rich, and independent."

However many sources of inspiration one can identify for Pippi Longstocking's appearance, powers, personality, and behavior, there is no more

important basis for the stories than the misanthropic, emotionally stunted age in which Pippi originated and developed. *Original Pippi,* which today is safely preserved in a case at the National Library—embalmed in shorthand—wasn't just a finger puppet for psychological or pedagogical philosophies. She was a cheerful pacifist whose answer to the brutality and evil of war was goodness, generosity, and good humor. When someone approached Pippi aggressively or threateningly—whether it be hooligans, social authorities, police officers, burglars, or a circus ringmaster and his strongman—she instinctively believed they wanted to play, dance, or fight just for fun.

The reader is introduced to Pippi Longstocking's resistance to all forms of physical violence in the second chapter of *Original Pippi,* where an unpleasant boy called Ove (renamed Bengt in the 1945 book) repeatedly mocks the girl. Each time Pippi reacts in the same peaceable way: she smiles broadly and obligingly, but says nothing. Her body language speaks for itself; she's neither fearful nor tentative. When Ove, provoked by her calm and passivity, yanks her braids, she gives another friendly smile and pokes Ove gently with her right index finger, sending him tumbling to the ground. Instantly a warlike glint appears in the boy's eyes. In the violent confrontation that follows, Lindgren pits blind strength—of which the world saw so much in the early forties—against gentle, nonviolent Pippi-power:

> "What do you think you're doing, you bumpkin," he shouted, and flung himself at Pippi with clenched fists. So Pippi took care of Ove. Grabbing him around the waist, she threw him high up into the air. But since she was a good girl who didn't want to hurt nasty little boys, she grabbed him again as he came tumbling down, catching him before he hit the floor, then threw him up again. . . . When he came down the final time, she gave him a teasing little shove, sending him into a ditch. She was still smiling a friendly smile at him.

Pippi Longstocking's first appearance as a figment of Astrid Lindgren's imagination occurred during one of the Second World War's most critical periods for the Allied Powers: spring 1941. Germany was preparing to invade both England and the Soviet Union, and the Nazi plan to wipe out all of Europe's Jews was entering an increasingly purposeful phase. Clippings and handwritten comments in Astrid's war diaries from 1941–43 indicate that Pippi was a response not just to the war but also to the people behind its lunacy. In several passages, the diarist developed small-scale psychoanalyses of Hitler, Stalin, and Mussolini, probing the personalities of the three despots until she reached the darkest corners of human nature, where instincts like the will to power and the urge to destroy and terrorize lurk. In 1945's *Pippi Longstocking,* there's a moment when Bengt and his little mob of bullies surround Ville and unleash the forces of darkness upon the smaller child: "On him, boys, so he daren't show his face on the street anymore!" Just as little Ville is frightened of the bigger, stronger boys, Astrid was frightened of the bigger, stronger military aggressors in the 1940s. At first it was Stalin who alarmed her, even more than Hitler. On June 18, 1940, she wrote in her war diary:

> The worst thing is that one hardly dare wish for Germany's defeat any longer, because now the Russians have begun to stir again. Over the past few days they've occupied Estonia, Latvia, and Lithuania on various pretexts. And a weakened Germany can only mean one thing for us in Scandinavia—we'll be overrun with Russians. And I think I'd rather be saying "Heil Hitler" for the rest of my life than have that happen. It's scarcely possible to imagine anything more terrible. . . . Dear God, don't let the Russians come over here!

Yet as the Nazis' territorial demand for "Lebensraum" turned eastward and the Swedes began to fear that their country might be the site of a final showdown between the world's most powerful tyrants, Astrid Lindgren's interest in and fear of Hitler's character and psyche grew. She began calling him "Adolf," just as she had called Mussolini "Musse"; Stalin, meanwhile, always remained Stalin. More and more newspaper clippings about Hitler were pasted into the diary as she tried to understand his persecution of a single ethnic group. On May 10, 1940, for instance, when German troops had crossed the border into Holland and Belgium, Astrid noted in

Astrid, Lasse, and Karin celebrated New Year 1943 at Näs with the other Ericssons. The snow was piled heavily outside, and the ice on Stångån, a nearby river, was thick enough to skate on. As in previous years, Samuel August and Hanna gave their four children one thousand kronor each as a Christmas present.

her diary that Germany most of all resembled "some malevolent beast, rushing out of its cave at regular intervals to pounce on a new victim. There must be something wrong with a people who alienate the rest of humanity at approximately twenty-year intervals." And in her comments on a longer clipping pasted across several spreads in the diary, which showed a picture of Hitler and reprinted his victory speech in the German Reichstag on July 19, 1940, she reached for a biblical image: "The lord of the world—the wild beast in Revelations—once an unknown little German craftsman, restorer of his people and (in my and many other people's opinions) a destructive, culturally corrupting force—what will he end up being? Will we ever find ourselves saying, *Sic transit gloria mundi*?"

One of Astrid's early stories about the "world's strongest girl" seems to draw on her fear and hatred of Hitler, along with her fascination with him, reading him as a parody of the world's strongest man. "Pippi Goes to the Circus," as the story was called in the *Original Pippi* manuscript in 1944, isn't as radical and sustained a caricature as Charlie Chaplin's film *The Great Dictator* (1940); nonetheless, the hot-tempered, aristocratically dressed ringmaster, who wields a sinister power, is almost as comical.

Schtrong Adolf

A blaring march, animalistic forces, uniformed circus folk, a German-accented ringmaster with a whip, and a large, responsive audience are the main ingredients in Astrid Lindgren's Hitlerian satire, whose dramatic arc is punctuated by a series of tests of strength. The ringmaster competes with Pippi, who is among the spectators. Initially he's presented as the vigorous, controlling ruler of his distinctive world. He sets himself apart from his uni-formed and tutu-clad subordinates by wearing full evening dress, lending him an aristocratic air. He's also equipped with a whip, a symbol of absolute power, and the reader is repeatedly reminded that the ringmaster "cracks" and "smacks" it as he wields his power. He holds the audience in the palm of his hand too, at least at first.

Pippi's increasingly flagrant disruptions of this dictatorial order begin when she leaps onto the back of a horse in the ring—inelegant and un-princesslike—and clings to the divinely beautiful Miss Carmencita, who nor-mally balances on the horse's back by herself. The audience thinks she's one of the acts; the ringmaster is furious, but keeps himself in check. The circus assistants are called out to stop the horse and get rid of Pippi, who gets her first glimpse of the ringmaster's true, choleric nature, as do the audience and the reader: "'Horripple girl,' hissed the ringmaster between his teeth. 'Ged aud-doff hier before zere iss an eksident!'—'There's already *been* an eksident,' said Pippi. 'I saw the horse doing something awful in the sawdust a minute ago.'"

The horse dung Original Pippi so cheerily mentions had been swept up and removed from the circus chapter by the time the first Pippi Long-stocking book was published in 1945. Lindgren chose to retain the line about the ringmaster "hissing between his teeth," however, which reveals that the great ringmaster is actually full of nothing but angry hot air. Things get worse still when Miss Elvira, a tightrope walker who is also the ringmaster's daugh-ter, tries to bring serenity and order back to her father's world. Again Pippi upsets the balance of power: leaping up onto Miss Elvira's tightrope, she plays a quick game of tag, then starts swinging on it. As a grand finale, she drops down and lands on the ringmaster's back. Having been made to look ridiculous, he retreats to "drink a glass of water and tidy his hair."

Why this specific detail? Perhaps because most people who'd seen film clips of the Führer in Swedish movie theaters couldn't help but be struck by the man's vanity, especially when it came to his hair. The dictator was constantly touching his pomaded side parting and adjusting the long hair that kept falling across his forehead while he gave his speeches.

When the freshly combed ringmaster returns to the ring, and to the audience he now has to win back, he plays his final, strongest card, which he presents in resounding circus German: "Laydeess und chentlemen! In a mowment you schall see ze grrreatest vunder off zis age, ze schtrongest man in ze vorld. Schtrong Adolf, whom no one hass effer defeated! Laydeess and chentelment, I giff to you: Schtrong Adolf!"

In a letter dated April 27, 1944, sent to Bonniers Förlag with a copy of the *Original Pippi* manuscript, Astrid Lindgren seems to hint that the chapter about Pippi's skirmish with the ringmaster and his strongman par-odied Nazism and its false gods. She mentions nothing about "Schtrong Adolf," but she does use the word "Übermensch." The letter includes the following passage:

> Herewith I enclose a children's book manuscript, which I
> confidently look forward to having returned at your soonest

possible convenience. Pippi Longstocking is, as you will discover if you take the trouble to read the manuscript, a little Übermensch in child form, set in a very normal environment. Thanks to her superhuman physical strength and various other circumstances, she is completely independent of adults and lives her life exactly as it suits her. In confrontations with adults she always gets the last word. In a book by Bertrand Russell (*On Education, Especially in Early Childhood,* page 85), I read that the most prominent instinctive trait in childhood is the desire to be grown-up, or perhaps more precisely the will to power, and that a normal child will fantasize about things that involve the will to power. I don't know whether Bertrand Russell is right, but I'm inclined to believe it, judging by the almost obsessive popularity of Pippi Longstocking for a number of years among my own children and their friends of the same age.

Even in 1944, big publishers preferred their prospective authors to be humble in their initial approaches. For this reason alone, Astrid Lindgren's sharp and lively presentation of her work must have attracted attention at Bonniers Förlag, which officially accepted the manuscript for consideration on April 30. Deliberations lasted longer than usual, perhaps because some people at the publishing house may have felt upset by the unknown author's use of such an inflammatory, adult, Nazified word—"Übermensch"—to describe her main character, a child. Especially so in the spring of 1944, when the horrifying master plan behind such fundamental Nazi slogans as "the final solution," "Lebensraum," and "blood and soil" had finally become apparent to the rest of the world. The letter, which ended with the cheery hope that the publisher wouldn't alert social services, is of literary-historical interest, because in it we learn from Astrid Lindgren's own pen that philosophy and psychology are indeed part of Original Pippi's DNA.

"Übermensch" was a central term and concept in Friedrich Nietzsche's philosophy. Originating in *Also sprach Zarathustra* (1885), in the 1930s it was thoroughly appropriated by the program of National Socialism. The result was a distortion of Nietzsche's vision, which Astrid

Lindgren was (maybe) parodying in her circus chapter, bringing the term back to its original Nietzschean meaning through the competition between the imagined Übermensch (the ringmaster) and the genuine Übermensch (Pippi Longstocking): the Übermensch as an ungovernable, impulsive being who wishes to be neither master nor slave but adheres to her own system of values and primarily uses her power for good.

A Bombshell on the Home Front

Summer 1944 proved to be anything but idyllic for the two adults in the Lindgren family. The fate of the *Pippi* manuscript was still uncertain, and while Sture and Astrid vacationed on wet and chilly Furusund, the bombshell dropped. One evening in early July, Sture stepped onto the balcony and made an announcement: he was in love with another woman, and had been for a while. It came as a shock to Astrid, and over the following weeks she was inconsolable, bereft of all energy and drive. On July 19, she tried to write about it in her diary:

> Blood is flowing, people are mutilated, misery and despair are everywhere. And I don't care. Only my own problems interest me. I usually always write a little about what's happened since last time. Now I can only write: my life has been caught in a landslide, and it's left me alone and shivering. I shall try and wait for better times, but imagine if better times don't come! Despite everything, I shall try and force myself to write a little about what's happening in the world. The Russians are advancing most alarmingly; they're already in the Baltic states, which the Germans are probably intending to give up. The Russians are on the East Prussian border. In Normandy things won't be quite as quick, but they're progressing there too. Representatives of the Finnish government have been to see Ribbentrop and further sealed their allegiance with Germany. The USA has therefore broken off diplomatic ties. I'm not up to remembering any more right now. I'm suffering the most dreadful pangs, my

Reading and literature were one of Astrid and Sture's shared pleasures. The couple subscribed to the *Dagens Nyheter,* and on their shelves at Dalagatan and Furusund stood books both classic and modern, including fiction and nonfiction, fairy-tales, poetry, and comedic writing like Sweden's Falstaff, fakir, and Denmark's Storm P.

> heart aches so much—how will I find the strength to go back to
> the city and pretend to live a normal life?

Sture and Astrid's marriage had always rested contentedly on mutual respect and shared interests. At least, that was what Astrid had believed. After many lonely, unhappy years as a penniless single mother, separated from her child, she had prioritized middle-class security and social stability since the beginning of their relationship at the Automobile Club,

War diary, October 30, 1944: "I write less and less frequently in this book. I have such a lot to think about and I've been in a state of nervous tension all fall, so I haven't got around to writing. Now it looks as though the worst crisis is over, but I'm still not sure it'll end happily."

when she had signed her letters to Sture, "Your own little stenographer."
Now her husband was demanding a divorce, only a few months after she
had written in a letter to her parents at Näs: "Dear Mother and Father!
Tomorrow Sture and I will have been married 13 years, just think! And
never a cruel word!"

Nor were there any now. Just the crushing news that he was in love
with another woman. She later discovered that, for some time, he'd had the
keys to an apartment where he went to meet his lover. All the gloom and
doom in her diary, which for the past few years had centered mainly around
the war and her family life, suddenly hinged on a single thing: Sture's infidelity and the possible collapse of their marriage. Ironically, Astrid had just
finished a manuscript she was planning to enter into a competition for
books aimed at girls, which was set in a blissfully happy Swedish nuclear
family. "Ah, joy of joys—the family gathered before the fireplace in the living
room!" as the book's sixteen-year-old main character gushes in a letter to
her pen friend. In the author's own life, meanwhile, this rose-tinted image
had been torn to shreds. If she got divorced, what would become of her,
Lasse, and Karin during peacetime, when Astrid's job at the censorship
office would end and she would lose full-time employment? She certainly
couldn't keep the apartment at Dalagatan, and life as an author—increasingly her dream—would be impossible as a single mother of two.

In early August 1944, when Astrid was back in Stockholm, Karin,
Lasse, and their maid, Linnea, remained on vacation, and Sture's location
was unknown, she reached for her diary and tried to make sense of
recent world events. But both memory and concentration failed her. She
couldn't maintain a sense of historical perspective; the war had suddenly
become a shadow in the background, while the tragedy in her own life filled
every corner of the foreground:

> Alone at Dalagatan with the bitterness of despair in my heart,
> Karin at Solö, Lasse at Näs, Linnea on vacation, Sture? Big
> things have happened, but I've been unable to write about
> them. Not even something as sensational as an assassination
> attempt on Hitler interests me. And today the newspaper said

the Finnish Ryti-Linkomies cabinet has resigned. Yes, that's right, I think Ryti was the president. But now it's Mannerheim instead. The new government will try to make peace with Russia, of course. "Turkey breaks with Germany," the billboards say this evening. So now it seems things can fall apart at any moment. Like they fell apart for me.

One stiflingly hot Sunday in late August 1944, Astrid and the children spent the day at Skansen, an open-air museum, with her brother-in-law Ingvar, Ingegerd's husband, who was passing through Stockholm. Nothing seemed real, and the hours slipped by as though she were in a daze. Some time earlier, Astrid had written a short letter to Bonniers, asking about the manuscript they'd received four months earlier. The letter was almost apologetic, far from the bold, breezy tone she had adopted in the original cover letter. On September 21, 1944, she finally received the response she had been expecting. The publisher apologized for keeping her waiting, explaining that the manuscript had gone to more readers than usual and justifying their rejection by saying that they already had their children's book list laid out for the next two years. Behind this flimsy explanation, it later emerged, lay a fundamental disagreement between at least one reader, the editorial department, and the publisher himself, Gerard Bonnier, who ultimately had to put his name to the product. As the father of small children, he believed Pippi Longstocking was too advanced. He recalled the incident many years later at a dinner party, to the literary researcher and author Ulla Lundqvist, who mentioned it in her afterword to *Original Pippi* in 2007.

Light in the Darkness

Amid all these setbacks, there was one light in the darkness, one that would eventually roar into a bonfire. Elsa Olenius, a children's librarian, phoned on behalf of the publisher Rabén and Sjögren to inform Mrs. Lindgren that her manuscript entitled "Britt Hagström, Aged 15" had won second prize in the competition she had entered. Her prize was 1,200 kronor, and the publishing house intended to release the book before Christmas. A few days later, Astrid Lindgren stood face to face with Olenius, who worked at the Hornsgatan branch of the City Library in Södermalm. She was head of the department for children's and young-adult literature, and also ran a children's theater at the library on Medborgarplatsen. Elsa Olenius looked back on this first meeting in Margareta Strömstedt's biography in 1977: "Even at our first meeting we had a strong connection, Astrid and I. I could see that she was unhappy about something. When I asked, she suddenly told me quite candidly how things stood. I remember I told my husband about her when I got home that evening."

Even after *Confidences of Britt-Mari,* as the book would be called in English, was published in November 1944 and the first positive reviews started appearing in the newspapers, Astrid struggled to feel pleased and proud. Yet she certainly had reason to be. Sweden's two most influential critics of children's literature, Eva von Zweigbergk in the *Dagens Nyheter* and Greta Bolin in the *Svenska Dagbladet,* both gave it positive reviews. Bolin called the book "dazzlingly funny, full of humor and quick irony, occasionally downright spiritual," and a week later Zweigbergk followed suit, declaring, "the book has both humor and heart."

Unlike the previous year, Astrid's birthday in November 1944 passed unmentioned in the diary. And when the annual Christmas parcel arrived from Vimmerby, containing meat, butter, eggs, sausages, apples, and a roast joint of beef, which were usually received with eager delight, it was opened without the customary fanfare. And the Lindgren family? They were scattered to the four winds:

> This dark November Sunday I'm sitting in front of the fireplace in the living room, writing, while Lasse is getting out of bed—at 3.30 p.m.—and Karin is sitting in her room, typing (no, she's just come in!). Sture's not home, far from being home. Karin and I went for a walk in Haga Cemetery this morning. Anyway, this is more or less how things stand in the rest of the world: appalling misery among the civilian population in northern Norway, which the Germans have evacuated on account of the Russian advance. Apparently there's awful hardship in

Holland, too, but where isn't there awful hardship? It's every-where, I think.

Short diary entries in December 1944 reveal Astrid's anxieties about her current situation and the immediate future. Would she be able to play the happy, cheerful wife and mother for the children and Sture's aging mother on Christmas Eve? She could, of course, and when the family cele-bration was over and New Year was approaching, the war diary came back out. It was time for her to take stock of the previous year. Astrid leafed back through the pages and read what she had written, picked up her pen, and tried to get to grips with the concept of "happiness":

Christmas Day, 1944: "I'm painfully aware that these may be the happiest years of my life; nobody can keep having such good fortune in the long run. I'm sure there must be trials in store for me." That's what I wrote on Christmas Day last year. I didn't know how right I was. Trials *were* in store for me—but I won't say I'm unhappy. It's been a hellish six months, this last half of 1944, and the ground beneath me is shifting. I'm disconsolate, down, disappointed, often in a sad mood—but I'm not really unhappy. There's still so much to fill my existence. By rights it ought to have been a dreadful Christmas—and I did shed a few tears into the herring salad as I was making it on the 23rd, but I was dead tired so it doesn't count. If happy is synonymous with doing well, then I suppose I'm still "happy." But being happy's not that simple. One thing I've learned, at least—if you're going to be happy, it has to come from within and not from another person.

Sture came to his senses at the beginning of the new year, after Astrid had taken three weeks' sick leave from the Central Post Office on the grounds of "neurosis with insomnia," as the doctor called it. We can assume it was also during this period that she began her book about the twins Bar-bro and Kerstin, which she continued to develop throughout February and

March. After a bracing spring cleaning, which was conducted in the best Småland style—dusting the bookcases, washing the floors, cleaning the windows, polishing the parquet flooring, and beating the carpets—the war diary came out again on March 23, 1945. She had accumulated a number of clippings about the collapse of Germany that had to be pasted in, including several articles about Hitler, who for inscrutable reasons wouldn't surrender, despite his and Germany's total defeat. Perhaps it was because he was ashamed of the judgment of history, wrote Astrid, before leaping suddenly from the war to the private sphere: "As far as the Lindgren family is concerned, I can say that 'Home is the sailor, home from the sea / and the hunter home from the hill.' We've spring-cleaned and made everything nice, and sometimes I'm happy and sometimes sad. Happiest when I write. Got a message from Gebers [another publisher] the other day."

Sture had begged for forgiveness and Astrid had given him an ultimatum, which he accepted. "Here he lies where he longed to be," goes another line of Robert Louis Stevenson's poem "Requiem," which Astrid quoted in English in the diary. Certain things had fallen into place, but not everything. In a long letter dated March 28 to Hanna and Samuel August, who knew nothing about the crisis in their daughter's marriage, Astrid seemed to be asking for her parents' understanding that she would be spending more time on fiction writing in the future. In the letter she cited particular sentences from an especially positive review of *Confidences of Britt-Mari*, and explained her and Sture's plans for the coming Easter holiday, when Lasse and Karin were going to Vimmerby.

Gullan and Gunnar, who knew significantly more about Astrid and Sture's marital problems, had invited the children to Näs so that their parents could have a bit of peace and quiet in Stockholm, and a chance to reconnect. In the letter to her parents, Astrid told them that Sture thought they should "have fun" over Easter, which meant going out and enjoying the nightlife Sture was so fond of, and which was part of his job. Astrid would have preferred to stay at home in Dalagatan, relax, read, and keep working on her book about the twin girls, which several publishers were showing interest in. As she also mentioned in her letter, the latest complimentary review of her debut novel had speculated about what the talented author—who was also a busy housewife—might achieve if she had more time. When she called this highly encouraging review "very strange," it was perhaps because it indirectly exhorted Astrid to do something she had dreamt of but never seriously dared to do: retreat somewhat from the role of housewife and mother and enter an altogether different sphere, one that revolved not around Sture, Lasse, and Karin but around her own desires and needs.

> The other day I was sent a copy of a Swedish school magazine with a review of *Britt-Mari*. It was a very strange review, and it began like this: "For a married woman with older children and an office job to write a book is no mean feat. If she's also won second prize in a competition for girls' books, well, that's deeply impressive. Astrid Lindgren is one such married woman." And it finished like this: "It is to be sincerely hoped that this merry and good book gets a sequel, and that the writer gives us many more hours of amusement in her next volume." (So I think it's really sweet of Gullan to take my children over Easter, so I can produce a few more "hours of amusement").

It's undeniable that Astrid occasionally felt trapped in her family, and sometimes isolated in her role as parent and child-rearer. In a letter to Stina in February 1944, a few months before Sture announced he wanted a divorce, Astrid called herself a "capable mother who sits at home and only keeps company with her children." Sture's unfaithfulness, his request for a divorce, and the subsequent six-month battle to keep their marriage together and avoid letting ten-year-old Karin's world collapse had given Astrid a different perspective on her situation. Whatever happened between her and Sture in the future, she needed to maintain her own identity and remember what she had written in her diary at Christmas: "If you're going to be happy, it has to come from within and not from another person."

SEVEN

Revolution in the Nursery

ON MAY 5, 1945, THIRTY-SEVEN-YEAR-OLD Astrid Lindgren sent one of her usual monthly letters home to Näs. These were addressed either to Hanna and Samuel August or Gunnar and Gullan but generally read by everyone at the farm. In the letter Astrid outlined her thoughts about becoming an author. She found herself in a strong position: Rabén and Sjögren, which had published *Confidences of Britt-Mari* in 1944, had been having financial problems, but had just been reorganized and consolidated. The publisher, Hans Rabén, had phoned to tell her so, and he also had said that the firm was looking forward to publishing her next book for girls. Yet Astrid was undecided. The small publisher's list was too unfocused, offering everything from *I Was Quisling's Prisoner* and *The ABC of Script* to a monograph on headaches, a biography of the Danish poet-priest Kaj Munk, a lexicon of Swedish authors, and a few children's books. Was it really the right place for her? She doubted it, as she wrote in her letter to Näs, and she was inclined to switch to the better-known publishing house Gebers, which was also trying to woo her: "I'll have to see how it goes. It might be better with a more established publisher, if I can manage to rustle up another masterpiece."

In the end, however, she stayed with Rabén and Sjögren, largely because Hans Rabén, a highly cultured man, was able to offer something his competitors couldn't: a visionary and audacious editor whose commitment and drive were a match for Astrid's. Her name was Elsa Olenius, and she was the children's librarian who had sat on the jury that awarded *Britt-Mari* second prize. Olenius worked regularly with Rabén and Sjögren, contributing ideas and taking on various editorial projects alongside her permanent post at the library on Hornsgatan. Many years later, in a book

Rabén and Sjögren released for its anniversary, Astrid Lindgren recalled the help Olenius gave her with her first ever proper manuscript:

> She was generous enough to devote two hours to me and my manuscript. . . . Elsa didn't think Britt-Mari would just launch into pouring her heart out to an unknown pen-friend like that. There had to be an introductory chapter to tempt the reader in. That way we could attract younger readers who were resistant to epistolary novels. Would I go home and write such a chapter, asked Elsa? I did. And I came back with it the next day, which Elsa thought was just me trying to put out the fire. But she accepted the chapter as bait. Afterward we danced a sort of *slängpolska* in the lobby before we parted. By that time we were friends for life.

Astrid had so much faith in her new friend that, after turning down Gebers and accepting Rabén and Sjögren's offer, she gave Elsa Olenius the manuscript Bonniers had refused to publish the previous year. Would she be interested in reading a story or two about the world's strongest girl?

Yes, she would. Olenius, who also taught drama and ran a small children's theater at the library on Medborgarplatsen, was the first person in the world to see the manuscript's potential and the literary power of its main character. During those euphoric days in May 1945, when people all across Europe were celebrating the end of six years of war and Astrid, Sture, Lasse, and Karin surged through Stockholm with the other blue-and-yellow-clad revelers, Elsa Olenius was busy reading *Original Pippi*. It was sensational, she decided, though certain changes would need to be made. Horse dung in a circus ring and a chamber pot full of urine getting thrown over people to put out a fire? That was too graphic.

Astrid had to share this positive response with her family in Stockholm and Småland at once. Everyone at Näs got to hear about it in her next letter. Then, however, the author was gripped by uncertainty: what would less progressive readers say to Pippi? She wasn't quite as sure of herself as her editor: "A few days ago I gave my book to Mrs. Olenius to read through, and two days later she called and was overwhelmingly enthusiastic about it. I was so excited to hear what she thought, because if she likes it I don't think it will be savaged, so you can understand why I'm pleased. I'm invited to lunch with her this week to pick up the manuscript, and then I'll deliver it to Rabén & Sjögren, since it looks like the publisher is back on its feet."

Forty-eight-year-old Olenius, who was a critic of children's and young-adult literature on Sveriges Radio, Sweden's national public radio broadcaster, as well as a librarian, drama teacher, consultant, and editor, didn't just love *Pippi Longstocking*—she was also prepared to midwife the birth of a children's book and literary character unlike any the world had ever seen. Olenius was so determined that in May 1945 she encouraged Astrid to submit the *Pippi* manuscript to Rabén and Sjögren's next children's book competition, for which Olenius herself was one of the four judges. First, however, a few changes had to be made. Astrid listened, got down to work, and slogged away at the corrections Olenius had suggested. On June 2, 1945, she noted in her diary: "It's such amazing fun being an 'author.' At the moment I'm revising *Pippi Longstocking,* if anything good can be made of that naughty child."

When, in August and September, the jury was choosing the winner of Rabén and Sjögren's competition (for books aimed at children aged six to ten), Olenius championed the *Pippi* manuscript, in which the anarchic girl had become a fraction more civilized. Only Gösta Knutsson, however, author of the best-selling Peter No-Tail books, shared her enthusiasm, and since the jury also included Gärda Chambert, a teacher, and Hans Rabén himself, the vote was tied. In a letter to Hanna and Samuel August dated September 8, Astrid reported the latest news from Elsa Olenius: *Pippi* would definitely be published but probably wouldn't win the competition. "I'm still more than happy and satisfied," she wrote. "On Thursday I'm having lunch with her, so I'll probably learn a little more then."

But, as it turned out, Elsa Olenius got her way. It seems she managed to sway Hans Rabén, and on September 14, 1945, the *Svenska Dagbladet* announced that a winner had been found: "According to the jury, the prize-winning manuscript, *Pippi Longstocking,* is in a class of its own, possessing an abundance of the qualities that characterize a good children's book: originality, excitement, and a totally disarming sense of humor."

When *Pippi* hit the shelves two months later, after having been rushed headlong through the production process—illustrating, printing, binding, and distributing the book—Elsa Olenius sang its praises on Swedish national radio, also taking the opportunity to plug two other new Astrid Lindgren publications: *Kerstin and I* and *The Main Thing Is You've Got Your Health,* a play for children, which Olenius had commissioned earlier in the year. Rabén and Sjögren was thus able to quote its own employee's gushingly positive review of the book in promoting it, even though Olenius had both edited the manuscript and been on the committee that awarded it a prize. Newspaper advertisements for the Christmas season featured a drawing of Pippi above the words: "Elsa Olenius: 'A bullseye.'"

Astrid Lindgren appreciated her editor's tireless and invaluable efforts in marketing *Pippi Longstocking* during this early phase. In a letter to Näs dated November 8, 1945, while she was still waiting for a copy of the printed book, the excited author reported the latest news:

> I've still seen nothing of *Pippi,* but surely it's got to be here soon. On Nov. 17 Elsa Olenius and somebody else are going to have a conversation on the radio, which will be called "*Pippi Longstocking* and the Rest." They're going to review a number of books, like last year. Elsa Olenius told me she's going to discuss both *Pippi* and *Kerstin and I,* and also my little amateur theater piece that Lindfors is publishing [*The Main Thing Is You've Got Your Health*]. So she's really doing all she can to put my name around.

Opposite: Ingrid Vang Nyman's brilliant cover for *Pippi Longstocking* in 1945, celebrating fun and games a few months after six cursed years of war. The celebration continues today: to date, fifty-six million copies of the Pippi books have been sold worldwide, and the stories have been translated into sixty-five languages.

Pippi

LÅNGSTRUMP

AV ASTRID LINDGREN

RABÉN & SJÖGREN

Nepotism or Networking

Was it nepotism, or was it simply networking? Both, and a little something extra. It was Elsa Olenius, with her many hats and her fingers in various cultural pies, who made sure that *Pippi Longstocking* was read aloud on Swedish radio week after week in early 1946. And it was Olenius who, on March 6, 1946—just three months after the book came out—staged an adaptation of the year's hottest children's title at her own theater in Stockholm's Medborgarhus in Södermalm. Astrid Lindgren had written the script, hastily cobbling it together from selected scenes in the book. It was published later that year by Rabén and Sjögren, allowing hopeful amateurs on school stages across the country to put on their own local production.

As a play at Medborgarhus, *Pippi* was an instant success. Such a success, indeed, that in March and April 1946 there wasn't enough space for all the children who had tickets to see *Pippi Longstocking* on stage, because to get into Olenius's children's theater, all you needed was a valid library card. That was the whole philosophy behind putting on plays in a children's library, after all: to turn mini-citizens into readers of good literature.

Rumor of an extraordinary piece of theater featuring talented child actors spread across the country—as did the book—and Olenius's youthful company performed in cities like Göteborg, Eskilstuna, and Norrköping later that year. Meanwhile, there were special performances of *Pippi* held in the capital, where a somewhat discombobulated ensemble even appeared onstage at Stockholm Concert Hall. Lindgren was present at a number of these shows, but she was chiefly visible as an author during 1946, appearing at various libraries and literary events around the capital and elsewhere. In a letter to her parents in spring 1946, she reported that the Swedish royal family's three small princesses were now fans of the antiauthoritarian *Pippi*:

> I'm going to Motala for Book Day, where I'll be plaguing the poor things with *Pippi Longstocking*. Apparently I'm now terribly famous. The Booksellers' Association is holding an exhibition at the Gallerie Modern at Dramaten [the Royal Dramatic Theater], and I'm going to do a reading from *Pippi* on the 20th. The child is turning into a national nuisance. Moreover,

Kungsbokhandeln, a new bookshop that's opened to much fanfare, is hiring either the Concert House or the Borgarskolan [a
local school] for Elsa Olenius to stage *Pippi* with her children's
theater. The Haga princesses themselves have been invited, so
they're really going all out with the publicity.

Pippi Longstocking's first year as a printed book and a piece of theater
was certainly accompanied by plenty of hype. A book day event held in
Avesta in December offers an illustrative glimpse. Five of the country's best-
known authors were reading from their new books, and Astrid Lindgren's
special contribution to the festivities was going to be a Sagostund—
Fairy-tale hour—for nine hundred schoolchildren in Avesta and Grytnäs.
Twice, her readings from *Pippi Longstocking Goes Aboard* were standing
room only at the city's largest movie theater. The local paper was also present, reporting the next day:

> The youth orchestra, under Mr. König's leadership, opened
> with music that did an excellent job of setting the fairy-tale tone
> that would later captivate the young audience. Local teacher
> Helge Ytterbom welcomed Mrs. Lindgren, and her subsequent
> reading—with Pippi Longstocking as the main character—was
> a tremendous experience for the children, who listened with
> rapt attention. Pippi's adventures, in the best Robinson Crusoe
> manner, executed in Mrs. Lindgren's captivating style, kept the
> children utterly gripped on that chilly December day, banishing
> all their troubles in the way that only such wondrously magical
> medicine can.

It hadn't been quite that rosy. Astrid evaluated a reading in Dalarna in
a letter home on December 7: it had been rather a challenge, with lots of
coughing and fidgety children, and she had been obliged to strain her voice
"until I went blue in the face, just so I could be heard."

Such was the atmosphere around the *Pippi* books in fall 1946. Noisy.
In record time, Pippi had crossed over into other media like radio and

theater, and Astrid was still planning several other books. It was as though the various incarnations of Pippi were multiplying of their own accord, propagating across different media and genres. Hans Rabén couldn't believe his eyes. The book, not initially his favorite to win the competition, had not only saved the publishing house from bankruptcy but was now steadily replenishing its coffers, once so distressingly empty.

In Hans Rabén's phone call to Astrid Lindgren in May 1945, when he'd persuaded her to stay at Rabén and Sjögren, he hadn't been entirely truthful. The publishing house's finances were nowhere near straightened out, as he'd claimed. In *Twenty-Five Years: A Chronicle* (En tjugofemårskrönika), Rabén admitted that the management had been reckless to put new books into production in the summer and fall of 1945, but argued that the seriousness of the situation—and a certain youthful desperation—drove them to it: "We were in the same situation as a gambler who keeps on betting, hoping for the big win that's going to let him sort everything out."

Right up until the day in mid-September 1945 when *Pippi Longstocking* was named winner of Rabén and Sjögren's competition, events could have gone very differently for the publisher, and for the first Pippi Longstocking book. The three-year-old company's financial circumstances were so dire, with so many expensive books left sitting on its warehouse shelves, that in August 1945 the publishers attempted to sell all the submissions they had received for the competition Astrid Lindgren took part in. Bonniers was offered more than two hundred manuscripts sight unseen, but declined. Among the piles of submissions were not only *Pippi Longstocking* but also another Astrid Lindgren book, entitled *The Children of Noisy Village*, which she had finished over the summer at Furusund. Astrid didn't think it was anything special, and in a letter to Hanna and Samuel August she referred to it as "a cheery book, although the text isn't so dreadfully good."

Bonniers turned down the offer from Rabén and Sjögren, which meant that the large, wealthy publisher had—without realizing it—rejected Astrid Lindgren and Pippi for the second time in literary history. Before the 1940s were out, *Pippi Longstocking* had sold about 300,000 copies in Sweden alone, making Rabén and Sjögren the country's leading publishing house for children's and young-adult literature. Again, the ever-present Elsa Olenius had a hand in it: in 1946 she whispered into Hans Rabén's ear that Astrid knew shorthand, could type, spoke several languages, and was in need of a part-time job. Rabén wasn't slow to take Olenius's advice. Mrs. Lindgren had, after all, turned Christmas 1945—which his employees and especially Rabén himself had long been dreading—into the most successful in living memory. Twenty-one thousand *Pippi Longstocking* books changed hands in two weeks. As Rabén wrote in 1967: "We were all in the warehouse until late at night, packing *Pippi*. I spent Christmas going round Stockholm's bookshops in a taxi. All Swedish children were going to have *Pippi* for Christmas that year."

Colomba and Corinna

The spread of Pippi fever in 1945–46 was the product not only of the initiative of Astrid's firebrand editor but of the book's first two pre-Christmas reviews in 1945, which were also the two most important: Eva von Zweigbergk's in the *Dagens Nyheter* and Greta Bolin's in the *Svenska Dagbladet*. These two respected critics also wrote columns about children's culture, education, and family life, under the pseudonyms Colomba (Zweigbergk) and Corinna (Bolin). They made frequent calls for innovation in Swedish children's literature, supported by Elsa Olenius, who had compiled the lists of books for Zweigbergk and Bolin's pioneering *Children and Books,* which came out that same year.

Together, Zweigbergk, Bolin, and Olenius made up a powerful trio in Swedish children's and young-adult literature of the 1940s. They were well aware of how to orchestrate their influence through the daily papers, radio, the publishing industry, and the library system. Astrid Lindgren, the new comet in the authorial heavens, benefited greatly from their efforts. Seeing them operate up close, however, she wasn't always enthusiastic about what they were doing, as she wrote to Hanna and Samuel August in August 1948: "Yesterday Eva von Zweigbergk phoned me and said that Bonniers was going to publish a new edition of *Tales One Never Forgets* [Sagor man aldrig glömmer], which Eva v. Zweigbergk edited. There was a story in it she wasn't very happy with and wanted to change. She wanted 'Nils Karlsson the Elf' instead. It was Elsa Olenius who put her up to it, of course. I know, I know."

In 1945, Pippi Longstocking was hailed by the two critics as a liberating force. The initial celebratory fanfare was sounded by Eva von Zweigbergk on November 28, 1945, in the *Dagens Nyheter:* "Pippi Longstocking has a major task in store for her, serving as a safety valve for ordinary children in an ordinary world where freedom is sadly rather limited." A week later, Greta Bolin followed suit in the *Svenska Dagbladet,* seconding Zweigbergk's claim that the character of Pippi liberated contemporary children from the pressures of authority and everyday life. Using her own family as an example, Bolin suggested that Pippi could provide a safety valve for grown-ups, too: "The book is quite simply a pyrotechnic display of jokes and horseplay. Our Jonas (aged seven), who heard some fragments, shrieked with laughter, and it's almost equally funny for adults."

Raising their voices in chorus, Corinna and Colomba praised the radical elements of Pippi's antics, setting the tone for other reviewers over the following days, weeks, and months. All this critical enthusiasm sent *Pippi Longstocking*'s Christmas 1945 sales skyrocketing, at a time when gifts increasingly reflected Swedish families' need to put the war behind them through laughter and merriment. And *Pippi Longstocking* delivered the goods. Is it possible to imagine a greater contrast with the sinister Nazis, who'd done their best to lay waste to the planet for six awful years? Even the jaunty, colorful jacket featuring Pippi and Mr. Nilsson promised rowdy fun, and inside were Ingrid Vang Nyman's congenial illustrations: Pippi in wacky clothing, with hair nobody could ever force into a steel helmet. A sense of comic distance emerged between Nyman's depiction and the depressing images of jackbooted military commanders and soldiers that had dominated the media for five or ten years.

Astrid Lindgren had never dared dream of such success. Since Bonniers' rejection in 1944, she had fundamentally doubted Pippi. Was the writing too provocative? Were people ready for the world's strongest child to be a girl? The pattern of children's reactions had always been unmistakable, but adults either loved it or hated it, like the Rabén and Sjögren jury, explained Astrid in a letter to Näs dated September 29, 1945: "I'm anxious to see what criticism Pippi will get; I'm sure there'll be a few dressings-down. There was a teacher on the jury and she didn't appreciate the book at all,

Few Swedish writers of the 1940s had such a natural and unintimidated approach to modern media as Astrid Lindgren, and she was one of the first people in Scandinavia to understand how essential it was to use platforms beyond paper-based ones to tell a good story. In the 1950s and 1960s, long before the term "novelization" came into use, she wrote radio and film scripts that were reworked rapidly into literary best-sellers.

because Pippi 'behaved so oddly,' as Dr. Strandberg told me when I met him at the publishing house yesterday. But Strandberg likes the book, and said that Pippi was a mixture of Huckleberry Finn and Superman."

Like Elsa Olenius, the journalist and travel writer Olle Strandberg took on various jobs for Rabén and Sjögren, and he didn't believe Astrid had any reason to fear criticism. Pippi—like Huckleberry Finn and Superman—was above all that, he thought. This view was largely borne out in the first six months after publication, when Astrid's little supergirl received nothing but complimentary reviews in the media, but in fall 1946 a few critical voices began to be raised, mainly among parents and educators.

The first of these belonged to a professor at Lund University, sixty-four-year-old John Landquist. An academic heavyweight who lectured in psychology, education, and literature, he was also a literary critic, author, and translator of Sigmund Freud. As a disciple of Freud, Landquist was obliged to adopt a skeptical attitude toward anyone who considered the will to power the most essential human instinct. The philosopher Bertrand Russell had outlined just such a position in *On Education, Especially in Early Childhood,* the book Astrid had referenced in her cover letter to Bonniers in 1944, and to which she alluded in the *Svenska Dagbladet* on January 15, 1946. *Pippi Longstocking*'s author was being interviewed because she had won one of the paper's annual literary prizes, and she described the main character's "almost frightening popularity" among children of her own acquaintance:

> "Tell us about Pippi Longstocking" was all I heard wherever I went, and I felt as though this fantastical character must have hit a sore spot in their childish souls. I found the explanation later in Bertrand Russell, who observes in his book *On Education, Especially in Early Childhood* that the most prominent instinctive trait in childhood is the will to power. Children are tormented by their own weakness compared with older people, and want to be like them. That's why normal childhood fantasies involve the will to power. According to Russell. I don't know if it's true. I just know that all the children I've tried Pippi on clearly love hearing about a little girl who's totally independent of all adults and always does precisely what she wants.

All this talk about the will to power as the primary driving force in a child's mind was a poor fit with Landquist's Freudian preconceptions, as became apparent in the August 18, 1946, *Aftonbladet,* where he hauled *Pippi* over the coals and criticized the *Svenska Dagbladet* for having lauded a mediocre writer. Entitled "Inferior and Prize-Winning," his article diagnosed Pippi as mentally ill and Astrid Lindgren as an "unimaginative dilettante." The elderly professor of education had read the book aloud to his daughter, and neither father nor daughter had liked the main character one bit. Pippi's antics were thoroughly nonsensical, indeed downright pathological, complained Landquist: "They don't make sense in terms of the situation or the mental world of childhood. They are mechanically, unimaginatively cobbled-together nonsense. For that reason they are also unsavory."

Indignant Voices

Astrid considered writing a retort, but chose instead to send long, heartening letters home to her mother and father in Småland on August 23 and September 1, sharing two pieces of good news: first about her new part-time job as an editor, and second about her latest top prize in a children's book competition, which this time had focused on detective novels:

> Tomorrow I shall begin my part-time job with Rabén & Sjögren, which I'm sure I've written about before. I'll be working 4 hours a day and have demanded 300 kronor per month. I haven't got hold of the *Aftonbladet* yet, so I can't show Mother the harsh telling-off I got from Professor Landquist. I haven't responded either, and perhaps I won't. . . . Not everybody thinks that *Pippi Longstocking* is uncultured and unsavory and unimaginative and everything else Landquist called it. P.S. Wouldn't you know it, I've won another prize! 1,500 kronor for *Bill Bergson, Master Detective.*

In the slipstream of Professor Landquist's critical attack on *Pippi Longstocking* in August 1946, more unsatisfied readers reared their heads in the media. And there was plenty for a grown-up to get worked up about: an impudent child who stuffed herself with cakes at morning coffee without asking permission, who didn't listen in school, who lied constantly and even scoffed at such an august institution as the police. A child who ate poisonous mushrooms, played with fire and loaded guns, slept with her feet on the pillow, blew her nose on her clothing, and encouraged other children to spell badly and speak inelegantly. "The book is quite simply riddled with unhealthy and unnatural childishness," said one column in the *Folkskollärarnas Tidning*, a teachers' magazine, and a reader signing as "Indignant" complained in one of the country's major dailies about the "deranged style" of the Pippi stories that were perpetually on the radio: "Isn't there anyone who can put a stop to this depraved program? . . . What do our educationalists say? Is there anything instructive or amusing about this Pippi Longstocking's exploits? In one instance she goes into a woman's clothing boutique and tears the arm off a mannequin, then after being told off by the saleswoman she answers: 'Yes, all right, take it down a notch!'"

Lindgren considered responding to her critics, but instead left the stage clear for reviewers of *Pippi Longstocking Goes Aboard,* which came out in October 1946. Several of them used their review to polemicize or to refute Landquist's article: Elsa Olenius, for one, who was standing in at the *Dagens Nyheter* throughout the fall as Eva von Zweigbergk traveled in the United States. Elsa seized the opportunity to promote her protégée and collaborator, whose new Pippi book she knew all about: Astrid had sent her the manuscript in May, asking for her opinion and any suggested changes, as we know from a letter to Hanna and Samuel August dated May 25, 1946.

As the *Dagens Nyheter*'s temporary critic wrote in her review on October 26, the latest Pippi book was far more internally coherent than the first, and in the majority of chapters Lindgren kept control of her "unique style of humor, without going over the top." Olenius concluded by advertising the play she and Astrid had adapted together, which they'd been staging successfully for more than six months: "The first book about Pippi Longstocking can now be seen in dramatized form. It is currently being performed at the City Library's children's theatre at Medborgarhus. The book is published by Rabén & Sjögren, and the price of a ticket to the little play is 65 öre. It's easy to perform and amuses all children."

One review that took a particularly wide variety of approaches to *Pippi Longstocking Goes Aboard* appeared in the *Aftontidningen* on November 16, 1946. Young Lennart Hellsing, himself an imaginative writer for children, with a knack for playing with rhyme and nonsense words, demonstrated his caliber as a reviewer by summarizing the past year's Pippi debates, criticizing the latest Pippi book for straining after effect, and finally applauding Pippi Longstocking as the torchbearer for a new era in children's writing. Writers such as himself, Tove Jansson, and Astrid Lindgren were among the avant-garde:

> Astrid Lindgren writes fairy-tales that are no less fairy-tale-esque than folk tales, but adapted to a modern environment. Her modern fairy-tales have the advantage of being written for children and understood by children, which is far from the case with folk tales. The deep wisdom and symbolism they contain is entirely missing from *Pippi Longstocking;* however, one may well ask what use young children have for an old man's insight. Isn't it more important that they (to put it in modern terms) are allowed to live in a healthy world of sensuality? With her Pippi Longstocking books, Astrid Lindgren has knocked a hole in the wall of moralism, sentimentality, and mawkishness that has enclosed Swedish children's literature for decades.

For the second year in a row, Astrid Lindgren did a roaring trade over Christmas, but she was struggling with her newfound stardom, and in her diary between Christmas and New Year 1946 she remarked: "I've become a teeny-weeny little bit 'famous.'" Something of an understatement. In the world of children's literature she was by far the year's highest flyer, having published four major books inside twelve months. Two years after her debut, Astrid Lindgren had two Pippi books on the market, as well as two novels for girls, two plays, and a children's detective novel; altogether they had sold 100,000 copies. She had also won four literary prizes, signed a film contract, and sold translation rights to *Pippi* to several countries. Unreal or not, it was time to remove the quotation marks in Astrid's diary from the words "author" and "famous."

The first big interview with "Pippi's mother" was striking in terms of its contrast between the careless Pippi and her stylish, elegantly dressed author. When *Vi* wanted to do an interview with Astrid Lindgren in the early summer of 1947, because her new book, *The Children of Noisy Village*, was going to be serialized in the magazine over the summer, the journalist couldn't hide a note of surprise at the sight of her: "A slim and graceful creature comes toward me, beautifully put together in brown and muted turquoise, with a merry twinkle in her calm, gray eyes."

So, what was the trick to her barnstorming success? *Vi*'s correspondent wanted to know. How was she so marvelously in tune with her small readers? "Well, I don't know that there's any trick to it," she said. "Maybe just remembering your own childhood well . . . how you felt and thought and talked when you were a child. It might sound obvious, but when your job consists of plowing through children's book manuscripts day after day, you discover how important simplicity is. No long or complicated sentences, no theoretical arguments, no incomprehensible words, no narrow-minded moral advice!"

For the first time, a broader public got to learn about Mrs. Lindgren's literary working methods. When she got the initial idea for a story, she explained, it was like she was in the hands of larger forces: "I prefer to write in bed, when I've been ill and I'm waiting to be rid of a fever, or in the evening after I've gone to bed. Or outside. Like *Bill Bergson, Master Detective,* for instance, which came into being in our rowboat in Furusund. And I work quickly, so I'm almost ashamed when I hear how lots of other people toil over their books. When I start writing I get a sort of happy feeling, like the book's finished already and I'm just there to get it down on paper."

Finally the journalist from *Vi* wanted to hear Mrs. Lindgren's thoughts on the debates about upbringing in Sweden, which had partly focused on the educational qualities—or lack thereof—in the Pippi Longstocking books. The question gave Astrid a welcome opportunity to respond to some of her critics:

I really wish we grown-ups would learn to respect children, to truly realize that "young children are also people," and to follow through on the consequences of that. I'd like to put in a word for freedom in children's education. Far too many people think that freedom in education is the same as freedom *from* education. When children get up to their monkey tricks, you can just shake your head and mutter something about irresponsible parents and "freedom." That's unjustified, and it delays and hampers developments in this important area.

Child Psychologists to Tea

Throughout her career, Astrid Lindgren carefully avoided associating herself and Pippi Longstocking with any particular school of psychology or pedagogical approach, which is not to say that she undervalued research and scholarship in those fields or was reluctant to engage with them. Quite the contrary. A few weeks before the interview in *Vi*'s midsummer issue in 1947, Astrid invited two Swedish child psychologists to tea at Dalagatan, along with Anne-Marie Fries and her sister Ingegerd, who had previously heard Joachim Israel and Mirjam Valentin-Israel lecture about the couple's controversial book, *There Are No Naughty Children* (Det finns inga elaka barn!). Their message was that adults shouldn't restrict children's freedom. Instead, they should learn to understand the nature of children and their needs at various stages of development. During the lecture, the psychologists had cited *Pippi Longstocking* as an example of an "antiauthoritarian children's book" that had a liberating effect on a child's psyche.

After the lecture, Ingegerd approached the speakers, introduced herself, and asked whether they could be persuaded to write a blurb for the Pippi book. They agreed, and ended up having tea one June evening at Astrid Lindgren's apartment. She was so pleased with the couple's blurb, which could also be used to promote *Pippi* overseas, that in May 1947 she sent Hanna and Samuel August an extensive quotation from it:

From a child psychologist at the Erica Foundation I've received the following recommendation: that *Pippi* "is among the best children's books published in the Swedish language. Unlike the

majority of children's books, it's refreshingly free of any kind of
finger-pointing or moralizing 'edification.' Its value, in my opinion, lies in its potential effect as a kind of safety valve for children who have been trammeled by the judgmental and punitive
kind of upbringing so often practiced. Children can identify
with Pippi, who is allowed to do everything they would like to
do themselves but either cannot or may not. This offers them a
socially acceptable outlet for the aggression all children feel
toward their parents, and which often manifests in problem
children in the form of various maladjustments and behavioral
disorders. For this reason I consider both books to be of great
value for mental health." What do you say to that! I had no idea
I was doing a good deed for mental health when I wrote *Pippi*.
The man, whose name is Israel, is an assistant at the Erica Foundation's department for remedial teaching, where they look after problem children.

Subsequent letters to her parents in Småland tell us that their chat
over tea on June 2, 1947, ended up revolving—unsurprisingly—around children's education, *Pippi,* and *There Are No Naughty Children,* a copy of
which the couple gave to their hostess with the dedication "To Pippi Longstocking's mother, with thanks from the authors."

Karin Nyman recalls the Israels' book making a strong impression on
her mother, and they frequently discussed it at home. After her encounter
with the psychologists in June 1947, it was as though Astrid Lindgren felt
emboldened to express her opinions about child-rearing and the impact of
childhood in the media. She did so several times in 1947 and 1948, in a series of articles about education and upbringing in the weekly magazine
Husmodern (The Housewife), where Astrid repeated what she had said in
her interview with *Vi* the year before and emphasized parental responsibility even more strongly: "Freedom in education doesn't preclude stability.
Nor does it preclude children feeling affection and respect for their parents.
Most important of all, it means that parents also have respect for their
children."

One chapter of *There Are No Naughty Children* may have especially interested Astrid Lindgren: the final one, "Education for Democracy," in which Joachim Israel and Mirjam Valentin-Israel put child-rearing in a broader, more universal human context: "Through sensible upbringing we must create a person who can safeguard the democratic society we hope will emerge—safeguard it against falling back into the barbarism of recent years."

It was this civilizing perspective on upbringing that Astrid Lindgren would utilize many times later in life, most clearly in her acceptance speech in 1978, when she was awarded the Peace Prize of the German Book Trade. First, however, she drew on it in the year she met the Israels and read their book. It was the fall of 1947, and Astrid was again featured in *Vi,* this time answering the question, "What is there in this era, in this world, that gives cause for optimism and hope?" Her positive answer—perhaps the most optimistic one Astrid Lindgren ever gave to this oft-repeated question—was as follows:

> We need happier people to create a world that's fit to live in. Although there may be many good reasons to be discouraged about the future, I, at least, can't help feeling a surge of optimism when I look at the people of tomorrow: the children and teenagers who are currently growing up. They're merry and breezy and secure in a way no previous generation has been. Taking a broad view, I think I can venture to say that they're also happier. This gives us cause to hope that a more humane and generous generation is developing, people who don't begrudge each other life. The sulky naysayers, the pig-headed, the privileged and the selfish—are they not the cause of all evil, both great and small? Their stunted souls have no room for generosity or human compassion. And if it's true that every single individual is the product of his or her childhood, then I think we can let ourselves look forward with a certain optimism. A reasonable degree of ill-will must surely disappear from the world when those who are now children and teenagers finally begin sorting out the mess our aged planet's in.

The Danish Connection

The first five years of Astrid Lindgren's career as an author were an explosion of artistic and commercial success. Three trilogies were launched: *Pippi Longstocking, The Children of Noisy Village,* and *Bill Bergson, Master Detective.* Counting the three short plays and two picture books she also found the time to write, Astrid Lindgren's publications numbered sixteen by 1949. Meanwhile, nine of her books had been sold for publication in Norway, Finland, Denmark, Iceland, Germany, and the United States, and many more such agreements were in the pipeline.

The majority of these foreign contacts in the 1940s were made through a literary agent in Denmark, Jens Sigsgaard, who had approached Astrid Lindgren in the spring of 1946, when the rumor that the world's strongest girl was Swedish made it across Øresund. Sigsgaard, who had a degree in psychology, was headmaster of the Fröbel Training College in Copenhagen, a hardworking author of children's books, and owner of the International Agency of Children's Books (IAC), which he had founded at the end of the war. He not only functioned as Astrid Lindgren's international outpost in the 1940s and early 1950s, a time when the European publishing industry had been blasted to smithereens and there was scarcely paper to print on, but proved an inspirational colleague and an exceptionally good friend. Correspondence spanning nearly fifty years testifies to their close relationship; today, their letters can be found at the national libraries in Copenhagen and Stockholm.

By the time they met, Sigsgaard was the author of several distinctive rhyme and picture books, including *Palle Alone in the World* (Palle alene i verden, 1942), which became a huge international success and ended up on Astrid's bookshelf at Dalagatan. In *Palle* we meet a boy whose internal life in many ways resembles that of his contemporary Pippi Longstocking. One day he finds himself dreaming that he's the only person left on earth. Palle can do whatever he wants, so he eats candy by the bucketload, drives a sports car, empties a bank, drives a fire engine with the sirens blaring, and takes a solo plane trip. But Palle also learns that the world is a dull place if you're all alone, and the boy's unrestricted freedom becomes a prison.

Illustrative of the mutually inspirational collaboration between Lindgren and Sigsgaard was an exchange of opinion in the fall of 1946, occasioned by his recommendation of Gyldendal's offer to buy *Confidences of Britt-Mari*. On September 26, the author responded: "Of course I'll accept Gyldendal's offer, with pleasure and gratitude. . . . What are the chances of placing Pippi in America? Perhaps the book wouldn't suit them there."

Agent Sigsgaard in Copenhagen replied promptly: "Pippi Long-stocking is in good hands in the USA with our new representative, Louise Seaman Bechtel. I've also just sent a copy of it to South Africa."

At the beginning of her writing career, Astrid Lindgren drew heavily on Sigsgaard's experience, frequently asking him for advice—in the fall of 1947, for instance, when she'd had several film offers for the Pippi Long-stocking books. Sigsgaard replied on November 7 that sales of film rights were something every author should consider carefully. It was crucial to maintain control of the characters they had created: "When it comes to an important question like a film adaptation of the book, I think you ought to take your time and not just accept the first offer that comes along. There's no doubt the book will become a classic, so it'll be filmed at some point."

Sigsgaard never did manage to sell Pippi on the American market. It was Elsa Olenius who made that coup, when she visited the United States in 1947. The news was immediately passed on to the Danish agent: "I'm afraid it's my sad duty to inform you that a good friend of mine who's been in America for a few months has sold Pippi to Viking Press. It was Mrs. Elsa Olenius, who'd been given a bursary to study children's theater there. It seems that America has a dearth of plays for children, so she recommended the Pippi piece (a little dramatization I wrote), and hey presto, Viking came along and bought the book. . . . Write a few lines and tell me you're not too crushed that I sold Pippi myself."

Sigsgaard was neither crushed nor bitter. He congratulated Astrid on the sale, adding a few words that in many ways epitomized the productive interaction between the literary agent and many Scandinavian children's book authors of the 1940s and 1950s, Astrid Lindgren chief among them: "I have previously emphasized that IAC's mission is not primarily business-oriented. Our main purpose is to make good children's books more widely known, and since Pippi is my favorite child, I'm pleased with her success."

Pippi Psychosis

Now that Astrid Lindgren had Jens Sigsgaard to promote her books overseas, the immensely busy author and editor had a little more time to keep an eye on things in Sweden. She was in constant demand. Both *Noisy Village* and *Bill Bergson* were triumphs, and Pippi fever looked to be chronic. It culminated during the week around Children's Day in Stockholm in late August 1949, when thousands of children and parents packed the large park at Humlegården. Everybody wanted a share of the magic, hoping to catch a glimpse of the most idolized child of the age and her horse, monkey, and house.

On the opening day, August 21, there were tumultuous scenes across the park. Children and parents crowded around the large mock-up of Villa Villekulla: partly to get a ride on Pippi's horse, partly to enter the competition for best Pippi outfit, and partly to grab some of the glittering golden coins that, as the program announced, came "tumbling down" from the sky twice a day. There were lines miles long for the park's mini-train, the Pippi Express, which puffed around Humlegården. On its first day it carried such prominent passengers as Carl Gustaf, the "Little Prince" of Sweden, and his older sister Christina.

"Pippi Longstocking Psychosis," read one of the capital's newspapers the next day, while the provincial papers came out with even more dramatic headlines: "Stockholm Children Storm Pippi—Crowds, Tears, and Fainting Fits."

The organizers of Children's Day were making huge profits, thanks to the skillful branding of Pippi Longstocking's universe. Astrid Lindgren wrote the program booklet, *Pippi Longstocking in Humlegården,* which was presented as a picture book about Pippi: The day before Child Welfare Day, Pippi goes into the big city to build a copy of her house, but first she has to clear the venerable old park of roughnecks and troublemakers. Ingrid

Vang Nyman did the illustrations for the booklet, each copy of which included a raffle ticket. She also designed the multicolored posters featuring three Pippi motifs, which were pasted all around Stockholm to attract the public. The money rolled in, filling more and more pockets. Pippi had become big business.

Christmas 1948 saw the premiere of a new short play about Pippi at the Oscar Theater in Stockholm, for which Astrid Lindgren had written the script. "A jaunty two-act piece in six tableaus, it is sure to become a fixture of the Christmas program for many years to come," said the hopeful theater manager Karl Kinch. Grown-up actor Viveca Serlachius played Pippi, ballet master John Ivar Deckner choreographed the exotic dances from Kurrekurredutt Island, and Per-Martin Hamberg, whom Astrid knew from her days at the censorship office and from the radio show *20 Questions,* composed the music, which was released the following year as a collection entitled *Sing with Pippi Longstocking.* In advance publicity, Astrid Lindgren made the following comment, which seems to indicate that the author was growing tired of all the fuss about Pippi: "Children like to fight, somersault, and throw pies, and I think they'll get plenty of that here. A new Pippi book? No, there'll never be any more. Three is enough."

But the world's strongest girl wasn't so easily held back. Demand was simply too high. More and more investors were knocking on Astrid's door, and first in line was film producer and media mogul Anders Sandrew, who assumed that securing the film rights as quickly and cheaply as possible would be a mere formality. But Sandrew, a farmer's son from Uppland—who also owned the Oscar Theater, where Pippi had played to full houses at Christmas 1948—soon learned that Småland farmers' daughters could be equally hard-nosed negotiators. In May 1949, Hanna and Samuel August received a letter that illustrated their daughter's flair for business:

> As Gullan may have told you, I've finally sold Sandrew the film rights to Pippi. He started off as a little greengrocer, but now he's a big cheese in the film and theater industry. He's known all

over the city and is terrifically rich. But he wanted to haggle over
the price. So we had a scuffle or two. Eventually he invited me
over for lunch one Sunday in his exceedingly beautiful home,
and I thought we were going to discuss the film script with the
director, but it was just him and me, and it was all so he'd have
a chance to haggle about the price. He drove me home and
stood in my doorway at least a quarter of an hour while he kept
haggling. But at last I got what I asked for—6,000 kronor.

Sandrew Productions mass-produced films in 1940s and 1950s Sweden, pumping out at least one a month, and *Pippi* was ready to premiere by
Christmas 1949. Astrid Lindgren hadn't been involved with the script,
which merrily embroidered the Pippi stories, partly to make room for various celebrities from the world of Scandinavian showbiz. The jazz musician
Svend Asmussen, for instance, accepted a role as a musical mailman who
plays a new instrument each time he appears onscreen with his mailbag.
Astrid managed to put on a brave face at the premiere, recalls Karin Nyman,
who sat in the front row beside her mother, but inside she was cringing. In
a letter home to Näs on December 21, she wrote, "I'm colossally disappointed in the Pippi film, although the critics were undeservedly easy on it."

One of the critical critics was Eva von Zweigbergk. Astrid wrote her a
long letter the day after the premiere, December 10, beginning by thanking
her for what Zweigbergk had written in the paper, then listing everything
else she could have criticized:

If I could've undone the film yesterday by paying back all the
money I got for the rights, I wouldn't have hesitated for a moment. I sat groaning in my seat, and just before the end I slunk
off, terrified somebody was going to come up to me and ask me
what I thought. And I asked myself: what in Heaven's name will
Eva Zweigbergk have to say about this? . . . I'm deeply grateful
for what you wrote about Pippi at the beginning of the review.
It's a great support for me, when I see what that film lot have
done to my poor child. . . . The Pippi film I dreamt of, a film

that should have been full of warmth and cheeriness and sunshine, is not what we've got, but in its slashed form it may still
be palatable for young, uncritical children.

Astrid Lindgren promised herself that in the future she would protect
her work better, just as Jens Sigsgaard had advised. Pippi Longstocking was
proof that a creature of the imagination could, like the shadow in Hans
Christian Andersen's fairy-tale, detach itself from the page and give its cre-
ator the slip. Since early 1946, Pippi had been constantly popping up in
new guises and commercial packaging. No longer merely a picture book
and a coloring book, a play and a film, she appeared as a magazine serial, a
paper doll, a gramophone record, and even in advertisements for a savings
bank and a pharmaceutical firm that was relaunching a vitamin pill for children. All with Astrid Lindgren's approval and—not infrequently—her cooperation. As she wrote to Hanna and Samuel August on February 1, 1947:
"Next week I shall be doing a gramophone recording of Pippi—it'll be the
episode with the burglars. Next there's bound to be Pippi dolls and Pippi
jigsaw puzzles."

A Star in Big Shoes

While Pippi was taking on a life of her own as a Swedish brand, Astrid
Lindgren had plenty to do herself. Her meteoric rise as an author had made
her one of Sweden's best-known and most popular voices on the radio: in
1948 she became one-third of the permanent panel on the country's most
popular radio program, *20 Questions*. The concept of the program seemed
tailor-made to her sharp intelligence, her sense of humor, and—not least—
her flair for oral communication. At a time when there was only one radio
channel serving approximately two million radio licenses, Astrid Lindgren
was as well known in Sweden around 1950 as Pippi Longstocking, increasingly appearing in magazines among other famous faces—always with a
sly smile, and ready with an answer as swift and funny as on the radio. In
one magazine in 1949, for instance, the children's book author was asked
the following complex questions: "What would you find it difficult to live

without? What would you find it difficult to live with?" To the first question Astrid answered: "Children and nature," and to the second, "Shoes that are too small."

In the spring of 1949, the *Vecko-Journalen* visited Astrid in Dalagatan to put a body and face to the popular radio voice: "Slender as a reed, with slim legs in American nylon stockings, brought home from her travels to the USA." Later that year, a journalist from a provincial paper traveled to the city to interview—or so he thought—a ruddy-cheeked fairy-tale aunt from Småland, but rapidly had to revise his opinion: "She looks like the efficient businesswoman she is, reasonably tall, slim, blonde, quick to laugh. What strikes you when you speak to her is that she's incredibly genuine. She never considers for a moment putting on airs. She's quite eager and curious, but you're warmed by her purely personal interest in things you thought would be trifles to a popular celebrity. She has no false modesty: She is aware of her importance and her utterly unique position as the only children's book author of major significance in the 1940s."

That the forty-one-year-old author and editor took life at a furious pace the *Vecko-Journalen* did not doubt. In previous years, they were told, Astrid Lindgren had not merely traveled up and down Sweden with her books but had also been on several long trips abroad, sometimes accompanying her husband on vacations and business trips to England, Italy, Finland, and Denmark, but also under her own steam, having visited the United States in 1948. Readers of the *Vecko-Journalen* learned nothing about the specific details of this overseas trip, however. It was somewhat complicated, because the journey had been financed by the Bonniers-owned publishing house Åhland and Åkerlund. The company had offered Astrid Lindgren an all-expenses-paid trip to the United States because—yet again—it was trying to steal Sweden's best-selling author from the competition.

Bonniers was struggling to accept its past blunders with *Pippi* and its "defeat" by a tiny publishing house on the edge of bankruptcy. Throughout 1946–50 it made various sneaky attempts to lure Astrid Lindgren away from Rabén and Sjögren and into its luxurious stable of authors at Sveavägen. In January 1946, two months after the publication of the first Pippi book, Astrid wrote home to Näs: "Yesterday I got a letter from Åhland & Åkerlund asking whether I would consider writing fairy-tales or stories for their Christmas magazines, which gave me a certain sense of triumph, seeing as Åhland & Åkerlund is owned by Bonniers, and Bonniers once rejected *Pippi*. Yes, yes, it's a very small triumph, but even so."

In 1947 Astrid Lindgren was offered a well-paid full-time job at Åhland and Åkerlund, where she would be responsible for everything to do with short stories. She mentioned it in a letter to her parents in May 1947, adding: "I don't want a full-time job. I much prefer hiding at the office and writing the rest of the time, so I turned them down—to their great astonishment."

She was, however, very tempted by the publisher's offer of a free trip to the United States in 1948, although she didn't like the thought of leaving Lasse and Karin and Sture for a whole month. The rather unusual offer, which involved sending Astrid over in her capacity as a journalist, was made in fall 1947 during a meeting between Astrid Lindgren and the editor in chief at the fashion magazine *Damernas Värld*. On behalf of Albert Bonnier Jr., she was supposed to ask whether Mrs. Lindgren would like to go to America and write something for *Damernas Värld* about "negro children." At first Astrid thought she had misheard, as she later wrote to Hanna and Samuel August: "I don't know what interest 'Damerna' can have in negro children, of all things. I was a little taken aback, so I haven't given them an answer yet. But a free trip to America wouldn't be the worst idea. Evidently Pippi is giving the gentlemen at Bonniers no peace—I'm getting one offer after another."

Six months later, on February 22, 1948, she told her father, mother, and Gunnar and Gullan at Näs that Albert Bonnier himself had been out fishing for her—at that she had taken the bait: "I've signed a contract with Åhland & Åkerlund for the America trip. I've booked a plane ticket for April 14, returning home on May 12. Albert Bonnier wrote a letter with the contract, writing that he signed the contract 'with a light heart' and that he believes in success 'for us both.' I, on the other hand, am not so certain, but I don't think I can let a chance like this pass me by, because it's an extremely good contract."

Astrid Lindgren ended up leaving for the United States on Bonnier's dime, and managed—with great difficulty—to write the agreed number of articles for *Damernas Värld*. She wasn't proud of the commissioned work, and in a letter to her parents dated December 10, 1948, she made it clear that as an editor she would never have accepted such hastily scribbled travel reportage "with a light sociological touch," as a reviewer later called it when the articles were collected and published, like the first *Kati* book, in 1950: "I've delivered a *little* part of my American articles to Abbe [Albert] Bonnier, and would you believe he thinks they're good. Personally I think they're so silly I get quite ill at the mere thought of them."

Astrid felt so guilty about these commissioned pieces that she refused point-blank when Albert Bonnier called her in 1950—for the last time—and asked whether she wanted to go to Egypt. At Bonnier's expense, naturally.

My Harsh Love

It was a busy and financially lucrative year for the Lindgren family. Not just because of Astrid's overwhelming success, but also because Sture's job at "M," the Swedish Motorists' Association, had kicked into high gear after the end of the war. People wanted to go out again, crossing countryside and borders, and increasingly they owned their own cars. When Sture Lindgren turned fifty in October 1948, his name appeared in newspapers across Sweden. Despite the period of war and crisis, he'd managed to turn M into Scandinavia's largest motoring organization, and according to press coverage on his birthday, the key to his success lay not simply in his insight into the international challenges of motoring and tourism but also in his extensive network, oratorical gifts, and remarkable memory. "Lindgren keeps the entirety of M in his head," wrote *Motor*. What the magazine neglected to mention was that the director's head also had room for books: he loved to read, and followed his wife's career closely. He even helped out with proofreading and comments such as "*Pippi Longstocking* isn't a book—it's an invention."

The books Astrid signed for Sture in the 1940s testify to her gratitude: "To my prophetic Sture, for his unflagging interest in Pippi. With a kiss on the forehead, from Astrid" and "To Sture (the prophet) from his adoring wife." Those were her inscriptions in the first two Pippi books.

Astrid accompanied Sture on many of his trips abroad, including to Italy in 1949. On the way home the couple stopped at Berchtesgaden and saw Hitler's "Eagle's Nest." Her family at home in Näs got a detailed account: "The building, high above the earth, must have been absolutely magnificent when it was in one piece. And the view over the German and Austrian Alps was incredible. Now only ruins remain, and nobody does anything about them. Presumably they're meant to stay there as evidence of what happens to tyrants."

In her 1949 collection of stories *Nils Karlsson the Elf*, however, her tone was a little more serious, and edged with an exclamation mark: "To Sture, my harsh love!"

Nils Karlsson the Elf was a sharply different Astrid Lindgren book, stirring a darker, more melancholy layer of the human mind. In depicting lonely children like Bertil, Göran, Gunnar, Gunilla, Britta-Kajsa, Lena, Lise-Lotta, Barbro, and Peter, she thematized longing in a way only fleetingly glimpsed in her earlier work, most clearly in the moving conclusion of the Pippi trilogy in 1948. Tommy and Annika, getting ready for bed, suddenly catch sight of the glow from Villa Villekulla's kitchen through the trees in the dark garden: "Pippi sat at the table, her head resting in her hands. With a dreamy expression in her eyes, she stared at a small candle flickering before her. 'She . . . she looks so lonely,' said Annika, and her voice trembled a little. 'Oh, Tommy, I wish it were morning, so we could go and see her right now.' . . . 'If she just glances up we can wave to her,' said Tommy. But Pippi stared straight ahead with dreamy eyes. Then she blew the candle out."

There was a minor mode to Astrid Lindgren's nature that the Swedish public of the 1940s knew nothing about, a gravity and thoughtfulness drowned out by her delighted studio audience's laughter and applause when they recorded *20 Questions* and ignored in her magazine interviews, which exclusively foregrounded the lively, happy children's book author. Behind the forty-year-old writer's jaunty, fearless façade was a well of melancholy and anxiety deeper than anyone suspected, and it had more than a little to do with her "harsh love," Sture. After their marital crisis in 1944–45, they tried to reconnect, but the demands of everyday life took their toll, especially on Sture. On top of long days at the office, he was frequently busy with trips, conventions and banquets, dinners and meetings, many of them at the Strand Hotel in Nybrokajen near his office, where they ate—and drank—until late into the night. Sture struggled with his weight and high blood pressure. As Astrid observed in her war diary in 1946: "I'm occasionally worried about Sture's health—and not without reason."

His poor state of health was inextricably bound up with his unwillingness to confront his alcohol problem. As Karin Nyman recalls: "My father drank too much. He tried to abstain completely, but not long after that he died. He never got blind drunk or drank until his personality changed, nor did he lose his job, but it was probably only a question of time."

This internal schism in the Lindgren family—between material prosperity and Sture's lack of willpower when it came to tackling his issues— was tough on Astrid. Sometimes, when she was alone, she would take out her diary and try to describe and explain her feelings of depression. On March 8, 1947, she came so close to the heart of the problem that, in the middle of a long passage, she decided to write one sentence in shorthand, one that encapsulated her concerns about her marriage—and about Sture. She didn't want to risk Lasse or Karin accidentally reading it if they happened to be flicking through the diary. After this sentence, Astrid switched

In 1947 Lasse passed his exams, and Astrid breathed a sigh of relief after many years of struggling to motivate her son in his studies. As she had written in her account book in the fall of 1937, when Lasse's problems at school had begun: "Lars will always be a daydreamer who forgets what he's supposed to do."

back into normal writing: "Now and then Sture has real problems with his heart—and he doesn't look after himself at all, which can be a trial sometimes. I don't like this winter. It's not as it should be, and sometimes I wonder whether *any* season will ever be as it should again."

But then Easter came, spring was just around the corner, and it was time to celebrate Lasse's school exams, which had caused his mother far more anxiety over the years than they had caused him. The day he graduated from Norra Latin—May 13, 1947—Astrid noted in her diary: "Lars, little Lars . . . When the doors opened and I saw my little boy standing in the back row with a cap on his head, singing the school song, it gave me such a start."

At the party back at Dalagatan afterward, they had to do without Sture, who was on a business trip to Portugal and sent his congratulations by telegram. Otherwise, however, all their Stockholm friends were present, including Esse, Lasse's old playmate from Håbets Allé. Astrid's family in Vimmerby couldn't leave the farm in the middle of spring, but they did receive a letter with a detailed, almost filmic account of the big day: it had revolved around Lasse, but it ended with an intimate and inspiring mother-daughter chat. Just as she had once come up with the name Pippi Long-stocking, it was Astrid's nearly thirteen-year-old daughter who, sitting on the edge of her bed, provided the inspiration for how the tale of Pippi, Tommy, and Annika should end:

> When Karin had gone to bed after Lasse's graduation party and I came in to say goodnight, she cried bitterly and said: "I never want to grow up." I think she felt it was too much responsibility to be an adult, and have to choose a job and all that sort of thing. "I don't want you to get old," she said, crying even more. When I'd chatted with her for a while, she said: "Now I'm talking to you, I'm not so sad—you'll keep living until I grow up!" And then she cried again, the dear creature. I remember being so afraid throughout my childhood that someone in the family would die. I always prayed to God that we'd all die on the same day.

Sorrowbirds and Songbirds

IF YOU VISIT VIMMERBY TODAY AND take a walk through "Astrid Lindgren's World," you'll find a theme park full of strong, kooky, happy children's book characters in a nice, warm, safe atmosphere. This image isn't false, but neither does it represent the whole truth about her work, in which rootlessness, unhappiness, and grief are nearly as pronounced as coziness, zest, and custard-pie comedy.

In fact, Astrid Lindgren's books are teeming with the lonely and isolated. Some of them are adults, but many are children and teenagers, like Pippi Longstocking, Nils Karlsson the Elf, Kajsa Kavat, Mio, Lillebror and Karlsson, Rasmus and Paradise Oscar, the children of South Meadow, Pelle from Seacrow Island, Emil, Rusky, Birk, Ronia, and many others. They may be fatherless or motherless, abandoned in a house or an apartment, tied to a sickbed, locked in somewhere as punishment, or roaming around outdoors. They may be only children, or children who have siblings and parents but lack the care and affection that family should bring.

The effects of loneliness on the children in Astrid Lindgren's work are as varied as its causes, but what most of them have in common is a longing for closer contact with other living beings. Usually the people in Astrid Lindgren's literary universe eventually manage to find one another, either in imagination or in reality. Or perhaps they find themselves, because while Lindgren was convinced that humans are naturally solitary creatures, she also believed we can find strength in acknowledging our own isolation. As children, as teenagers, and as we age, we must all learn to be alone.

This theme, which runs throughout her work, emerges in the final scene of the Pippi Longstocking trilogy, when Tommy and Annika glimpse

Pippi through the kitchen window and wonder at her sovereign isolation as she gazes into the candle flame, before she blows it out and the book ends. One year later, several isolated children appeared in the story collection *Nils Karlsson the Elf,* which heralded a change in Astrid Lindgren's work. After eight novels, she returned to the kind of short prose she had written around 1940 for various magazines. In a few of the stories in *Nils Karlsson the Elf,* she also cemented the stylistic breakthrough—the child as first-person narrator—she had introduced to the world in *The Children of Noisy Village* in 1947: "I'm Lisa. I'm a girl, as you can tell from the name. I'm seven, and I'm turning eight soon. Sometimes Mamma says, 'You're Mamma's big girl—won't you be a sweetheart and dry the dishes today?' And sometimes Lasse and Bosse say, 'We don't want little girls playing Indians with us. You're too small.' So I'm not sure whether I'm big or little. When some people think you're big and other people think you're little, then maybe you're just the right age."

Writing a children's book as if it were drawn directly from a child's mind, foregrounding the child as the book's only narrator, was neither common nor considered entirely proper. Even in the 1940s, children were still supposed to be seen and not heard, and there were remarkably few precedents in world literature for a child like Lisa from Middle Farm, who describes herself and her surroundings without ever mentioning something a child wouldn't know, and—equally important—without being interrupted by an adult. Her most important forerunner is *Huckleberry Finn* (1884), but the first attempts at writing a fictional "child's voice" were actually made fifty years before Mark Twain's classic novel, in the Romantic era: in Hans Christian Andersen's *Fairy-Tales Told for Children* (1835), lots of boys and girls are given a chance to speak; earlier still, in 1826, Andersen had experimented with this revolutionary perspectival shift in his poem "The Dying Child," which from start to finish is narrated from the deathbed of a little child, a child soon to be taken up to God, totally alone. After the Romantic period, it was mainly within the genre of memoir that writers used child narrators, and children's characters and voices had to settle for appearing within a framework prescribed by an adult narrator—as in Laura Fiting-hoff's *Children of the Moor* (Barnen från frostmofjället, 1907), for example, which is about seven orphaned children and their extraordinary flight from famine, generally considered the first major realistic children's novel in Sweden.

The Children of Noisy Village was therefore an epochal book, although no Swedish critics in 1947 paid any heed to the small, sensational pronoun that began the book's first two sentences: "I'm Lisa. I'm a girl, as you can tell from the name." Voices like Lisa's deepened the world of childhood significantly, making it more alive and authentic. Via an underage narrator, the grown-up author could venture further into the nature of children, depicting fundamental, universally human emotions like happiness, curiosity, sorrow, and loneliness. This process is clearly apparent in Astrid Lindgren's work around 1950, when Lisa's first-person voice spread to another *Noisy Village* book in 1949 and to *Nils Karlsson the Elf* the same year. The latter contained nine short stories about contemporary children, all connected by feelings of isolation and the longing for care and attention.

The two short stories in *Nils Karlsson the Elf* that begin with the words "Now I'm going to tell you" both have girls as narrators, Barbro and Britta-Kajsa, and each is about an isolated child who lacks a friend her own age. Although each narrator has a mother and father who live with her, the message in both stories is that two grown-ups are rarely enough to fill a child's emotional life, and certainly not if the parents disregard their child's emotional needs. This important issue preoccupied Astrid Lindgren throughout her life, and in September 1952 she wrote a long opinion piece about the relationship between parents and children in the journal *Perspektiv*, entitled "More Love!" In it she argued that nothing later in life would or could ever replace the love a child *didn't* get before the age of ten:

> A child that doesn't feel loved by its parents and can't find anything else to love and be loved by will grow up to become an unhappy and often loveless person, who may do much harm on the path through life. Nothing is more certain than that the fate of the world is decided in the nursery. There it is decided whether the men and women of tomorrow will become people with healthy souls and good wills or stunted individuals who

From the beginning of her career as an author, Astrid spent time among her primary readership. Diligent and committed, she took part in events like Book Day all around Sweden, giving readings, signing books, and talking about being an author. Seen here in 1950, she always emphasized that she wrote primarily for her own inner child.

use every opportunity to make existence a little more difficult and burdensome for their fellow human beings. Even the politicians who will control people's fates in the world of tomorrow are small children today.

It's the heedlessness characteristic of too many parents' interactions with children that the two first-person stories in *Nils Karlsson the Elf* are about, although the parents in both stories are relegated to the periphery. In "Mirabell" we meet Britta-Kajsa, an only child who lives in a small cabin far out in the woods with her hardworking, poverty-stricken parents in extremely modest circumstances. Her parents don't have the money to buy her a doll, so Britta-Kajsa simply imagines having one. One day, however, she finds a doll called Mirabell poking out of the soil in the garden, where she had sown some mysterious seeds given to her by a wizard who appeared when her mother and father were at the market. Out of the girl's profound loneliness, a fairy-tale is born: Mirabell grows and grows until she can be snapped off at the root, like one of the plants Britta-Kajsa's mother and father are more interested in than they are in her. The doll is both a welcome toy and a manifestation of the girl's need for closeness, friendship, and affection.

In another short story, "Dearest Sister," Barbro makes a friend out of the reader by telling us about her secret twin sister Ylva-li: "Don't tell anybody! Not even Mother and Father know." Like Britta-Kajsa, Barbro lives an isolated life, but here the primary cause of the girl's terrible loneliness is a change in the family makeup: "Father likes Mother best, and Mother likes my little brother best, who was born in the spring."

A child's loneliness can have many faces and expressions, and Astrid Lindgren was painfully aware of the misery an older child can feel when abruptly sidelined within the family, partly because she had witnessed it firsthand in 1934, upon arriving home at Vulcanusgatan with Karin as a newborn. Lasse's sadness that day etched itself into her, and in a letter dated February 11, 1944, to her sister Ingegerd, who had been through a similar experience with her newborn son Åke and his older sister Inger, she described the situation and atmosphere:

For all children who have siblings, I think, there will be periods of sorrow. I shall never forget the time when I came back with Karin in my arms and said, "My little Karin," and Lasse heard it while he was sitting on the toilet at Vulcanusgatan. I sensed I should go to him, and I did, saying, "My little Lasse." And then when I was sitting in the nursery a while later he came rushing in, kissed me on the hand (the only time he's done that) and said, "I was just wondering why you weren't saying 'My little Lasse!' and then you came and said it. You're so sweet!" Every time I think of it I get tears in my eyes, because I understand he was sad, and that he was incredibly relieved when he didn't have to be sad anymore.

In the story about Barbro from 1949, her mother doesn't remember to say, "My little Barbro!" so the girl creates not just an imaginary friend who calls her "my dearest sister!" but a special language that belongs to the sisters alone. Barbro spins a whole fairy-tale realm out of her imagination: beneath a rosebush in the back garden, which she names "Salikon," is the entrance to this parallel world, where her sister Ylva-li lives in a golden castle with her poodles Ruff and Duff and her horses Goldfoot and Silverfoot, which the sisters ride through the "Big Nasty Forest where the Evil Ones live" and the "Meadow where the Good Ones live." In this fantastical universe, Barbro's life is rich and meaningful, because here everyone pays attention to her and treats her with affection.

With its glittering metals, muted, beautiful tones, and mysterious language, "Dearest Sister" foreshadows the novel *Mio, My Son* (1954), which emerged out of an earlier, epic short story, "He Travels through Day and Night," written in 1950 for the magazine *Idun*'s Christmas issue. The complete text was repurposed as the first major chapter of *Mio, My Son,* in which the reader discovers the social and psychological backdrop to the narrator's imaginative journey. In both the 1950 story and the 1954 novel, the boy is nine years old, named Bo Vilhelm Olsson but nicknamed Bosse, and has spent his childhood with emotionally stunted foster parents. Fleeing into his imagination, he searches for his unknown and sorely missed father.

Like her earlier stories featuring Britta-Kajsa and Barbro, *Mio, My Son* is about a profoundly lonely, introverted child's ability to use his mind and the depth of his longing to retreat from sorrow and pain, creating a fantasy world complete with parental figures, brothers, sisters, relatives, and friends, all of whom acknowledge his existence.

Vulnerable children and teenagers interested Astrid Lindgren. In her opinion piece in *Perspektiv,* "More Love!," she described an experience during a performance at the theater, where a mother with two children a few rows down was unable to hide her infinite love for her younger son even as she demonstrated a total lack of interest in the older one: "It's as though he doesn't exist. He just sits there, looking somehow lost. Isolated, curled in on himself, unable to make contact with the others. Throughout the performance he exchanged not a word with anybody. There's a wall of loneliness around him. His abandonment is so vast it makes you despair."

It was this wall of loneliness that Astrid Lindgren wanted to breach on behalf of all vulnerable, isolated children when she wrote *Mio, My Son* over two spring months in 1954. In it, the reader meets a boy who is "curled in on himself and unable to make contact with others." With the aid of his fertile imagination Bosse tells us the story of Prince Mio, who finds his father, the King, and proves his worth through valiant deeds. In reality, however, the orphaned boy is sitting alone on a bench in a dark, deserted Stockholm park, staring at the lights from the surrounding apartments, where children with proper mothers and fathers sit at proper dining tables and have fun together. At the house of Bosse's best (and only) friend, Benka, for instance: "In the houses all around there were lights everywhere. I could see there were lights in Benka's window too. He'd be sitting indoors now, eating pea soup and pancakes with his mother and father. I imagined children sitting with their fathers and mothers everywhere there was light. It was just me sitting out in the dark. Alone."

Sture's Death

The word *ensam,* which in Swedish can mean lonely, alone, single, and solitary, crept into Astrid Lindgren's diary around 1950, and would appear there many times over the decades, as her life changed repeatedly and she reflected

In the *Expressen* on December 12, 1992, Astrid reflected on her marriage: "I really, really liked him. He had a wonderful sense of humor and was kind, but I was never in love with him. I've never experienced grand passion in the way most people seem to have done, although I don't feel it's something I've missed out on. . . . Sture was only 53 years old, I was 45, and I took it with equanimity. I've always been able to manage on my own."

deeply on her own family and the family as an institution. When a family member moves or disappears, it always alters something in the atmosphere of the home. As Astrid wrote in her diary at Easter 1950: "A family is a curious constellation. Each time a member breaks away or vanishes, the family unit is utterly changed. Sture + Astrid + Lars + Karin is something very different from Sture + Astrid + Karin. I hope to God it never becomes Astrid + Karin. Let it be Sture and Astrid, in the end, with the other two happy wherever they are. Perhaps one day it'll be Astrid + nobody. Right now I feel like anything could happen. Life is such a fragile thing, and happiness so hard to maintain."

There were still no signs of change in Sture's alcoholism. It's clear from Astrid Lindgren's admonitory words to the young Sara Ljungcrantz in their correspondence during the 1970s that it had been a problem for many years: "I know such an enormous amount about alcohol. . . . Take good care of the clear, sensible, logical brain you have, and don't soil it with spirits."

Her fear of one day being alone, which Astrid never mentioned to her parents in her letters home to Näs but increasingly discussed in her diaries after her marital crisis in 1944, became a reality one June day in 1952, when Sture suddenly began to vomit blood. Though rushed into medical care, he died two days later at Sabbatsberg Hospital. The cause of death was a ruptured vein in his esophagus, resulting from cirrhosis of the liver. When Astrid got back home on June 16 after two traumatic days at the hospital, she sat down with her diary and reviewed the final hours of her life with Sture:

> I lay on an ottoman by his side, holding his hand. Eventually I fell asleep, but I woke when, in my sleep, I heard his breathing change—it had been strong, but it grew slower and slower, and just after eleven o'clock in the evening the end came. Stina had been with me earlier, but she had gone home shortly before then, so I was alone with Sture when he passed away. I wrote some lines on a piece of notepaper as I sat by my unconscious boy's side. This is what I wrote:
>
> June 15, 1952: "While strolling out an afternoon in June." That's what my darling used to sing. And that's what he's doing now—strolling out an afternoon in June. He's dying before my eyes. "Birds were singing everywhere," he also sang. Well, now they're singing in the trees outside Sabbatsberg. And my darling is dying. He can't hear me anymore, see me anymore. Or I would have thanked him for his goodness and kindness—it's a *sweet* person who's passing away this June evening. He was a child to me, and I loved him deeply. I've always held his hand, but where he's going now I can't follow and hold his hand.

God, please help him find the way! I would so dearly like to hold his hand always!

Karin, who had just turned eighteen, was on vacation in Paris. She returned home immediately. Today, when she looks back on her father's sudden death, she remembers it as an unpleasant surprise, but not a huge shock. Everyone in the Lindgren family was aware of Sture's fragility, and for several years before it happened Astrid had known where things were headed, believes Karin Nyman: "We were very worried about him, and when he died—somewhat unexpectedly, within just a few days—that worry was lifted. I mean, it was a relief. When I came home from France (Lasse fetched me) the three of us spent several days together in the apartment, which I remember being filled more with lovely conversation and good memories and relief than with tears and sorrow. Astrid grieved afterward for the husband she'd not had much time with, the husband she'd had so much fun with, and a good sex life, I think, but probably for a long while she had associated their life together mainly with disappointment and worry."

Shortly after the funeral, Astrid took a trip to the Stockholm archipelago, trying to live as normally as possible, although she was constantly thinking of Sture, and even talked to him when she was alone. On July 9 she wrote to Elsa Olenius, who'd been a huge support, both at the hospital and in the days afterward: "It *is* empty without him here. Because he was around us all the time out here on Furusund, of course, and here there was no reason to worry. But I suppose you're right—it's probably best for little Sture to sleep. Oh, I was so glad you were with me at Sabbatsberg! I'm so glad to have you!"

In letters home to Hanna and Samuel August, Astrid forced her mind in other directions, telling them how the vacation was going, and about Lasse, his wife, Inger, and their little son, Mats. All three had come to visit in early July with Karin and their cousin Gunvor, and the girls were a big help when strangers suddenly dropped in. One day Astrid Lindgren's Dutch publisher knocked on the door with a copy of *Pippi Langkous,* and Greta Bolin from the *Svenska Dagbladet* also dropped by to interview Astrid about

In November 1952, Astrid wrote home to her mother: "On Sunday evening, after waving goodbye to Gunvor, Karin and I went to Northern Cemetery and lit a candle on Sture's grave, since it was All Saints Day. There were candles burning on almost all the graves, and they glowed so beautifully in the dark. And you can be sure, Mamma, that I'm looking at ALL the death notices to see how old the deceased person was. It's as if I want to convince myself that more lives than just Sture's have been cut short before their time—and goodness me, there are many, many!"

life and literature. On July 31, 1952, an article appeared in the newspaper about the author's grief: "Right now Astrid Lindgren needs nature as a healing force, because she has recently lost her husband and life partner. The wound is still so fresh that it scarcely seems more to her than a bad dream. She is not alone, however; she has her sweet daughter Karin and her son Lasse and the best solace of all, her grandson Mats, who is one and a half. 'The world's most beautiful grandchild,' says Astrid Lindgren . . . and she begins to tell the loveliest tale, one that will never be printed, because it's the tale of a grandchild who steals his grandmother's grief-stricken heart."

Grief wasn't usually something Astrid shared with the outside world. Life had to go on. Back in Dalagatan in August, she continued work on the upcoming radio series about *Bill Bergson, Master Detective,* carried out her part-time job at Rabén and Sjögren, began to take driving lessons, sat in the recording studio as they tackled a new, entertaining series of *20 Questions,* and prepared for the publication and launch of her new book. Just before Sture's death, Astrid had completed the third and final volume about the children of Noisy Village, sixty thousand copies of which would be printed by the end of the year. Keeping up a brisk pace on the treadmill of life was Astrid's best defense against grief and depressive thinking. So were the walks she took through Northern Cemetery in Stockholm, where she could reassure—if not exactly comfort—herself that other people had died at the age of fifty-three. Christmas 1952 was carefully recorded in the diary: "I usually list all the Christmas presents in this book to aid my memory—on Christmas Eve 1952 Sture got a wreath of Christmas roses on his grave. . . . 'I want to live at least until you get inducted into the Swedish Academy,' he used to say, that little optimist. A wreath of Christmas roses, he got for Christmas 1952."

Every year between Christmas and New Year in the 1950s, Astrid Lindgren took stock of the previous twelve months in the small black or brown notebooks she had once called her "war diary," which now numbered more than fifteen volumes. As well as listing that year's haul of gifts and recounting the Lindgren family's ups and downs over the year, Astrid had also started to take a sharper look at herself and her role as a woman. How would her life work without a man at her side? Could she live alone in Dalagatan once Karin moved out and twenty-five years of family life irretrievably vanished? Such thoughts surfaced every year between Christmas and New Year, including in 1957: "I want to try not to be afraid anymore. . . . It's fear of everything that's the real misfortune. So let life bring what it will, and let me be strong enough to accept what it brings."

Mother and daughter lived together in Dalagatan for six years during the 1950s, before Karin got married and moved in with Carl Olof Nyman. Those final years in her childhood home are clear in Karin Nyman's memory: "Our lives didn't change much. Financially not at all, because it was Astrid who earned the money we needed. We could remain in the apartment, she and I. But Astrid's existence altered gradually, and she developed more of a social life and entertained more than when she had to live with Sture's expectation that she would stay home, and that he wouldn't have to socialize. It was nice for her that I kept living at home until I married—we lived as a twosome for several years. She could write as before, of course."

Mio, My Son

Toward the end of the 1950s, Eva von Zweigbergk and Astrid Lindgren were asked to collaborate on *Friendly Criticism* (Vänkritik), a book dedicated to Olle Holmberg, a professor of literature, and consisting of a series of conversations between Swedish literary critics and Swedish authors. Each pair chose a single work by their respective authors to discuss; Lindgren and Zweigbergk selected *Mio, My Son*. Zweigbergk posed the following question: "I'd like to know how Astrid Lindgren, the nimble, quick-witted person we all know from the radio, having grown up with a gaggle of siblings, is capable of depicting childhood loneliness with such great sympathy and insight."

Lindgren answered honestly—and cautiously. She explained that the lonely children might represent the author's unconscious longing for the lost paradise of childhood and for closer contact with the natural world. Beyond that she wanted to leave it up to the readers themselves to interpret the book. "What do I know?" she asked.

Mio, My Son is thus a book open to many interpretations. A biographical approach affords a further potential explanation for Astrid Lindgren's special "insight" into Bosse's loneliness: *Mio, My Son* was written on a wave of grief. Underneath the surface narrative, where Bosse dreams of finding his father, lay another emotional drama, in which the author's loss was reflected in the boy's loneliness and longing.

No other book in Astrid Lindgren's oeuvre feels as crushing and claustrophobic as *Mio, My Son*. From the moment Bosse's imagination takes hold and he assumes the guise of Prince Mio, venturing with his friend and squire Jum-Jum into the gloomy realm of the dead, where a knight called Sir Kato reigns, the language centers around a handful of particular words: "solitary," "alone," "black," "dark," "death," and "sorrow." These words are repeated over and over with small variations, often within the same passage or extended sentence. The first time Mio sees the lake and enchanted birds outside Sir Kato's eerie castle, for instance: "I dream sometimes of vast black waters opening before me. But never have I dreamt, never has any human dreamt, of water as black as that I saw before my eyes. It was the bleakest, blackest water in all the world. Around the lake were nothing but tall, black, desolate cliffs. Birds circled above the dark water, many birds. You couldn't see them, but you could hear them. And I have never heard anything as sorrowful as their cries."

If you count the author's use of the words "black" and "dark," you'll find that they appear almost a hundred times over the course of the sixty-odd pages Mio and Jum-Jum spend amid the soul-like cliffs of Outer Land, while words like "solitary" and "alone," "death" and "sorrow" are repeated altogether more than fifty times. No other words in the novel are used even remotely as often as these, and they all help tighten the novel's grip on the reader's throat, intensifying the claustrophobic atmosphere so characteristic of many scenes in *Mio, My Son*. Yet the sorrowful, evocative language involves more than just repeated words. Another important tool is the invocation recited by Jum-Jum whenever the two boys need a miracle. It's spoken eight times on the way to their final confrontation with Sir Kato, varied each time, depending on the danger or challenge the young heroes face. One fixed, recurring element in the invocation is the final phrase: "If only we weren't so small and alone." These words are repeated eight times in all, becoming a kind of refrain in the novel and underscoring humanity's insignificance on a cosmic scale. One of the final times Jum-Jum pleads for help is when Sir Kato has captured him and Prince Mio, and they've been condemned to rot slowly in prison: "If only death weren't so heavy, so heavy to bear, and if only we weren't so small and alone."

This particular variant of Jum-Jum's invocation is difficult to imagine in the mouth of a nine-year-old. Even in a fantasy novel, the words are better suited to an adult voice. Perhaps these eight invocations had their own resonance and import for Astrid Lindgren amid the torrent of words and images that flooded onto the page in spring 1954—with astonishingly few corrections in comparison to her other novels.

In 1945, while Sture and Astrid's marriage was in crisis, she noted in her diary that the initial creative phase of working on a new book was a special place where she always found peace and solid ground: "Sometimes I'm happy and sometimes I'm sad. Most happy when I write." From the beginning of her career as an author in 1944–45, the writing process provided a counterweight to Astrid Lindgren's personal worries, her melancholy and fear. As she scribbled down her fiction in shorthand, she felt, as she put it, "inaccessible to all sorrows." But when it came to working on *Mio, My Son* in 1954, sorrow was, for once, not shut out from the writing process. On the contrary. From the first twilit scene in Stockholm to the dark dreamscapes of Outer Land, sorrow and the sustained agony of loss and misfortune are the dominant mood in *Mio, My Son*. Not even at the end of the novel, when the sun finally casts its rays into its murky universe, does the reader escape being reminded of sorrow: "At the top of the highest silver poplar sat Sorrowbird, singing all alone. I don't know what he was singing about now that all the missing children had come home again. But I thought Sorrowbird probably always had something to sing about."

The big black bird accompanies Mio throughout most of his journey, reminding us that sorrow is a condition of life, on an equal footing with happiness. No one can avoid it. Astrid Lindgren liked to explain it with the aid of a Chinese proverb, which she would repeat to dejected or anxious friends, for instance Elsa Olenius, whom she comforted in 1959: "You can't prevent the birds of sorrow flying over your head, but you can prevent them building nests in your hair."

Presumably Astrid Lindgren did exactly that when buried in *Mio, My Son* in the spring of 1954: let the birds of sorrow flap around her head as she wrote and wrote, taking care the big black bird didn't build a nest. Many thoughts, memories, associations, and ideas crossed paths during those two spring months. Yet even then, it didn't take much to remind her suddenly of Sture. In a letter Astrid wrote to a German friend on Walpurgis Night—Witches' Night, April 30—in 1954, she described the loss of her husband

and her work on the book, which was currently absorbing most of her time
and energy:

> On exactly this date two years ago I was home [at Näs] for a few
> days. It had just properly turned spring, and I was sitting on a
> hill one evening as the sun shone and birds chirped, and we
> sang: "Life may never again invite you to celebrate." When I got
> back to Stockholm, my husband was ill, and he didn't live much
> longer. So I think about all that on Walpurgis Night. Inciden-
> tally, I'm writing like a madwoman at the moment, perhaps I
> already told you? In fact I'm doing nothing but writing (and
> going to the publishing house a few hours a day). It'll be fun
> when the time comes to send you the book and hear what you
> think. But that will be a while yet, of course.

It wasn't very long, however, before Astrid—alongside her young narrator in *Mio, My Son*—had struggled through the darkness and emerged
into the light. Summer had arrived, and she had finished yet another book,
which was due to come out before Christmas. Meanwhile Rabén and
Sjögren sent her a check for five thousand kronor as thanks for her extraordinary efforts as an editor over the past year. Astrid intended to use the
unexpected windfall to buy a car, although she still didn't have a license—
hence she took the overcrowded boat from Strandvägskajen to Furusund.
In front of her stretched a gloriously long summer holiday, with plenty of
writing and visits from family and friends, Astrid's new friend from Germany included.

Louise the Songbird

Their friendship sprang up in the fall of 1953. In late September, Astrid
Lindgren and Elsa Olenius embarked on an extended journey around
Europe, the primary purpose of which was to visit an international
children's literature conference in Zurich, where authors, publishers,
librarians, teachers, journalists, and people in radio—250 participants in

all, from twenty-seven nations—had convened to set up IBBY (the International Board of Books for Young People). On the final day of the conference, Erich Kästner gave an unforgettable speech, which was later quoted in the magazine *Svensk Bokhandel*. In the same issue, Astrid Lindgren "interviewed" herself:

> "And did Mrs. Lindgren meet many nice people?"
>
> "Yes, a whole lot of them. Erich Kästner was there, and Lisa Tetzner, and from England came Pamela Travers, the Mary Poppins woman, you know. And we mustn't forget Jella Lepman, head of the International Youth Library in Munich, which was built with American money. It was Jella Lepman who took the initiative in this kind of international cooperation, which one may venture to hope will promote good books for young people. Yes, there's something happening on that front, and that's a good thing. After all—as Erich Kästner so rightly said in his admirable concluding speech: 'Die Zukunft der Jugend wird so aussehen wie morgen und übermorgen ihre Literatur' [The future of youth will look like their literature does tomorrow and the day after tomorrow]."

Kästner's perspective on the future of young people and contemporary literature for children stuck with Astrid on her way home from the conference, as she left Elsa and traveled alone to Hamburg, Bremen, and Berlin to promote her books, which had been translated into German. A small up-and-coming publisher in the form of married couple Friedrich and Heidi Oetinger had acquired the German-language rights to *Pippi Langstrumpf* in 1949, after five larger publishers had kindly but firmly turned them down. Now the Oetingers were poised to take Pippi's mother out to dinners and banquets in Hamburg and Bremen, where there were readings and Astrid Lindgren spoke about the importance of laughter and smiles in the postwar period. Her trip then took her to Berlin, where she had been invited by the city's Hauptjugendamt—which, according to the interview in *Svensk Bokhandel*, corresponded to the Swedish Barnavårdsnämnd, or Child

Louise Hartung (1905—65) had Goethe in her blood, and couldn't imagine life without *Faust*. She explained as much in a letter to Astrid, even putting *Pippi* up on the same pedestal, because the two loners fitted together so well. Hartung, a powerful figure at the Hauptjugendamt, had replaced all the children's librarians in Berlin and decreed that *Pippi Langstrumpf* should be on every reading group's program each Monday.

Welfare Authority. It was a branch of the Berlin administration dedicated to finding creative ways to help children from broken homes grow up reasonably normal and happy:

> "So Mrs. Lindgren was invited as a kind of mental vitamin injection?"
>
> "Hmmm, that might be putting it too strongly. I think the Hauptjugendamt had got the idea that a little Longstocking wouldn't hurt German children, and wanted to convince booksellers of that. They'd invited all the children's booksellers in

the whole western sector to a meeting at the 'Haus der Jugend' in Berlin-Dahlem. And we sat comfortably on a green lawn in the sunshine and had a lovely time. I read a little story from one of my books, and Ursula Herking, Germany's most distinguished female cabaret star, read from *Pippi Longstocking, Kajsa Kavat,* and *Kati in America,* and all the booksellers were so sweet and encouraging. But booksellers mostly are, don't you think? And afterward the energetic ladies from the Hauptjugendamt took the opportunity to appeal for the booksellers' help making the books more popular among children."

One of the energetic ladies from the Hauptjugendamt in Berlin was Louise Hartung. A few months earlier she had written to Astrid and offered her the use of her two-room apartment in Rudolfstädter Strasse in Wilmersdorf while the Swedish author was in town. In early October 1953, Astrid waded boldly into the complex world of German prepositions and came up with a polite thank-you note: "Liebe Frau Hartung, vielen Dank für Ihr freundliches Schreiben und für die Einladung. Natürlich will ich so fürchterlich gern nach (oder zu?) Berlin kommen." [Dear Frau Hartung, Many thanks for your friendly note and for the invitation. Of course I'd be delighted to come to Berlin.]

During her trip Astrid not only gave readings and chatted with her readers but visited various booksellers, schools, and care homes for children injured in the war. On her last evening in the city, Louise Hartung took the Swedish author on a secret sunset mission. They drove across the as yet unguarded border between the Federal Republic and the German Democratic Republic into the old, bombed-out districts of the East, where as a young, talented singer Louise had given concerts, made records, taught photography, and until 1933 lived something of a bohemian lifestyle with such artistic souls as Kurt Weill and Lotte Lenya. Immediately after arriving home on October 28, 1953, Astrid sat down and told Hanna and Samuel August about Berlin: "It was one of the most dismal things I've ever seen. I saw the place where Hitler's bunker was—it's just a ruined heap, and everywhere the streets are lined with ruins, ruins, and ruins. It was like being on another planet. On the few undamaged houses the Russians have put giant flags and painted incomprehensible slogans. Poor Louise Hartung went around crying. It was once the grandest part of Berlin, and she didn't even recognize her city. She had to read the street signs to find out where we were."

This tour through the streets where Louise had lived as a young woman—where she had survived the battle for Berlin in spring 1945, where only months before Astrid's visit Soviet tanks and troops had beaten down the first people's uprising in the GDR—was the beginning of a long, sensitive, and intellectual friendship. As Karin Nyman recounted: "I remember Astrid coming home in 1953 and being fascinated by this German woman who had experienced the war firsthand, who took her on secret excursions into the East and told her about the social situation for children after the war in Germany and about 'die Halbstarken,' gangs of criminal teenagers who, according to Louise, had seen their mothers raped. Louise was a highly gifted woman, passionate about culture, and she showed a strong interest in Astrid Lindgren's books. Astrid found her positive and insightful criticism productive. But also a bit exacting."

The two women managed almost six hundred letters in eleven years, before Louise Hartung died in 1965, shortly after Astrid Lindgren had visited her on Ibiza. It was the highly emotional Louise who wrote most and longest, but Astrid kept up her end, considering the colossal number of letters she produced during those years, both in private correspondence and in her capacity as an editor. She wrote approximately 250 letters to "Louisechen," spread evenly from 1953 to 1964. The first were in German, then a few in English, but the rest in Swedish, once Astrid discovered that Louise—who wrote only in German—was able to read Strindberg in his own language. From the first, Astrid addressed her as "Louisechen," a diminutive of Louise, which over the years came to be inflected with affectionate humor: "Louisechen mein Freundchen," "Louise meinchen," "Louisechen Hartungchen Berlinchen," and—when the space race began at the end of the 1950s—"Louisechen, mein Satellitchen, Sputnichen."

In the vacuum after Sture's death, Astrid's friendship and correspondence with the gifted and cultured Louise Hartung was an intellectually challenging window onto another, bigger world than the one in which Astrid moved day to day in Stockholm. The women exchanged huge numbers of literary tips, as well as opinions about authors and their work, from the youthful passions of Goethe to the lusts of the aging Henry Miller. "What are you reading at the moment?" Louise asked at regular intervals, and Astrid would tell her about all the books she dreamt of wedging into her packed schedule. There were times when her work as a writer and editor hemmed her in, spiritually as well as temporally. In a letter written on New Year's Eve 1958, she aired her frustrations: "I have so little time, and such a great hunger to read, yet I simply can't manage novels any longer, apart from a few old classics I reread. But I prefer to read history, philosophy (although I'm horribly unversed in that department), poetry, biographies, and memoirs. Nothing gives me deeper satisfaction than philosophy and poetry, I think. Have you read any Swedish poetry?"

From their first long letters in 1953–54, there existed a colossal openness and intimacy between them. Neither of them seemed afraid to speak honestly about herself, and Astrid's concluding words in a letter dated February 22, 1955, were illustrative of the mode of dialogue they sought and found. The two women genuinely *spoke* on the page, often as though they were sitting at some café in Berlin, Budapest, or Vienna. Their letters were never hermetically self-involved, but engaged inclusively and curiously with the other correspondent. In February 1955, Astrid wanted to hear Louise's opinion on the meaning of life and existence: "Sometimes I wonder why I'm alive, why people are alive in the first place. But I only say this to you— I don't go round hanging my head so other people see it. If you know why people are alive, then write and tell me."

The year before, on April 30, 1954, in the series of letters that were becoming increasingly like self-portraiture, she had compared herself with her German pen friend, who wrote such wonderfully original, profound letters and was generally one of a kind, unlike the uniformly dull and ordinary Astrid: "I'm simply as ordinary as one can be, utterly normal and well balanced, albeit a little melancholy, which those around me probably never notice. I've probably never had much zest for life, although I can be very jolly when I'm with other people. I've had to carry this little melancholy since I was young. I was really happy only as a child, and maybe that's why I'm so fond of writing books where I'm able to reexperience that wonderful state."

Over the following years Astrid added more strokes to her tepid portrait of herself: as a person who was often sad, with an enormous need to "sit completely alone and stare at my navel." She also told Louise about her stressful editorial job, where she was pushed and pulled in all directions, and on February 13, 1957, she described a recurring dream about being transformed from a person in the big city into a solitary little animal far out in the woods: "I lay awake at night, coming up with a terribly beautiful poem that began like this: 'Oh, but she who / could be allowed to be / a lonely little animal in the woods . . .' No, this doesn't mean I always want to be *mit mir allein*. It just means I've had a difficult time with people who are fighting with each other and constantly want me to take sides."

Among the many things she shared about herself and her personality, things that clearly originated in a remote, deeply private space far away from her daily life in Sweden and her family and friends, Astrid also mentioned her exaggerated loyalty, which she called "a streak of madness in myself." Loyalty was a virtue, of course, but it could also be a yoke, and had often proved such in several of Astrid Lindgren's close friendships. She never found a solution to this problem, as Karin Nyman recalls: "Her devotion to her friends was huge. Astrid cherished strong feelings for people. But she had friends whom she felt pressured by, tired by, because they were so pushy and demanded so much validation, wanting 'sole rights' to her time and attention. What Louise was for her, I think, was above all a person she relied on when it came to judging what she wrote, the only one, as far as I know, that she really consulted for advice. And she was totally fascinated by Louise's life story, by everything she told her about the war and postwar period in Berlin, and a specifically 'European' identity."

Advances

If Astrid hadn't noticed during her first hectic visit to Berlin in October 1953 that Louise was more attracted to her own gender than to the opposite sex, she swiftly realized once back in Stockholm. It wasn't just the emotional, romantic letters from Louise that tipped her off; she also began to receive a stream of packages from Germany, containing everything from bouquets, flower bulbs, books, and gloves to chocolate, jellies, bowls of fruit, and a plane ticket to Berlin. Louise was doing her best to capture Astrid's heart, although she already had a girlfriend in Berlin: Gertrud Lemke, a doctor with a practice in Bundesplatz in Wilmersdorf, where the plaque on the door read "Psychotherapist."

As spiritually liberating and intellectually compelling as their correspondence was initially, it rapidly took an exhausting turn. Especially after the two women met on Furusund in July 1954, when Louise parked her car outside Astrid's red wooden house on her way to Lapland. The trunk was full of Berlin bulbs and roots that could be planted in Astrid's garden. Three days of long hikes and German conversations followed. These conversations were so many and so long that Astrid jokingly began to call Louise "Scheherazade." But Louise's heart harbored love as well as stories, love of the idealistically romantic kind. Gertrud Lemke described her girlfriend's ten-year infatuation in a letter dated July 1, 1965, when she returned Astrid's letters after Louise's death: "Louise created a kingdom out of you and around you, beaming all her powers of imagination into it and shielding it from all banalities and pedestrian facts. You were the right person to awaken this fascination and fulfill its expectations. Yet she intended something else, too, beyond perceiving you simply as this 'queen of closed boxes, of blissful dreams, of unfulfilled longings, of unnamable blisses.'"

Although Astrid regularly made the boundaries of their friendship clear, Louise's infatuation was a sore, largely unspoken point throughout their correspondence. After Louise left Furusund for Lapland and the Arctic Ocean on July 16, 1954, Astrid wrote her a letter: "Louisechen, Louisechen, I'm really not as wonderful as you believe, and you mustn't be so completely devoted to another person—not to me and not to anybody—because it makes you defenseless and leaves you at the mercy of someone else's caprice. I'm so very fond of you, and we shall be friends all our days, but you mustn't idealize me at the expense of the other people I know need you as a tonic and source of strength."

Louise in her youth. She was the eighth child in a family that lost four sons in the First World War. Louise was considered something of a wunderkind, she later recalled. As a child she was able to play Schubert's "Die schöne Müllerin" on the flute, and as a young woman in Paris and Berlin she tried to make a living as a concert singer, making a record she later played for her Swedish friend.

Astrid's protestations usually fell on deaf ears, and it rapidly became apparent that she would have to be clearer, without hurting her friend and pushing her away: "You say I'm 'playing with fire.' What fire? And how would I behave if I *weren't* playing with fire? Liking another person and being friends with her, is that playing with fire?"

Yes. When the other person was Louise Hartung, it was. The stream of affectionate letters and fresh flowers continued—roses, tulips, irises, and pinks, all ready to put in a vase. Then, at Christmastime in 1954, Astrid suddenly received a thick letter from Germany with a plane ticket to Berlin and a fairy-tale about a lizard and an oyster, written by Louise. It was a love story, the product of many hours spent wondering how to make Astrid open up

("Astrid zum Reden bringen könnte"). The answer came quickly, in the form of a fairy-tale about an ungrateful and anxious oyster "who got too much affection from too many people and shut herself into her shell." Astrid's fairy-tale was about all the people at home in Sweden who projected their needs and desires onto her, among them a male lizard who was apparently willing to abandon his lizard wife and lizard children for her and who threatened to commit suicide if he didn't get his oyster: "But she still didn't want to share her oyster bed with him, because she had such a need for solitude. She wouldn't share her inner self and her oyster bed with anyone. There were other lizards too, male lizards and female lizards, and all of them demanded they be the one the oyster liked best. That made the oyster very anxious, and she said: how can I choose a single one and say 'nur du und ich' [just you and me]?"

Having laid out her increasing struggle to honor the various expectations placed upon her by men and women demanding love and friendship, Astrid then brought Louise into the fairy-tale. She took the form of a vivacious female lizard from the banks of the river Spree, who also laid claim to the much-sought-after oyster up north:

> The oyster was so fond of her and wished she could be happy. But the way was so long and the water between them so deep, and the oyster thought: "Kleine süsse Eidechse [Sweet little lizard], find yourself an oyster on the banks of the Spree, an oyster who can make you as happy as you deserve. Es gibt für alles Grenzen [There are limits to everything]. You can't sit there far away on your bank and call to me, because I can't come to you or you to me—the water that separates us is too deep. . . . Don't ask too much of me, kleine Eidechse, because I'm an oyster who's locked herself in her shell. I'm sitting here on my oyster bed, watching life go by."

Not even this heavy hint discouraged Louise's efforts. In fact, the number of letters and packages increased steadily throughout 1955 and 1956, and the following winter Louise launched a new verbal offensive.

This time she skipped the fairy-tale and expounded her belief that genuine closeness in a friendship between two women rested on "körperliche Vertrauenheit." In other words, being not just spiritually but physically intimate. On February 13, 1957, Astrid Lindgren replied categorically:

> All kinds of love have a right to exist. But if someone—like me—is absolutely heterosexual and not even remotely bisexual, you can't be gripped by "love" for a person of the same sex, if by love you mean "Komm in meine Arme" [Come into my arms]. But I can definitely feel a deep sense of intimacy and admiration, or whatever you want to call it, for a woman, as I do for you. Much of what you think is strange about me is because I think it's a bit difficult to understand why you're so devoted to me, and that I can't really live up to your expectations. You can never be satisfied with giving love and only getting friendship in return.

Here the stream of letters and gifts might have ended, but it didn't. The two women kept seeing each other at least once a year, either in Stockholm or in southern Europe, often at secret meeting places in Germany or Switzerland. They were worried that if the Oetingers in Hamburg found out about these visits, they might rope their star Swedish author into doing extra publicity in Germany. Astrid enjoyed these getaways, although Louise could be a chore. When she returned home after a brief visit to Stockholm in April 1957, Astrid cried crocodile tears, and wrote in a letter to Elsa Olenius: "The next day The Great Trial broke out, in the form of Louise Hartung, who is the world's most intense person, and she talked for hours without stopping. She asked if she could stay here and I couldn't bring myself to say no, because she offered me room and board when I was in Berlin. But by the end I was absolutely dizzy and my poor head was fit to burst. I've never felt greater relief than when she left to make her flight. . . . I lay straight down to sleep and realized all the German words were seeping out of my tormented head."

Yet the fact remained that Louise and Astrid had inspiring conversations about art and literature for adults and younger readers. Both women worked in the field, after all; and being a shrewd, cultured reader, Louise Hartung proved an ideal sparring partner, consultant, and adviser on Astrid Lindgren's work and the European fate of her books. Particularly on the lucrative German market, where Astrid Lindgren's work shored up the Oetingers' finances in the 1950s, saving the publishing house just as the Pippi books had saved Rabén and Sjögren.

Louise Hartung loved getting involved in questions of translation. In 1955, for instance, she became incensed on the author's behalf when she saw how many editing changes Friedrich Oetinger wanted in *Mio, My Son*, given the sensitive German children's book market during the traumatized postwar period. On November 24, 1955, a grateful Astrid wrote to Louise, "Ah, you're so active when it comes to my books. . . . You really are a force of nature." In subsequent years she often announced how glad she was to have Louise's thorough and authoritative judgment of her manuscripts: "You're the only person who can give me a proper, honest assessment. . . . I bow completely to your opinion, but to no one else's."

In the 1950s and early 1960s, Astrid sparked many inspiring discussions by sending copies of a manuscript or book to her fellow reader in Berlin. Louise was enthusiastic about *Mio, My Son* (1954), *Karlsson-on-the-Roof* (1955), and *Rasmus and the Vagabond* (1956). But then came *Rasmus, Pontus, and Toker* in 1957, which triggered a crisis in their friendship: The book's shabby villain is the sword-swallower Alfredo, who speaks circus German, likes beer, and calls the book's two blond boy-heroes "verdammte little louts." Alfredo vividly describes his straggling central European family, which included a mother with small, iron fists she used assiduously on her eighteen children and an uncle who was an anarchist and ended up blowing himself to bits.

This was a bridge too far for the sensitive Louise. She felt deeply hurt, and accused Astrid of "Nationalhass" (national hatred), at a time when the German people needed trust and tolerance. When Astrid read Louise's indignant letter, she also felt hurt, but as an artist in a country that permitted freedom of expression:

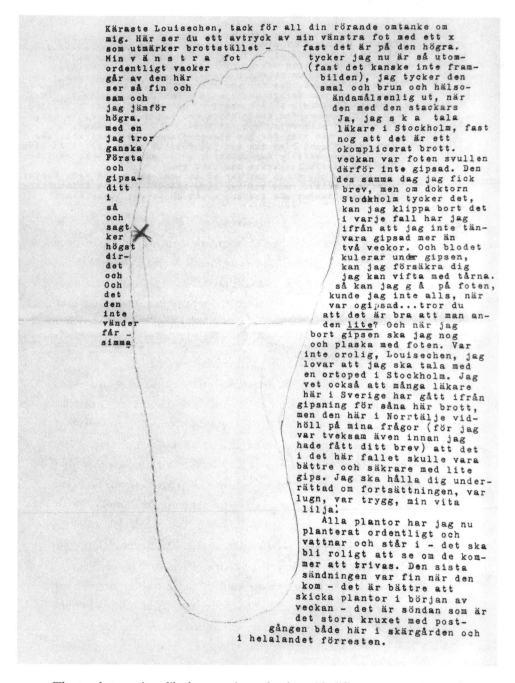

Käraste Louisechen, tack för all din rörande omtanke om
mig. Här ser du ett avtryck av min vänstra fot med ett x
som utmärker brottstället - fast det är på den högra.
Min v ä n s t r a fot   tycker jag nu är så utom-
ordentligt vacker   (fast det kanske inte fram-
går av den här   bilden), jag tycker den
ser så fin och   smal och brun och hälso-
sam och   ändamålsenlig ut, när
jag jämför   den med den stackars
högra.   Ja, jag s k a tala
med en   läkare i Stockholm, fast
jag tror   nog att det är ett
ganska   okomplicerat brott.
Första   veckan var foten svullen
och   därför inte gipsad. Den
gipsa-   des samma dag jag fick
ditt   brev, men om doktorn
i   Stockholm tycker det,
så   kan jag klippa bort det
och   i varje fall har jag
sagt   ifrån att jag inte tän-
ker   vara gipsad mer än
högst   två veckor. Och blodet
dir-   kulerar under gipsen,
det   kan jag försäkra dig
och   jag kan vifta med tårna.
Och   så kan jag g å på foten,
det   kunde jag inte alls, när
den   var ogipsad...tror du
inte   att det är bra att man an-
vänder   den lite? Och när jag
får   bort gipsen ska jag nog
simma   och plaska med foten. Var
                             inte orolig, Louisechen, jag
                             lovar att jag ska tala med
                             en ortoped i Stockholm. Jag
                             vet också att många läkare
                             här i Sverige har gått ifrån
                             gipsning för såna här brott,
                             men den här i Norrtälje vid-
                             höll på mina frågor (för jag
                             var tveksam även innan jag
                             hade fått ditt brev) att det
                             i det här fallet skulle vara
                             bättre och säkrare med lite
                             gips. Jag ska hålla dig under-
                             rättad om fortsättningen, var
                             lugn, var trygg, min vita
                             lilja!
                                 Alla plantor har jag nu
                             planterat ordentligt och
                             vattnar och står i - det ska
                             bli roligt att se om de kom-
                             mer att trivas. Den sista
                             sändningen var fin när den
                             kom - det är bättre att
                             skicka plantor i början av
                             veckan - det är söndan som är
                             det stora kruxet med post-
                    gången både här i skärgården och
             i helalandet förresten.

The two letter writers liked to surprise each other with different perspectives and
funny anecdotes. In one of Astrid's letters from Furusund in the summer of 1958,
she reported a broken left foot in a rather original way, arranging the text around a
drawing of the foot and assuring Louise that she'd planted all her bulbs and roots.

Louisechen ... you are the most intelligent person I know,
and I thought you knew me. Yet you think I have "tief eingewür-
zelte Abneigungen gegen alle Deutsche, gegen alles fahrendes
Volk und gegen alle Ausländer" [deeply engrained animosity
against all Germans, against all traveling folk and against all
foreigners]. This was harsh and bitter to hear for someone who
abhors all forms of nationalism as deeply as I do. I thought
you knew that. I thought you knew I hate every form of human
classification by nationality or race, all forms of discrimination
between black and white, between Aryans and Jews, between
Turks and Swedes, between men and women. Ever since I
was old enough to start thinking independently, I've loathed
that blue-and-yellow greater-Swedish adulation of the father-
land. . . . It seems as repulsive to me as Hitler's German
nationalism. I've never been a patriot. We're all people—that's
always been my particular way of putting it. So it hurts me more
than I can say that you read the polar opposite in the Rasmus
manuscript.

Rasmussing

In the spring of 1958, Astrid traveled to Florence to receive the Hans Christian Andersen Award, known familiarly as the "Nobel Prize for Children's
Literature," the greatest international honor that can be bestowed upon
a children's book author. It was due to be presented in the magnificent
Palazzo Vecchio, among medieval paintings by Leonardo da Vinci and
Michelangelo and before an audience of people from across the world,
including publisher Hans Rabén, who was president of IBBY in 1956–58
and was instrumental in awarding the Andersen medal to his own author.
One month earlier, Astrid had written to Hanna and Samuel August to tell
them about this prestigious award, but emphasized that they mustn't spread
the news around Vimmerby just yet: "I believe the whole thing is still a secret, so don't say a word to anyone. But it's a terribly grand international
honor, awarded to the best children's book published in the previous two

years. Not that I think Rasmus is *that* good, but if they don't have anyone better there's nothing else to do but say thanks."

Astrid Lindgren's less than wholehearted enthusiasm for *Rasmus and the Vagabond* may have had something to do with her brisk rate of production in the 1950s, when she seems to have ignored her German friend's advice: "Only write when you want to, and never because you feel obliged." Each year throughout that decade brought another Lindgren, featuring new or familiar characters, which would immediately be repackaged into new formats and for other media. It was a lucrative business for everyone involved. Astrid's term for it was "rasmussing," because three of her main characters during those years were called Rasmus, and the name also appeared in the Swedish titles of three books: *Bill Bergson and the White Rose Rescue* (Kalle Blomkvist och Rasmus, 1953), *Rasmus and the Vagabond* (1956), and *Rasmus, Pontus, and Toker* (1957).

This convoluted state of affairs was largely due to six-year-old Eskil Dalenius. In 1951, Astrid Lindgren had turned the first two books about Detective Bill Bergson into a radio serial, broadcast every Saturday evening during prime time and featuring the naturally gifted child actor Eskil Dalenius in the role of Rasmus. The boy had an inimitable voice and a real knack for firing off retorts like "*Fy bubblan* [an expression of disgust coined by Astrid Lindgren], you're such a dummy," which passed directly into Swedish slang in the 1950s. *Bill Bergson and the White Rose Rescue* became an overwhelming success among listeners, and Astrid Lindgren was immediately asked to write a sequel. The director was Elsa Olenius, and the child actors once again came from her theatrical talent factory at Södermalm, where they had also found Eskil Dalenius. After the sequel, Astrid was asked to produce a film script as soon as possible. It could be about anything, but it had to feature Eskil Dalenius in the main role, and his character's name had to be Rasmus.

The film, premiered in 1955, was titled *The Vagabond and Rasmus.* Astrid later reworked it into a radio serial and—squeezing a third use out of it—the book *Rasmus and the Vagabond.* Commercial rasmussing now kicked up into high gear: they needed to hurry, because Eskil Dalenius wasn't getting any younger. In 1956, Astrid Lindgren agreed to write another film script for Eskil, which was given the title *Rasmus, Pontus, and Toker.* Like the previous Rasmus stories, it was repurposed first as a radio serial and later as a book. Only after five years' nonstop rasmussing did the now eleven-year-old Eskil Dalenius finally take a step back.

Rasmus and the Vagabond may not have been "Nobel Prize" material, but it was certainly the best book to come out of all the Rasmus madness in the 1950s. In it, we meet another unhappy, wistful boy, who like Bosse in *Mio, My Son,* is an orphan who knows nothing about the sense of safety and identity a family can give a child. Blond, spiky-haired Rasmus Oskarsson is growing up in an orphanage, and he's repeatedly passed over when wealthy, childless parents drop by to pick and choose from among the well-scrubbed, neatly combed children, always emerging with a sweet, even-tempered, curly-headed girl. As Rasmus observes: "If you're an orphan with straight hair that nobody wants, you might as well be dead."

At the beginning of the book, we meet the melancholy boy up his favorite tree, where he's sitting alone in his den and planning to "run off into the world and find somebody who wants me!" His nighttime vanishing act—when he leaves the orphanage, his friend Gunnar, and the superintendent, "the Hawk," behind—is both hair-raising and poetic. Creeping off in the dead of night, Rasmus leaves not only the orphanage but his childhood, and he's momentarily gripped by fear of the dark, the future, and a reality he has never properly experienced. "All alone in the world," says Rasmus, with a lump in his throat, but he finds strength in a verse he remembers from school: "The verse was about a boy who was also out alone in the evening."

Rasmus and the Vagabond depicts one of the strongest and warmest friendships between an adult and child in Astrid Lindgren's oeuvre. It turns out the next day that Rasmus, still barefoot, and wearing the homespun trousers and blue-striped shirt given him by the orphanage, has spent the night in a hayloft with a vagabond without realizing it. In the morning the wanderer introduces himself as "Oscar—paradise vagabond and the Lord's trickster." He explains to the frightened boy that God determined long ago that everything should exist on earth, including vagabonds. When Paradise Oscar starts preparing to leave the hayloft, Rasmus makes a decision:

"Oscar, I'd like to be a paradise tramp too." Oscar answers that Rasmus is only a child and ought to stay at home with his father and mother, to which the boy replies succinctly and quietly: "I have no father and mother, but I'm looking for some."

Astrid Lindgren's pairing of these two people setting out into the world—the involuntarily solitary orphan and the voluntarily solitary vagabond—is notable because Rasmus and Oscar personify two different perceptions of what it means to be alone in life. These two kinds of isolation—voluntary and involuntary—had begun to haunt Astrid Lindgren. In her letters to Louise, Astrid often expressed the desire to be alone, liberated from her work and other people, while in her diary she wrote about fearing the emptiness around her when Karin left home. As she noted on September 5, 1958, when the day finally came:

> Perhaps this was the first day I really felt that "one little piggy stayed at home." When Karin got married I went to Furusund, where a piggy can be alone for ages without realizing it. Since I got back on Sunday I've been with "some people" every day. But today I ate lunch alone with Nordlund [her housekeeper], spoke only about illness, and longed for Karin to be sitting there instead. But I am aware, of course, that it's only a temporary atmosphere. I'm not sitting here in mourning. But thank God I have an occupation, a calling, a job—how do people cope when they're alone and don't have that?

Children of South Meadow

If you asked posterity which Astrid Lindgren book from the 1950s should have won the Nobel Prize for Children's Literature in 1958, the answer would most likely be *Mio, My Son*. Few people would suggest the short-story collection *South Meadow* (1959), although in many ways it's equally gripping. In tone and mood it was markedly different from her books of previous years: *The Children on Troublemaker Street, Karlsson-on-the-Roof,* and various iterations of the Rasmus books.

The four tales in this collection are set in the eighteenth century, when poverty was widespread in Sweden. Written in a deliberately old-fashioned fairy-tale style, they confused and affronted many literary critics, who compared the author's sentimentality to Selma Lagerlöf's—which they did not mean as a compliment. At Rabén and Sjögren, where for nearly fifteen years they had been counting on one Astrid Lindgren best-seller per annum, they grew uneasy at this abrupt stylistic shift, and indeed *South Meadow* was not a commercial success. For once, Astrid Lindgren seemed to have miscalculated what stories children—or perhaps the adults purchasing on their behalf—wanted to read. Fellow author Lennart Hellsing, one of the critical voices when the book came out in 1959, considered *South Meadow* a backward step for Swedish children's literature, which Astrid Lindgren had helped modernize, rather than simply an unexpected change of tack. As Hellsing wrote in the *Aftonbladet* in December 1959: "It would be absolutely dreadful if *South Meadow* found imitators; folk fairy-tales now belong once and for all in a vanished age. This narrative mode belongs to the world of adults."

Perhaps it was Hellsing's criticism of Lindgren's choice of genre that was old-fashioned. Certainly he was unable to see that, in *South Meadow*, Astrid Lindgren was treating the subject of loneliness in a way that was ahead of its time. The tales describe the kind of fear whose object is unknown, in a language true to children, reflecting their inner experiences. Few writers had accomplished this in children's literature before, and it would be more than ten years before child-psychological research, aided by fairy-tale studies—especially Bruno Bettelheim's *The Uses of Enchantment* of 1976—noted that fairy-tales often depict in symbolic form the conflicts that arise in children at various stages of development. One example might be fear of rejection or abandonment, which the tale would address through plot and language, producing a therapeutic effect in the child's unconscious mind. Via this elevated form of imaginative play, children can work through things that aren't always possible for individuals to work through in reality, claimed child psychologists and scholars of fairy-tales in the 1970s. Astrid Lindgren made a similar argument as early as the late 1950s.

"Children can't be alone in the world, they have to be with someone."
Thus writes Lindgren at the beginning of *South Meadow*. The book capped
a decade filled with great sorrow, fear of loneliness, and frustration with her
enormous and ever-increasing workload. It had taken her a long time to get
over the loss of Sture; then one day the pleasure she took in her grandchild,
Mats, was suddenly overshadowed by Lasse and Inger's divorce. Like so
many of the children she wrote about, the boy was stuck in the middle between his mother and father, left feeling as abandoned and alone as if he had
no parents at all. At least, that was Astrid's interpretation, as she confided to
her diary on Christmas Day 1957: "No sorrows hit you as hard as the ones
that hit children."

Mats ended up spending a lot of time with his grandmother at the end
of the 1950s. Astrid brought him to stay with her as often as she could, at
Dalagatan, Furusund, and Långbersgården in Tällberg near Siljan, the lake
where she had begun to spend her winter holidays, often inviting family
down too. In March 1959, she and her now eight-year-old grandson went to
stay at Siljan by themselves—Astrid not neglecting to bring her pencils and
stenographic pads, because in the mornings she worked on her new book.
As she lay in bed and wrote, Mats and the other children at the boardinghouse would play on the snowy hills, which offered a view far over Siljan
and toward a cluster of lakeside houses known as Sunnanäng (South
meadow).

The tales in *South Meadow* take the subject of "childhood loneliness"
as far as it will go. The four stories are about either orphaned, sick,
extremely vulnerable, or isolated children with familiar Swedish names like
Mattias, Anna, Malin, Stina, Maria, and Nils. Coming from another age,
they were in that sense the forerunners of all lonely children in 1950s
Sweden, including the brood of boys and girls Astrid Lindgren had
depicted in her previous books: Bertil, Göran, Britta-Kajsa, and Barbro in
Nils Karlsson the Elf, Kajsa, Eva, and Märit in *Kajsa Kavat,* Bosse in *Mio,
My Son,* Lillebror and Karlsson in *Karlsson-on-the-Roof,* and, not least, Ras-
mus in *Rasmus and the Vagabond.* All have recognizably the same core, but
the crucial difference is that the children in *South Meadow* are destitute.
Each has had almost everything in life taken from him or her, yet is left with

humanity's greatest source of riches: the imagination to rise above the meaninglessness and malevolence of existence and into a paradise of community and joy. As Malin, who has lost her parents and ended up in the poorhouse among the parish's other rejects, expresses the spark of hope that nobody can take from those with imagination: "With faith and longing, it shall be done!"

The Poetry of Bright Nights

WHILE MORNINGS AT HOME IN DALAGATAN were blissfully peaceful—a time when the author could lie in bed and write her new book until the housekeeper turned up, the telephone began to ring, and the mail was dropped through the slot—the peace was shattered shortly before one o'clock, when the editor disappeared through the publishing-house doors at Tegnérgatan 28 and climbed the stairs in small, swift bounds. She usually had a packed schedule ahead of her, and was frequently interrupted by journalists and photographers. In spring 1953, it was the *Vecko-Journalen* that came to visit her office:

> You see a genuine female editorial desk, which is practically sagging beneath the weight of manuscripts for children's books, suggestions for children's books, and finished children's books stacked high. Amid all the mess is a much-worn Royal and a Dala horse that has also seen better days. "I usually sit here between one and five, but today I'm going to the radio station at four o'clock for a recording" . . . (here the telephone gives a muffled ring somewhere among the piles of manuscripts) . . . "No, thank you, I don't want to advertise any skin cream, that definitely wouldn't be a good ad . . . not with my skin, I can assure you" . . . (puts the phone down) . . . "And after the radio station I'm nipping down to the Oscar Theater to see *Bill Bergson, Master Detective* on his latest adventures."

The most essential part of Astrid Lindgren's job as an editor—she headed Rabén and Sjögren's department for children's and young-adult literature from 1946 to 1970—was assessing manuscripts by Swedish writers, the hardened as well as the hopeful, and reading foreign books for potential purchase, translation, illustration, and, like all their other publications, packaging in an attractive jacket. This didn't mean, however, that she spent all day reading or talking on the phone behind a closed office door; she was in constant motion every afternoon, contacting all sorts of people both inside and outside the publishing house: authors, editors, consultants, translators, illustrators, proofreaders, printers, and booksellers.

Private conversations with publisher Hans Rabén usually took place in the morning, when he called Astrid at home to ask for advice and to chat about the tasks that lay ahead that day. She would read all the Swedish manuscripts and foreign books in the evening, once she was back at Dalagatan.

This exacting schedule as an author and editor was rigidly compartmentalized, hour by hour, throughout the day. As Astrid wrote in a letter to Louise Hartung in June 1959, when the busy woman down in Berlin asked how the busy woman up in Stockholm was doing, and what she was currently working on: "Writing constantly in the mornings, going to the publisher, going home and working, sleeping, waking, writing, going out and back, etc., in an unbroken circle."

Astrid Lindgren's role at Rabén and Sjögren was one of great power and influence. In 1949 the firm's offices had moved from a gloomy suite on Oxtorgsgatan to nicer, brighter surroundings in Vasastan, near Tegnérlunden Park. Together with Hans Rabén, Astrid helped shape two and a half decades of Swedish publishing and literary history, a period that is now considered a second golden age in children's and young-adult books. It was an era that coincided with postwar economic growth in Sweden, when a series of social reforms in the 1950s had a positive impact on children's culture, encouraging a rising birthrate, higher living standards, and greater purchasing power. This meant there were more and more children's books on the shelves of Swedish libraries.

For Rabén and Sjögren, this was a period of constant expansion, based primarily on its numerous competitions in the 1940s, which had attracted new authors to the publisher—Astrid Lindgren chief among them. This was reflected in the number of publications per year, recalled two of Astrid's closest colleagues during that period—Kerstin Kvint and Marianne Eriksson—in their book *Dearest Astrid* (Allrakäraste Astrid). In the mid-1950s they were publishing forty titles per year, rising to sixty in the following decade and around seventy by the time Astrid Lindgren and Hans Rabén retired in 1970.

As we have seen, Astrid read the majority of the manuscripts at home in Dalagatan, having neither the time nor the necessary peace and quiet to do so at the publishing house. There, on the other hand, Astrid could practice all the office skills she had acquired over the course of her career, including letter writing. A significant amount of her daily correspondence was directed at illustrators, translators, and the consultants who functioned as an editorial second opinion. This permanent out-of-house staff included, among others, Stina and Ingegerd. Stina, especially, took on numerous translation jobs for Rabén and Sjögren over the twenty-five years her older sister was the senior children's book editor, while Anne-Marie Fries was drawn into the ranks of consultants and freelance editors, which also included Elsa Olenius. As Astrid wrote to Näs on February 27, 1947, the year after she had been employed by Hans Rabén: "Stina and I are translating for Rabén & Sjögren, and Anne-Marie is proofreading. 'Just set to, just keep at it,' I tell them."

And keep at it they did. In the spring of 1955, even the youngest literary scion of the family tree—and her partner—were co-opted into working for the publisher. As her contented mother wrote in a letter to Hanna and Samuel August: "Karin and Carl Olof are currently translating a French book for Rabén & Sjögren. Soon I'll probably have all my relatives busy in the publisher's service."

Her numerous and often extensive letters to other authors have become part of Astrid Lindgren's mythology as a senior editor. She rarely put off a task, had a flair for constructive criticism, and helped many unfinished books and stymied authors to progress by suggesting changes and offering encouragement. The most difficult letters to write were rejections to aspiring authors. Astrid took a lot of care with these, having once been coldly rebuffed herself. As she remarked to Louise Hartung in the summer of 1960: "I've just written a three-meter-long letter to a poor dear who hasn't quite got the command of language that she ought. . . . There's nothing worse than robbing people of hope."

Another necessary duty, one that weighed almost as heavily, was her mornings spent writing and dealing with various related obligations. There were meetings in Stockholm's best restaurants with famous children's book authors from abroad like Erich Kästner and Lisa Tetzner; there were private get-togethers at home in Dalagatan for the publisher's leading Swedish authors; and there were the annual booksellers' meetings, where the next season's publications were presented. Finally there were overseas trips to book fairs, conventions, or seminars, where Astrid represented all the house's authors, including herself. Something of a balancing act—and perhaps also a conflict of interest? Certainly the question was raised in Sweden, where some authors felt that Astrid Lindgren was taking up too much space, in name and in person, at the country's largest children's book publisher. Who was judging and editing her books?

The answer was Astrid Lindgren herself, and no one else. Her successor, Marianne Eriksson, a colleague of Astrid's for many years, recalled in an interview that she was always "utterly certain about her own manuscripts, and didn't need any help." Similarly, Karin Nyman remembers that financial issues regarding her mother's books while she was employed at the publisher were always negotiated directly with Hans Rabén, and no other editor was ever involved in working on one of her books. Astrid even did her own proofreading. To her colleagues and the many other people who queried this shuttered way of doing business, Astrid Lindgren gave the following response, in the magazine *Barnboken* in 1985: "Sometimes I've heard nasty insinuations that because I also write children's books, I might have been sitting in my editorial chair and keeping all my dangerous competitors at bay. I wasn't, not at all! Nobody was more overjoyed than I was when a good manuscript landed on my desk. And having to reject a manuscript, that was—as every editor knows—torture."

Rabén, Sjö-, and Lindgren

That there was relatively little public criticism of Astrid Lindgren's problematic dual role was thanks to her dazzlingly skillful handling of her responsibilities as a writer and editor. She maintained a difficult balance.

Partly by pitching in and never being above humbler, more routine tasks at the office, like writing back-cover blurbs and marketing text for the catalogue, or drafting advertising copy or sales sheets for booksellers. She liked to use her name to help other, lesser-known authors, and in correspondence with booksellers she was careful to emphasize that the recommendation was "coming from Astrid Lindgren." She was also unafraid to challenge readers, as we can see from some draft advertising copy that today is held in the Astrid Lindgren archive: "There are two types of people. The ones that love to read and the ones that never dream of picking up a book if they can help it. Which type do you want to be?"

And if the publishing house suddenly found itself in need of a writer, as was the case in 1956, when the photographer Anna Riwkin needed one for a photographic picture book about Japan, Astrid Lindgren leapt into the breach, although she had plenty to keep her busy already.

Eva Meets Noriko-San was the start of a twelve-year collaboration with Riwkin. Their overall project, many years before anyone had started thinking in terms of globalization, encompassed eight picture books from vastly different regions. The photographer usually traveled without her writer, since there was neither the money nor the time for both to go. The books were hastily produced, and Astrid Lindgren struggled with the sense that she was compromising her high standards of quality. As she commented to Ulf Bergström in 1991, in his monograph on Anna Riwkin: "You could say I was forced into working with Anna. You've got to do it! the publisher told me. In hindsight I can say that I'm not fond of all the books we did."

A similarly ad-hoc task came up in 1959, also leading to several successful books, although this time it was Astrid's own doing. Before anyone else at Rabén and Sjögren, she spotted a potential moneymaker in Harald Wiberg's atmospheric illustrations for Viktor Rydberg's classic poem *Tomten* (The Christmas gnome). In fall 1960 a picture book came out in Swedish featuring Rydberg's poem. It was simultaneously published in Germany, England, and Denmark in foreign-language editions, for which Astrid Lindgren had turned Rydberg's poetry into prose that could be more easily translated. In a letter dated December 7, 1960, to Louise

Hartung, who she knew would be a fervent advocate of this concentrated shot of Nordic Romanticism, Astrid recounted the story behind the international coeditions:

> Here in Sweden we have a well-known poem you probably haven't read. It was written by a long dead bard, Viktor Rydberg. . . . A Swedish artist has illustrated the poem, and a picture book has come out of it that left the Swedes gasping with delight. It would never have happened if several publishers hadn't taken part. Once last year, when we had Scandinavian publishers visiting, I ran into the middle of their meeting and said, "One moment, gentlemen!" Then I showed them the pictures and read the poem at the same time, and I said, "Would you help publish this picture book?" And would you believe it—in the course of five minutes I'd sold 20,000 gnomes. But there was one condition. Rydberg's poem is difficult to translate into other languages in a way that really works, so these publishers insisted *I* should write a prose text for the images. I've done so: a short, not especially brilliant text. Rydberg's poem contains a few metaphysical meditations, and I've scrupulously left those out.

In German, *Tomten* became *Tomte Tummetott,* in English *The Tomten,* and in Danish *Nissen.* How loyal Astrid Lindgren's prose reworking was to the original poem, which wasn't actually mentioned in the coeditions at all, is debatable. In big letters on the front page of the Danish edition were the words "A story by Astrid Lindgren," while the artist had to be satisfied with smaller letters underneath: "With illustrations by Harald Wiberg."

Astrid Lindgren's business idea became a huge sales success, especially in the United States, and a year later it was followed up with her Smålandic paraphrase of the nativity story, *Christmas in the Stable,* titled *Jul i stallet* in Danish, in exactly the same format and again with illustrations by Harald Wiberg. In 1965 it was followed by a third stab at commercial success, *The*

Tomten and the Fox, based on a classic poem by Karl-Erik Forsslund. Astrid again turned poetry into prose for the coeditions, while the Swedish version kept Forsslund's original.

Was this a fraction too shrewd? Certainly it was typical of Astrid Lindgren's excellent business instincts, and the money kept rolling in. With all due respect to the second founder, Carl-Olof Sjögren, the firm should have been called Rabén, Sjö-, and Lindgren.

Less lucrative, but an exciting Scandinavian initiative nonetheless, was Astrid Lindgren's idea to commission Tove Jansson to illustrate a new translation of J. R. R. Tolkien's *The Hobbit* in 1959–60. The two great Scandinavian children's book authors had met only once or twice, but Astrid used all her rhetorical powers to win Jansson over. Boel Westin's biography of Jansson reproduces her letter of November 1960, in which Astrid tried to convince Jansson to abandon her Moomins and large-format canvases: "God bless you for Toffle!! But who shall comfort Astrid if you don't agree to the suggestion I'm laying out here? . . . When I read the book I see the illustrations drawn by Tove Jansson, and I say to myself that this will be the children's book of the century, which will live long after we're dead and buried."

Tove Jansson needed only a few days to think it over before she got down to work, and in 1962 *Bilbo: A Hobbit's Adventure,* in Britt G. Hall-qvist's translation, was ready. When Astrid Lindgren saw the finished illustrations and how beautifully they fit into the book, she was pleased, and proud of what they had achieved together: "Dear admirable Tove, if you have a cloak hem, then send it to me so I can kiss it! I'm so delighted by your wonderful little Hobbit that I can't put it into words. This is exactly the kind of little, wily, moving, kindly person he should be, and he's never been depicted that way in any other edition."

Literary critics and Tolkien fans were less enthusiastic, however. "The children's book of the century" ran to only one printing, and must be considered one of Astrid Lindgren's greatest flops as an editor. Yet Jansson's little hobbit ended up framed on the wall of Astrid Lindgren's study, where it hung until her death, and today the book has become a cult collector's item.

Lunch with the Crones

Whenever Hans Rabén was traveling, vacationing, or sick, Astrid had to take charge, and as Samuel August and Hanna learned from a 1950s letter, their daughter thought it was "fun" to sit in the boss's chair, overseeing everything and taking on all that responsibility. Others had glimpsed this flair for leadership much earlier. Even at the *Vimmerby Tidning* in the 1920s, the eighteen-year-old journalism trainee was tasked with answering the phone and keeping an eye on local news when the editor in chief had an errand to run. And later, during the war, when Astrid Lindgren was working at the mail censorship office in Stockholm, she became a role model for the others on her shift. So much so that even the highly educated academics who worked there nominated Astrid when they were asked to choose someone to represent the mail inspectors. As she wrote in a letter home to Näs in June 1943:

> I can also tell you that I've been chosen as chair of our staff association. They thought I was "well liked among the staff and favored by the cage [the head office]." I immediately turned them down gratefully but firmly, because I think it should be a man, for the simple reason that we'll have a harder time getting our way if a woman has to talk to the bigwigs, ministers, and so on. So yesterday we chose a man as chair. But I'm rather proud of myself, because there are loads of Ph.D.s and university graduates of both sexes on our staff, and like all academics they're tremendously conceited about their education, so it's genuinely remarkable that they suggested a woman who only has a secondary school diploma as their chair.

This quotation reveals a strong, independent woman with a keen awareness of power dynamics in the workplace: a thirty-five-year-old who knew how to obtain the maximum possible influence, how to express herself, and, most important, how to thrive among powerful men, not by being rebellious and anarchic like Pippi Longstocking but through pragmatism, loyalty, and the scrupulous execution of her duties. In that sense Astrid Lindgren was the archetypal example of a modern "businesswoman" in the

Alva Myrdal mold. One who knew that every woman had to stand up for herself and command respect if women were going to forge a path into society and change the structures of their male-dominated world.

According to Myrdal, the route to women's liberation wasn't through hard-hitting, outward-looking struggle but through the forces working behind the front lines and inside each individual woman. It was this kind of transformative force that Lotta Gröning called "collaborative feminism" in her book about Myrdal, arguing that women should gain ground in the workplace by forging alliances and negotiating, not by kicking up a fuss. Astrid Lindgren mastered this art throughout her working life, and it was only after her retirement in 1970 that she began to sound like an activist and started banging her fist on the table so that everybody could hear it.

From the outset of her dual career in the book industry, Astrid Lindgren came into contact with many professionally talented, inspiring, and extraordinarily powerful women. Surrounding herself with the right people was something else she had a nose for. Elsa Olenius was a network in and of herself, and via her web of connections Astrid grew more closely acquainted with Greta Bolin and Eva von Zweigbergk, who in the 1950s were Sweden's two leading literary critics. They often reviewed Astrid Lindgren's work, interviewed her, and furthered her cause as best they could through their media-industry connections. Greta Bolin—and Zweigbergk, to a lesser extent—were frequently invited to the Dalagatan meals Astrid Lindgren was fond of calling "crones' lunches." These meetings, bringing together different groups of colleagues, good friends, and relatives, were both professional and social in nature. As Karin Nyman recalls: "Her sisters were a group by themselves. Then there was a group consisting of Anne-Marie Fries, Marianne Eriksson from Rabén & Sjögren, and the authors Barbro Lindgren and Maud Reuterswärd. They took turns inviting each other for lunch and felt like close family. Margareta Strömstedt and Astrid often ate lunch together in the years after 1970, either by themselves or with some other 'crone,' Margareta's sister, for example."

No crones' lunch was complete without touching on the subject of "korkade karlarna": stupid men. Even an Alva Myrdal-esque collaborative feminist could get sick of diplomacy and need to vent her frustrations. Louise Hartung was sent a representative example in a long letter dated January 18,

1963, in which Astrid described the New Year's tiff she'd had with Hans Rabén. The row was about an author who, for fiscal reasons, asked to be paid in the New Year instead of in December. This was a commonly accepted form of creative accounting, but it required Hans Rabén's approval, and this had been quite impossible to get after the New Year. Astrid had been turned away repeatedly by the boss's secretary with the message that Dr. Rabén (she never omitted the title) still hadn't taken a look at the author's accounts, which the senior children's book editor had checked and could vouch for:

> I don't know whether I've made it clear to you what hurt me so indescribably. It was that I—who after all am the boss's right-hand woman and hold a very responsible position—should be forced to run around like an idiot asking for permission I wasn't getting. So I went home. But now I've forgotten everything. For the boss it was a question of prestige, of course. He wanted to show that "it doesn't matter who's coming and asking for something, I'm the one who decides." Yes, I know, it's all ridiculously petty, but in the moment it drives you nuts. And I rarely go nuts. . . . God, men can be stupid, and they're so especially touchy about their silly prestige you think they must be pulling your leg.

Astrid Lindgren got embroiled in a second power struggle with leading male figures in the book industry at the end of the 1950s, when she felt that Gyldendal, a prestigious Danish publishing house, was damaging Danish children's literature by chronically underpaying its authors. In 1958 the house wanted to reissue her *Noisy Village* books, but was told that the author absolutely could not agree to the 5 percent royalty Gyldendal was offering. She stuck firmly to 7.5 percent, which was the industry standard. The Danish publisher responded that it couldn't go any higher, despite being as generous as possible in its calculations, because it would have to raise the price to four kroner per book. Danish parents wouldn't pay that much, even for a book by Astrid Lindgren, claimed Jokum Smith, head of the publishing house. At this, the already irate Swedish author erupted. Was it really the case that Gyldendal was pursuing a cultural policy that entailed

squeezing writers as much as possible? Astrid Lindgren's protest was sent
on Rabén and Sjögren letterhead on April 22, 1958:

> I don't want to be difficult, so I accept the terms you suggest.
> Yet I can't help asking: was Gyldendal not intending to spear-
> head a new movement in Danish children's and young-adult
> literature, lifting it out of the decline your librarians complain so
> bitterly about? . . . You will never put out any good Danish
> manuscripts with that sort of royalty. A decent writer ought to
> write no more than one book a year, and he will earn—as a
> rule—1,000 kroner from it, so you can easily work out what that
> means. If he has any brains he'd rather take a job in a butcher's
> or a ladies' hairdresser's, or he'll start churning out books on an
> assembly line to get a reasonable income. Trust me, Denmark
> will never have a strong culture of children's literature if you
> don't get people used to the idea that even children's books cost
> money. . . . With a policy like that, you'll *always* end up with
> cheap stuff. . . . Sorry, sorry I'm saying all this, I don't mean any
> harm. Quite the contrary. But as I said, I accept the terms you
> suggest, and I gratefully look forward to receiving the gold.

Gut Feelings

That Astrid Lindgren spent nearly twenty-five remarkably friction-free
years as a senior editor at Sweden's largest children's book publisher, all the
while producing books of her own, is due in no small part to her cultural-
political efforts on behalf of all children's literature and children's book
authors. Her letter to Gyldendal was an example of this, and it was rooted
in her unshakeable view of children's books as both a product and an art
form. She consistently avoided ossifying her opinions about children's literature into rules, dogmas, and objectives, as Gurli Linder had done in
1916, for instance, with her book *Our Children's Free Reading* (Våra barns
fria läsning), Greta Bolin and Eva von Zweigbergk had done in *Children
and Books* (Barn och böcker) in 1945, and Astrid's fellow author Lennart

Hellsing did to some extent in 1963 with his collection of articles *Thoughts on Children's Literature* (Tankar om barnlitteraturen).

Even after retirement, Astrid Lindgren was often asked: what is a good children's book? Her standard response was always cautious, defensive, and—some might say—close to saying nothing at all: "It must be good. I can assure you I've racked my brains over this for ages, but I can't come up with any other answer: it must be good."

Astrid Lindgren's answer makes sense given the multiplicity and variety of children's and young-adult literature she nurtured and championed. How could anybody believe it was possible to restrict literature to a formula? As a consequence, children's books at Rabén and Sjögren tended to have much in common with Astrid Lindgren's work, but this still left a broad field. After all, Lindgren wrote for both sexes and various ages, as well as in many genres and formats: humorous novels, crime novels, fairy-tales, fables, books for girls, fantasy, comedies, and dramas. Her work was also a model example of the way in which books could be repurposed for other media, such as film, theater, radio, and television. For a younger children's book writer it was hard not to be inspired, impressed, and left slightly in awe of the way Astrid Lindgren orchestrated her role as an author. The artistic and commercial dynamo's broad spectrum of literary work reflected a visionary artist's resistance to being pigeonholed, and this fundamental desire for artistic freedom and diversity in art saturated her perspective on the children's book industry. As the recently retired Lindgren said in an open letter to authors and publishers in the magazine *Barn och kultur* in 1970:

> If you want to write a harrowing book for children about how difficult and impossible it is to be a human being in our world, you have the right to do so. If you want to write about racial subjugation or class struggle, you have the right to do so. And if you just want to write a poem about a flowery island in the archipelago, you have the right to do that without necessarily having to think: now which words rhyme with waste water and oil spill? In short: freedom! For without freedom, the flowers of poetry will wither wherever they grow.

Astrid Lindgren's fundamental ideology, including in art, originated in the culturally radical movements of the interwar era, particularly trends within modern pedagogy and child psychology, which explored the notion of "the whole person." Children's books should do the same, she felt. Instead of protecting and lecturing children they should be challenging them, thereby including young people among humankind as a whole. Rarely did she put it as clearly as in an interview in the *Dagens Nyheter* on September 8, 1959, when she stated that children's book authors should, as a matter of principle, write about whatever they wanted, including issues that were taboo and suppressed:

> If it's done in an artistically defensible way, a story should be able to speak earnestly about death, and children simply have to cope with that. Death and love are the biggest things humanity experiences, and they concern all ages. I don't want to frighten children out of their wits, but just like adults they need to be shocked by art. You've got to shake a soul that's used to being asleep. Everybody needs to cry and be scared every once in a while.

By making this sort of pronouncement in newspapers and magazines, constantly underscoring the child's sovereignty and emphasizing children's literature as a distinct art form, Astrid Lindgren proved colossally significant for the artistic self-confidence of a generation of Swedish children's book authors, who both before and after the war fought for reasonable fees and access to an authors' association.

Also of immense symbolic value was Olle Holmberg's 1954 review of *Mio, My Son* in the *Dagens Nyheter,* which brought the children's book into the realm of high culture. Never before in Swedish literary history had a professor of literature treated a children's book on an equal artistic footing with books for adults. Well before publication, the author had been laying the groundwork in letters and conversations with the critic. After a lunch in Dalagatan for Holmberg and his wife in September 1954, Astrid had encouraged the professor to prise the review assignment out of Eva von Zweigbergk's hands. A letter from Astrid to Olle Holmberg and his wife Maj, dated September 16, 1954, makes clear that he had already read the first proofs of *Mio, My Son,* and during the lunch at Dalagatan he expressed his enthusiasm for the book. Something the writer had hoped for, of course, when she sent him the proofs: "I'm pleased as Punch that Olle says he likes Mio. No fall rain can dampen my happiness about it. . . . Maybe I didn't say it clearly enough on the phone. I'd a million times rather have a review by Olle than one by E.v.Z., but she might get spiteful and make things awkward."

In the wake of this historically and culturopolitically important review, Olle Holmberg worked over the following decade to make Astrid Lindgren a member of De Nio—a literary academy founded in 1913 in Stockholm, whose purpose from the start had been to promote literature, peace, and women's issues. The members of De Nio ("the nine") were chosen for life; four places were always reserved for women and four for men. In 1963, while Holmberg was chairman of De Nio, Astrid Lindgren was voted in, a decision that had great symbolic significance for Swedish children's and young-adult literature. Not just anybody could be voted into the gender-balanced society, of which both Ellen Key and Selma Lagerlöf had been members. Among the eight current ones were several faces Astrid knew extremely well. Apart from Holmberg in chair no. 1, in chair no. 2 was the lawyer Eva Andén, who had helped young Astrid Ericsson get to Copenhagen in 1926, and in no. 9 was John Landquist, who in 1946 had tried to kill off Pippi with his hatchet job criticizing the book and its author.

Lindgren took every opportunity and platform at her disposal to use her national profile and position in Swedish cultural life to strike a blow for the usefulness of children's books and for the importance of reading for future democracies inside and outside Scandinavia. In doing so she wasn't addressing a literary academy but speaking directly to parents, schoolteachers, trendsetters, and political decision makers, asking the polemical question, "Do we need children's books?"

Astrid Lindgren had plenty of examples of the power and usefulness of books in the hands of a child from when Lasse and Karin were young, and later from spending time with other children. When, in February 1960, she once again took her grandchild Mats on a winter vacation to Dalarna, she realized that literature could close a protective ring around a child, creating a parent-free zone. As Astrid wrote to Louise Hartung on March 6, 1960, from Långbersgården in Tällberg: "Mats reads a lot, and when he reads he hears *nothing*—you have to shout pretty loudly to get any reaction whatsoever. I said to him, 'You don't listen to what people say to you when you're reading.' To which he answered, 'No, and that's a good thing. When Mamma's angry it's better if I just sit and read.' I'm so very glad that children find ways to cope with die verdammten Erwachsenen [the goddamn grown-ups]."

Astrid Lindgren never lost faith in the conviction that children's ability to create new worlds in their imaginations would eventually come to save civilization. She mentioned this in her famous acceptance speech in 1978, when she received the Peace Prize of the German Book Trade. The first time Astrid Lindgren got the international media talking about her humanitarian message, however, was in 1958, when she was awarded the Hans Christian Andersen Medal in Florence, and warned against letting books lose ground against modern media like film and TV, whose influence, she believed, made children passive, or was perhaps even degenerative:

> There is no medium that can replace the book as fertile soil for the imagination. Contemporary children watch films, listen to the radio, watch television, read comics—all this can be amusing, certainly, but it doesn't have much to do with imagination. A child alone with a book creates his or her own images somewhere in the secret places of the soul, which surpass everything else. These kinds of images are necessary for humanity. The day children's imaginations are no longer capable of creating them will be the day humanity grows poor.

Seacrow Island by Helicopter

In the years 1962–64, with books like *Karlsson Flies Again, Emil in the Soup Tureen,* and *We on Seacrow Island,* Astrid Lindgren took her writing to new heights. Quite literally: in September 1962 she took a long and noisy flight that even Karlsson with his propeller would have envied. Louise got a full report in a letter dated October 4: "The other day I flew in a helicopter to Furusund. I'm writing a script for a film set on the archipelago, and the production company transported me by helicopter to the islands at the far end to see where the film will be set. Afterward they dropped me off at the jetty in Furusund. I absolutely loved flying by helicopter. You feel like a bird, hovering over the treetops and the archipelago, and the red foliage on all the trees was fantastically beautiful from above."

While the producer Olle Nordemar and the director Olle Hellbom puzzled over choosing an island, finding a friendly St. Bernard, and picking seven of the eight thousand children who had shown up to the casting call, Astrid Lindgren began a new and challenging writing process. It would end up spanning eight months, forcing her to deviate from her normal working rhythm of books and film scripts: this was a TV series consisting of thirteen twenty-eight-minute episodes, and shooting for the six-hour-long epic would begin before its author had even come close to finishing. Astrid had to write some of the later episodes first, so that the crew could film the spectacular Christmas episode before icy winter conditions made it impossible for the boat from Stockholm to reach the island's jetty. Instead, they set down the equipment and passengers on the edge of the ice, a hundred yards from solid ground.

This stressful phase of writing—when "the film boys" Nordemar and Hellbom kept asking for instant changes or additions—alongside her usual editing work, became an unforgettable year in Astrid Lindgren's artistic life. In Berlin, Louise could follow along via her friend's many letters:

November 6, 1962: I'm working on my Seacrow Island film. It's a big job, and it's going very slowly—I never have enough time to settle down to work on it.

February 2, 1963: The work is fun. I've begun to thrive on this fantasy island, Seacrow Island, and with the people there. They're really pleasant to be around, I think, but what they'll become once a director's gotten his hands on them I don't know—might lead to some nasty surprises. At the moment I'm busy with Christmas on Seacrow Island. A little child puts out a bowl of porridge for the gnomes, and when night falls over the houses and all the lights are out, a fox comes and sticks his snout in the porridge. If it turns out the way I *imagine* it, it'll be really charming, but it probably won't. I should probably be writing a book—at least then nobody will come along and change anything.

March 26, 1963: The winter episode on Seacrow Island has been recorded, with the boat at the edge of the ice and everything. How it'll turn out, I don't know. I just know I'm working really hard, and that all the episodes, i.e., the scripts, must be finished by May 10. Voj, voj.

The Finno-Swedish exclamation "voj, voj" (roughly "oh dear, oh dear") illustrated Astrid's discomfort with the tight production schedule, which involved many different people, an infinite assortment of technical equipment, and such unpredictable factors as the weather. Her skepticism proved unfounded, however. A fabulous script, a number of good performances by the actors, a professional film crew, and, not least, the weather— everything came together to create one of the national public broadcaster Sveriges Television's most successful series ever, *We on Seacrow Island.* A film in thirteen chapters, it brought the nation together every Saturday evening at seven o'clock from mid-January to mid-April 1964, and it was generally perceived as an homage to Swedishness and the Swedish archipelago. Viewers were charmed by its nostalgia and idyllic summer-holiday-at-the-seaside atmosphere. The series earned gigantic ratings and won widespread artistic recognition. Maria Johansson as Tjorven became Sweden's biggest TV personality, while Torsten Lilliecrona, in the role of butter-fingered father and author Melker, won an award for best male actor. In 1964, *We on Seacrow Island* was selected as Best TV Program of the Year.

Sweden wasn't allowed to keep the TV series to itself: its neighbors wanted to watch too. The consensus was that the TV series—to use one of Tjorven's oaths—was "pretty infernally good." Even in flat, archipelago-deficient Denmark, children and adults could identify with the sense of community in *We on Seacrow Island*. This pan-Scandinavian enthusiasm pleased the author. She would happily confess that she felt Swedish to her marrow, but usually remembered to add that nationalism was alien to her. Nature in Sweden should be perceived beneath a Scandinavian sky, and in the light of Scandinavian fairy-tale traditions, as she explained in the *Dagens Nyheter* in September 1959:

> There's something in me that loves Swedishness. There are so many wonderful, enchanting fairy-tales in the world, but I have my roots in Swedish nature. I would never be able to live abroad. I'd miss the earth, I'd miss the scent of Sweden. Scandinavian folk tales are essential, with all their folk wisdom and nature, like shadows among the elves, nixes, wood spirits, and brownies. All people from Sweden, Norway, and Finland have something in common: the poetry of bright nights. In the background there will be a path through a pine forest, a thrush's song, a sunset.

Nordemar and Hellbom selected the small island of Norröra for filming, three nautical miles east of Furusund. Astrid Lindgren borrowed the name Seacrow Island (Saltkråkan) from the family sailboat, which she had bought from Hans Rabén, and which was moored at Furusund beside the family's skiff *Syltkrukan*. After Lasse was given his speedboat, *Mio*, in the 1960s, the family had a veritable fleet, which was used frequently in the summer months when the children and their growing families stayed at the other two Furusund houses Astrid had acquired.

The atmosphere in the Lindgren household during the bright nights of the early 1960s, as well as old gossip and tall tales absorbed over twenty-five summers on the archipelago, became woven into *We on Seacrow Island,* which was subsequently reworked into the longest novel Astrid Lindgren ever wrote: 360 pages spanning one year, summer to summer. The omnipotent narrator weaves in and out of the thoughts, dreams, and longings of all the island's inhabitants. Even the animals on the island are ascribed human feelings and comprehension.

The thirteen episodes in the TV series and chapters in the novel are built on the schism between urban and rural life, with which Astrid Lindgren lived her whole adult life. On the one hand there was her stressful, burdensome everyday life in "Ninevet," as she was fond of calling Sweden's capital in letters to family and friends. It was an expression that stemmed from Samuel August, and referred to the Middle Eastern metropolis God laid to waste in the Old Testament because of the populace's ungodly behavior. On the other there were the peaceful vacations and old-fashioned rhythm of working she adopted on Furusund, beneath the open sky, close to nature, near woods, fields, and sea.

The Summer with Malin

The restorative effect nature always had on city-dwelling Astrid Lindgren was also felt—in both body and soul—by the Melkerson family in *We on Seacrow Island.* When the four children and their single father arrive at the farthest jetty on the archipelago route, they're a little alarmed by the damp weather, the apparently deserted island, and the ramshackle cabin their naïve artist father has rented for a year. It doesn't look much like a summer idyll, but it soon proves a paradise that has a permanent effect on all five Melkersons. Nineteen-year-old Malin, who assumes the role of mother to her three younger brothers and clumsy father, finds the love of her life on Seacrow Island. The two older boys meet their ideal playmates, the youngest, Pelle, gains a beloved pet, and Melker finds the most inspiring place to work any writer could imagine. What kind of literary work is he constantly tinkering with in Snedkergården? The reader never learns. Perhaps a novel about living happily on a small island in the archipelago, a motherless family coming back to life, and people and animals interacting with each other naturally and freely? That's what Astrid Lindgren imagined, anyway: a kind of robinsonade about big-city folk arriving on an island that turns out to be populated by all sorts of people at various stages of life, with a clear balance of temperaments, character types, and genders.

This fantasy island in the Stockholm archipelago was the closest Astrid Lindgren ever came to depicting a matriarchy. An hour's sail from the patriarchy on the mainland, among remote prehistoric cliffs, strong, dynamic women like Märta, Tjorven, Stina, Teddy, Freddy, and Malin blossomed among soft, sensitive men like Nisse, Björn, Peter, Melker, Pelle, Johan, and Niklas. Tjorven's big sisters, the twins Teddy and Freddy, are described in the novel as tomboys, and referred to several times as "amazons." Typical of the gender and power balance in the book is a lengthy passage in which Seacrow Island's vibrant core, seven-year-old Tjorven, is stranded on a rock with Pelle, a city-bred boy of the same age. Hardly have they reached land before Tjorven assigns Pelle a supporting part as Man Friday, while she herself—bypassing democratic discussion—assumes the role of Robinson Crusoe in a pinafore: "She had decided to be a Robinson with an altogether normal, cozy household, one who ate wild strawberries for dessert. She could see them growing thickly in the grass outside. If Friday had been an ordinary person, he could have taken Teddy's old fishing rod, which stood outside the shack, and gone down to the lake to catch a few perch."

But Pelle, fond of animals and protective of the environment, feels sorry for the fish and the live bait. Thus the pattern continues throughout the novel: with a few gruff exceptions, the male characters frequently reveal their feminine sides, often regarding environmental issues. The novel indirectly raises this particular topic when Snedkergården unexpectedly finds itself in danger of being bought and modernized by a destructive capitalist, who arrives in a large, polluting speedboat. Astrid Lindgren's interest in environmental issues is evident in an interview she gave while working on the script in 1963. In it she described the stressful process of writing, playfully adding that she had to get a move on "before the environment is destroyed by plastic boats and other so-called technological advances."

That Astrid Lindgren was ahead of the curve of various paradigm shifts in the mentality of 1960s Scandinavia is clear from the atmosphere of freedom, tolerance, and respect that surrounds all the children on the island. All the people on Seacrow Island—no matter their age or gender—are allowed to be themselves, to feel, think, and, to a large extent, do what they want. Much of what takes place on the island over the course of two summers and a Christmas vacation is governed by this principle. In addition to the straightforward narrative, the novel includes various undated entries from

Malin's diary. July 18 is the only date specified, but it's an important day, when Melker Melkerson repeats to his family the following words of wisdom: "This day, one life." The same words, a quotation from the eighteenth-century Swedish poet Thomas Thorild, had made such a deep impression on seventeen-year-old Astrid Lindgren in Ellen Key's home in 1925. At the breakfast table, Melker explains to his children what the words mean: "It means you should live today as if that's all you've got. That you should pay attention to every single moment and feel that you're really living."

The conversation that follows, about "heightening the feeling of living," has been sparked by Pelle's old comb. He removes one tooth every day, keeping count of how much of the glorious summer they have left on Seacrow Island. His dreamy father thinks he's torturing himself, so he throws Pelle's comb into the trash: "It's wrong to dread the days to come. You should enjoy the day you've had." Pelle is astonished by the vehemence of his father's reaction, and by the grown-ups' long conversation about "the feeling of living." Where do you feel it? he asks Malin, who answers, "In you, I think it's in your legs. When you say you've got a lot of wriggle in your legs, that's the feeling of living!"

The children of Seacrow Island circa 1964, meant to represent the Swedish men and women of tomorrow, feel this restlessness deeply, and they make sure to savor every single moment on the archipelago as if it were their last. They set off on grand adventures on foot and by boat, sometimes ending up in dangerous situations if the weather suddenly changes. These experiences are part of the novel's underlying Thorild-esque philosophy. "This day, one life" means knowing and acknowledging that death will always exist in life. Nothing lasts forever. This lesson is illustrated brutally when a fox kills Pelle's rabbit, savages Stina's lamb, and comes close to finishing off their dog, Boatsman. In one split second, intense joy is transformed into deep, coal-black grief. Pelle and Tjorven are too young to really grasp it, yet the author spares neither them nor the reader. It falls, inevitably, to Malin, the novel's mother figure, to teach them this Lindgren-esque lesson about the reality of sorrow and the necessity of loneliness: "Life, you see, is sometimes difficult. Even small children, even a little boy like you, will have to go through things that hurt, and you have to go through them all alone."

We on Seacrow Island, a pleasant dream about an environmentally friendly community of children, adults, and animals living as equals on an island in the sea, became an important factor in Swedish and, to an extent, Scandinavian self-perception in the 1960s. Though gender roles hadn't yet begun to shift significantly and "environmental awareness" was a foreign concept, when *We on Seacrow Island* appeared on black-and-white television screens on Swedish, Norwegian, Danish, and Finnish channels—and was simultaneously released in book form in all Nordic languages—the consensus regarding children's rights was undergoing far-reaching changes, and these were reflected with particular clarity in the social legislation and school reforms of the 1960s.

Lindgren's careful social criticism based in environmental issues and the balance of power between men and women, and between adults and children, was not limited to the TV show or novel. Over the next ten years, many of Astrid Lindgren's books, TV programs, and films, set against various historical backdrops, called into question the patriarchy: the system didn't take sufficient care of nature, it was always itching to declare war, and it continued to oppress women and children. In *We on Seacrow Island,* and especially in her books about Emil from Lönneberga, which developed during the epochal year of 1968 into a trilogy about antiauthoritarian sons rebelling against their fathers, Astrid Lindgren began the final, great chapter of her life and career as an author, coming into her own as a humanist, critic of civilization, and political activist.

An Uprising in Lönneberga

In a surprising change of scene, Astrid Lindgren turned her attention in May 1963 from the contemporary Stockholm archipelago to Småland at the close of the previous century. She registered the shift in her diary on May 23: "Today I wrote the first words of what may become a book about Emil from Lönneberga." She had come up with an idea for a collection of stories about a Småland farm boy with so much "wriggle in his legs" that these days he'd be diagnosed with ADHD and handed a bottle of pills.

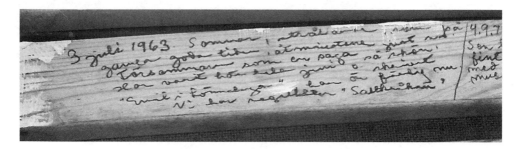

On a wooden bench on the balcony of her house in Furusund in 1955, Astrid began to keep a rather unusual diary. Every year she summed up the previous summer in pencil on the underside of the bench. On July 3, 1963, she wrote something about *We on Seacrow Island,* but first: "Summer, beaming like in the good old days! Early summer, at least, was as lovely as a fairy-tale! Been here all June and written Emil in the Soup Tureen. He's finished now."

    The name Emil arose in the same haphazard way as Pippi Longstocking had, when Karin plucked a name out of thin air and Astrid built a character around it. Now it was Karin's firstborn, little Karl-Johan, who provided a spark of inspiration by throwing a few nasty tantrums in the summer of 1962. On several occasions it had been impossible to pacify the three-year-old, and something had to be done about it, explained Karl-Johan's grandmother on Book Day in Klagstorp in 1970: "Then one day I hit upon something, and I screamed even more loudly than he did: 'Do you know what Emil from Lönneberga did once?' The name just flew out of me, but Karl-Johan fell silent, because he wanted to find out what Emil from Lönneberga had done. Afterward I used that trick every time, so he had to keep his mouth shut. It hadn't occurred to me to write a book about Emil, but suddenly I began to mull it over: Who is this Emil, and how is he getting on in Lönneberga, and before I knew what was happening I'd begun writing about him."

    Yet the Emil character had been more years in the making than it might seem. Other lively boys in the author's past and present contributed to the creation and development of the only character in Lindgren's oeuvre who could always match Pippi Longstocking's vitality and popularity. Over the years, Astrid had been eager to use some of Samuel August's impish stories from his Småland childhood in a literary form more extensive and ambitious than free-standing short stories like "A Småland Matador" and "A Bit about Sammelaugust," which were published in 1950. The idea became more insistent after her mother's death in 1961, when Astrid was afraid her father wouldn't live long without his beloved, indispensable Hanna from Hult.

Her brother Gunnar and his childhood hijinks at Näs, which Astrid had witnessed, also contributed to the character of Emil. One time he had crawled up onto the roof just as Samuel August came round the corner. "Come down from there, Gunnar," said his father, and the little boy immediately obeyed. Ten minutes later his father walked past again, and Gunnar was sitting high up on the roof, exactly as before. "Didn't I tell you to come down?" "Yes, but you didn't say I couldn't climb up again!"

Certain unforgettable episodes and remarks from Lasse's childhood in the 1930s and his son Mats's in the 1950s also fed into the character of Emil. By 1963 Mats was no longer a little boy, but he was still as affectionate as he'd been in the winter he and his grandma had spent together in Dalarna, when he suddenly and spontaneously announced, "The most important thing is that we're together . . . ever!" In the 1960s five new grandchildren were added to Karin's and Lasse's families, always a source of joy, wonder, and inspiration. In fact, Astrid drew inspiration from lots of children around her, as well as from other people's stories about children, recalls Karin Nyman:

> Astrid would pick up on authentic, fragmentary remarks she had heard from children or episodes she had witnessed and give them to one of the children in her books: "Herring on a Sunday, yuck!" said the child of one friend. "I've got so much wriggle in my legs" came from Ingegerd's son Åke, and a boy in another family we knew used to stand on a heap of manure when it rained so he'd grow faster. But apart from that, Mom believed that all her sources of inspiration came from her childhood, her all-important childhood. It wasn't uncommon for people to want her to meet and see their children: "Oh, you'll be so inspired by this child," but she was always very clear that

that wasn't how she got inspiration. I think it's true that, as Astrid said, Emil was modeled on Samuel August and Gunnar—and maybe her nephew, Åke, a kid who landed his parents in the most hopeless situations when he was small.

It was little Karl-Johan, however, who inspired the name Emil in 1962–63 and provided the most direct impetus for Astrid to begin the three stories that would become the first installment of a whole saga. For this reason, Astrid Lindgren chose to dedicate the book to her grandchild. "Till Karl-Johan" was written at the bottom of the first blank page in the initial 100,000-copy print run of the Swedish edition of *Emil in the Soup Tureen* (simply titled *Emil i Lönneberga* in Swedish).

Astrid never grew tired of studying and hearing about Karl-Johan, who was thoughtful and imaginative and owned a "mössa" (woolly hat) he sometimes slept with. For some inexplicable reason the boy called his mother "Little Mrs. Nyman," and one evening in 1963, as Karin and Carl Olof were sitting at the dinner table, the four-year-old suddenly stared at his parents and said, "I know you, but you don't know me." He was similarly cryptic when he showed up unannounced with some siblings and cousins on Astrid's doorstep in Furusund, as she recounted in letters to Anne-Marie Fries, Elsa Olenius, and Louise Hartung: "'Do you have any food for the little ones?' asked Karl-Johan in his sweetest voice. And when I said 'yes,' he said just as sweetly, 'That's good, because they'd like some.' And they do. Rather often. So I make quite a lot of food for 'the little ones.'"

Karl-Johan declared that he would be getting married to his infant sister Malin when he grew up, and the two would have three children named Leif, Mats, and Kadolf. His sister was still too young, but her big brother rehearsed the ceremony after attending a family wedding at a church. One of Carl Olof's brothers was getting married, and Astrid was babysitting. Initially things went well, thought Grandma. Malin slept most of the time, and Karl-Johan followed the ceremony with interest, right up until the priest intoned in a ringing voice, "Let us pray!" Karl-Johan then shouted in an even louder voice, "Help! Help!," which distracted several churchgoers, as Astrid reported in a letter to Louise Hartung in February

In fall 1963, Grandma read aloud from her first book about "Emil from Lönne-berga" for Karl-Johan, left, and his little sister Malin.

1963. When they came home from church and were eating dinner, Karl-Johan inquired after his parents with the words: "When are those goddamn people coming home?"

But there were many other children among Astrid's acquaintance and in her memory banks who contributed to the character of Emil: Samuel

August, Gunnar, Lasse, Mats, Åke, and, not least, Astrid herself, who was born on Emil's name day in November 1907 and whose middle name was Emilia. The boy she had always had inside her was eager to leap into action in 1963, providing enough stories for a whole trilogy—the installments came out in 1963, 1966, and 1970—which was rounded off with another three stories in the 1980s, gathered in the book *Emil and Ida in Lönneberga*. In this book Emil dedicates his enormous collection of carved wooden figurines to future generations, and finally bids farewell to the reader and to his workshop in Katthult. The work as a whole is so coherent and framed with such an elegant device (Alma Svensson writes down Emil's many escapades over the years) that the fifteen stories can be read like an episodic, picaresque novel à la *Don Quixote*.

If we look at the first three Emil books, which reflect the spirit of the 1960s, when various popular impetuses toward freedom broke out across the entire Western world, including the civil rights movement, student protests, the flower-power movement, and demonstrations against nuclear power and the Vietnam War, we find that beneath the humorously noisy surface is the sincere and heartfelt urge to say something about the thirst for freedom, civil courage, and "the democratization of the family," as Astrid Lindgren termed it in a Danish newspaper in 1977.

In one of her books about Astrid Lindgren's work, literary scholar Vivi Edström wrote that in the role of Emil's father in the 1971 film adaptation, the Swedish actor Allan Edwall "lacked a certain glint in his eye as he marched out to the woodworking shed, frightening the children with his shouting." This is debatable. Didn't Edwall perfectly embody the books' hollowed-out father figure who resembled the ailing authorities in so many European democracies in 1968–70? The illustrator Björn Berg, himself a son and father, always depicted him as an absurd patriarch at the head of the Svensson family table, and Astrid Lindgren never objected to this interpretation during their ten-year collaboration. In Berg's expressive drawings, Anton Svensson repeatedly emerges as precisely what he is throughout the Emil saga: a foolish figure the reader both laughs at and pities. But not too much! On the final page of the trilogy in 1970, after Emil's act of heroism during the snowstorm, while his father stays home in the warmth, feeling sorry for himself, Astrid Lindgren puts words in Anton Svensson's mouth that underscore how petty he is: "Well, I'm not so sure now he'll be chairman of the parish council, Emil. . . . Still, we'll make a decent fellow of him yet. If he's allowed to live and keep his health, and if God wills it."

The principal conflict throughout all three books is the power struggle waged between father and son, manifesting both in the father's fear that his son will soon be taller than he and in the son's uncontrollable urge to boss his father and mother and all of Katthult around, even Lönneberga as a whole. At last, paradoxically, he ends up doing exactly that—as chairman of the parish council, no less. In all fifteen stories, which span a year and a half in Emil's life, this power struggle surfaces whenever Emil reveals himself to be cleverer, craftier, braver, more compassionate, and more imaginative than his father, and again and again he ends up being locked inside the little workshop. Yet as he sits alone in the shed, which is somehow both distressing and exhilarating, Emil grows inside. The boy's world expands as he sits bent over his carvings, and the door to freedom swings open, letting the antiauthoritarian rebel continue to spread horror, goodness, and glee in his straightforward, somewhat thoughtless way.

In the final story of the saga, the spirit of youthful rebellion Emil represents is elevated beyond its immediate context. Once again he defies his father, risking his young life for the sake of another person. In a crippling snowstorm, Emil rescues his ideal father figure—farmhand Alfred—from dying of blood poisoning. Alfred, Emil, and Lukas, a horse, are on the verge of death when the boy heroically squares up to the natural forces raging around him. "You find the strength when you *have* to," he shouts, the same article of faith that got Astrid Lindgren through the worst periods in her life.

It's this reminder of humanity's moral courage and Emil's love for the man he wishes were his father that hold the book's exuberant humor and its many hilarious scenes together, raising the Emil stories to the level of classic world literature for children. The work's greatest stroke of genius is its humanistic undercurrent. This quiet, urgent echo in the wake of the laughter reminds us who we are, and what we as human beings must always remember: to do unto others as we would have them do unto us.

In Memory of Samuel August

Astrid Lindgren's father never got to read the final Emil book. On July 28, 1969, when the summer and its bright nights were drawing to a close, Samuel August Ericsson died. He was ninety-four. Ten days later, Astrid Lindgren made an entry in pencil underneath a bench on her balcony in Furusund, where she kept an alternative diary year by year: "Heatwave all summer. Insanely dry. A summer of despair, Lasse deeply depressed, sick, no job. Father died July 28. Not long before that, the first people set foot on the moon. Have written Pippi songs. Busy with Karlsson."

The third volume of stories about Emil came out in 1970, titled *Emil and His Clever Pig*. The little jack of all trades from Katthult was still full of beans and shenanigans, but the primary source behind the character was gone forever. As with his great-grandchild Karl-Johan in 1963, the book paid tribute to him on its first blank page: "In memory of Samuel August." He'd followed Emil's exploits with avid interest, and fizzed with ideas, remembered Lindgren, speaking on Book Day in Klagstorp in the fall of 1970:

> In his final years my father identified so much with Emil that I almost thought he believed he really existed. A while before he died, I told him about Emil's successful transactions at the auction in Backhorva, and it amused my father vastly because he was so good at dealmaking himself. He thought Emil should go to a few more auctions, and he asked me every time we saw each other whether Emil had been to a new one. He also wanted me to write a book about what happened when Emil really did become chairman of the parish council. My father was a church warden for many years, happy and kind and generous, a real "välmänske," a friend to all the world.

"Välmänske" was a Småland word, explains Karin Nyman, which her mother used to refer to people who spread positivity and created a good atmosphere without making a show of it—people who did nice things for others, who pitched in and helped out when needed, often spontaneously

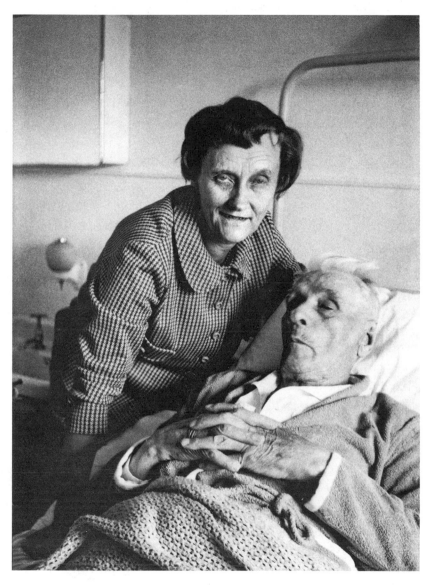

Father and daughter, 1969.

and on instinct, like when Emil gave his teacher a big kiss on the lips in front of the whole class before explaining to the blushing and bewildered woman what he was doing: " 'I think I did it out of goodness,' said Emil, and it's since become something of a phrase in Lönneberga. ' "I think I did it out of goodness," said the Katthult boy when he kissed his teacher,' they used to say, and perhaps still say today, for all I know."

Samuel August Ericsson had been just such a välmänske, but now he was gone. Within a decade, Astrid, Gunnar, Stina, and Ingegerd had lost both parents, two strong personalities who had laid down firm but liberating guidelines for their four children and always managed to set a good example. Not least as a happily married couple, in an age when the concept of love was in transition, and more and more families were dissolving in unhappy divorces. As Astrid Lindgren said in an interview in the *Expressen* on December 6, 1970: "They meant so much to each other that in a way we kids ended up in the background. My father loved my mother madly, and told her every day how exceptional she was. . . . When she died I was sure he would completely lose the will to live. But he kept thinking it was wonderful to be alive, and waited confidently to die. Hanna was in Heaven, and he would meet her again. That was for sure, and there was no more to be said about it."

When Hanna had a brain hemorrhage in spring 1955, entering a long period of illness, Astrid asked Louise Hartung whether she ever thought about her relationship with her mother. Astrid did, and she had come to a clear realization: "I've always loved my father more than my mother, but I admired her for her clear head and extraordinary competence." And when Hanna died in May 1961, Astrid repeated in a letter to Louise that she had never had a "special bond" with her mother.

This also becomes apparent in Astrid Lindgren's biographical sketch of her parents, *Samuel August from Sevedstorp and Hanna from Hult,* based on her parents' youthful letters to each other, which was first published in the weekly magazine *Vi* in 1972. There is no coldness or distance in her depiction of the reserved and pious Hanna, but her description of "välmänske" Samuel August glows with empathy, so that this portrait of her parents becomes primarily a declaration of love for her father, and of her gratitude for everything she felt she owed him: "He had a remarkable faith in life, a joy in it, and a sure conviction in the life hereafter, so not even Hanna's death could break him. He continued to love her and talk about her and praise all her virtues. He even continued to do so at the age of ninety-four as he lay happily and contentedly in bed at the nursing home, his last stop here on earth."

Näs would never be the same without Hanna and Samuel August, just as the Lindgren home in Dalagatan had taken on an utterly different shape and structure in the 1950s and the holiday home in Furusund was in constant flux during the 1960s, depending on whether Astrid was there alone or with family. "Solitude seems to be a peculiar fluid, which fills the house with a strange sense of refreshment," she remarked in a letter to Louise in August 1963, in which she expressed astonishment that solitude could be so invigorating. Yet at the same time she felt guilty about not missing her children or grandchildren at all after they returned home. She would never marry again, that much was clear. As she wrote to her German friend in July 1961, when she was enjoying the summer weather, picking mushrooms, and reading Maurois's biography of George Sand:

> I totally agree with you that it's a mystery how people can live in a marriage. You have to be very young, I think, when you get married, but then again there are those fools who keep marrying and marrying and marrying over and over again even at a more advanced age. One thing I do know . . . there's no man on earth who could tempt me into another marriage. Getting the chance to be alone is a quite extraordinary pleasure, looking after yourself, having your own opinions, acting by yourself, making your own decisions, arranging your own life, sleeping by yourself, thinking for yourself, aaaaah!

TEN

The Battle for Fantasy

ANGELS, PIXIES, DRAGONS, AND WITCHES weren't welcome in Scandinavian children's literature in the 1970s. "What is fantasy? Is it talking animals and elves and trolls?" asked the Swedish author Sven Wernström during a seminar at the Nordic Folk Academy (Nordens Folkliga Akademi) in Kungälv at the beginning of the decade, which set a new agenda for children's and young-adult literature in Scandinavia: "For me, fantasy is something very different from animals and angels, trolls and dragons. Fantasy is being able to imagine something that's not there. But there are two kinds of things that are 'not there': a) things that aren't there because they're impossible (such as gods, angels, talking animals); and b) things that aren't there but are still possible (such as a socialist Sweden or a democratic school)."

Sven Wernström, who wrote books for children and young people about the Cuban revolution, Jesus as a partisan, and the thousand-year history of the Swedish workers' movement, became a prominent role model for many authors in Scandinavia around 1970. "All literature is political" was the watchword of the literary left wing, in which socialist children's books were considered a weapon in the class struggle, elevating children and young people into a Marxist world cleansed of supernatural fantasy creatures.

Yet on the farm at Näs in eastern Småland, they continued to vote for the Center Party and keep faith in spirits. Hanna and Samuel August's old kitchen in their red house was regularly visited by a witch, who took Hanna's worn baker's peel, covered it with small pieces of chocolate, and stuck it through the kitchen door for the children. The ones who gave in to temptation and grabbed the peel were hauled into the kitchen and squeezed into the firewood box. In a hoarse, horrible voice, the witch told them she was going to take her shears and cut off the beastly children's beautiful hair. Sometimes the witch ignored the peel and simply chased the boys and girls around the house instead. There was only one spot—under the bed in the guest room—where they could take a breather and comfort their smaller siblings and relatives, who huddled in the dark and cried with fear.

Life could be scary when Aunt Astrid came to Vimmerby and played the witch in her childhood home, which she had bought, renovated, and furnished so that it resembled down to the last detail the house she, Gunnar, Stina, and Ingegerd had grown up in. Her games lasted a long time and were remarkably realistic, author Karin Alvtegen recalls. One of Gunnar and Gullan's seven grandchildren, she occasionally ended up in the firewood box, but like all the others she would manage to sneak away when the witch's back was turned (it always took her an inordinately long time to find the shears on the top shelf).

"That was where she lived when she came to Näs, and that was where she played at being a witch with us nephews and nieces. I mean, there's playing and then there's playing. That was the fun thing about Astrid. We were never quite sure whether she had turned into a real witch, she was so good at it. Grown-ups weren't, mostly."

Astrid had started these games at Furusund in the early 1960s, when she took Karl-Johan and a girl of the same age into the woods to look for trolls and pixies hiding behind the trees. The children would usually sit in a handcart and follow Karl-Johan's grandma with their eyes while she crept around and tried to catch the woodland spirits. Later, when the children were bigger and there were more of them, she assumed the role of a spirit herself, this time armed not with a baker's peel but with an eerie Japanese mask—a gift from a distant admirer. She would put it on and give chase, recalls Karin Nyman, adding: "Astrid took for granted, I think, that fear and tension were a necessary element of games. People of all ages will recognize that and agree with it, so it's not something she could claim to have invented."

Astrid Lindgren also liked to frighten her readers. She did so in much the same way as the adults in Nangilima scare their children, with "really eerie, horrifying fairy-tales," as it says at the end of *The Brothers Lionheart*.

A kindly grandma on the heels of her grandchildren on Furusund in 1968. "Children are balm for the soul," wrote Astrid Lindgren to Louise Hartung at the beginning of the decade. "You see what the Lord was really thinking when He made people, that they should be good and laugh at life."

Astrid, Gunnar, Stina, and Ingegerd had often been similarly terrified by their grandma, recalled Astrid in the *Dagens Nyheter* in September 1959:

> My father's mother, who was the gentlest person on earth, told us quite scary things, myths and ghost stories. I remember, for instance, one about Skinny Jack in Rumskulla Church. He was a man who'd crept into the church long ago, disguised as a ghost,

to frighten the bell ringer. But then he got locked into the church overnight and fear turned him solid—"his blood froze to ice," said my grandma. He wasn't alive, but nor was he dead, so he couldn't be buried, and they had to leave him standing in a niche. A hundred years later the priest had a maid, the type who wasn't scared of anything. One night she was flirting in the vicarage with an itinerant tailor, boasting about her fearlessness. He made a wager with her. If she went into the church and carried Skinny Jack out on her back, he'd give her a piece of fabric for a dress. She left and came back into the house and threw Skinny Jack down on the floor. "I didn't promise to take him back again." So the terrified tailor made more promises, persuading her to take him back. Just as she had gotten back into the church with him *he grabbed hold of her*—grandma said that bit so that we shuddered—and demanded in a ghostly voice that she carry him out to the bell ringer's grave. From the grave came a hollow sound: "If God forgives, so will I." Then Skinny Jack collapsed and turned into a heap of ashes, and afterward he could be buried in consecrated ground. . . . Yes, that's the kind of story we got, my brother Gunnar and I and our other siblings.

It wasn't unlike Astrid to surprise her loyal public with a book whose form or content they wouldn't see coming. If by doing so she could annoy literary critics of the type who liked to dictate what children's literature should be, then so much the better. Astrid Lindgren wasn't much for political correctness, and even before the battle for fantasy in Scandinavian children's literature properly took hold, she made her opinion clear. In an essay in the magazine *Barn och kultur* in 1970, Astrid Lindgren gleefully made fun of the social-realist style of books by Sven Wernström and others, hinting that she too could whip up a socially minded children's book if need be:

Take 1 piece of divorced mother, a plumber if possible, although a nuclear physicist is also fine—the main thing is she doesn't "sew" and isn't "sweet," blend the plumbing mother with two

parts sewage and two parts air pollution, a few spoonsful of star-
vation, and several parts parental oppression and fear of teachers, carefully arrange the whole thing layer by layer with a few
handfuls of racial conflict, a few handfuls of gender discrimination, and a pinch of Vietnam, sprinkle liberally with sex and
drugs until you get a good, strong stew that would give Zacha-
rias Topelius a dreadful start if he tasted it. . . . No sensible person believes that good children's books come out of sitting
down and writing from a recipe.

Yet this was precisely what many younger Scandinavian authors were
busy doing, with stout encouragement from equally young academics at
universities, where books for children and young people had become ob-
jects of study. At Copenhagen University, older writers were flayed alive for
"doggedly continuing to write about individual problems," as the issue was
phrased in one of 1970s Scandinavia's trendiest scholarly publications:
Children, Literature, Society (Børn, litteratur, samfund), a collection of
writings by such left-leaning firebrands as Pil Dahlerup, Søren Vinterberg,
and Ove Kreisberg. Unlike Astrid Lindgren, they had nothing against de-
fining what a good children's book should be in the year 1972: "A good
children's book is a book that uses the situation of children to ask questions, and that gives socialist answers."

Emil and Ikea

Back on the Swedish side of Øresund, three literary historians—Eva Adolfsson, Ulf Eriksson, and Birgitta Holm—were attacking Astrid Lindgren's
work. In the journal *Ord och Bild,* Emil from Lönneberga was labelled a
future "agrarian-capitalist," while the books about Pippi, the children of
Noisy Village, Nils Karlsson the Elf, Mio, Mardie, Lillebror and Karlsson-
on-the-Roof were characterized as a series of broken promises of "liberation from the performance ideology of our society."
    Around the same time as the Marxists at *Ord och Bild* were recasting
the ungovernable, unpredictable boy from feudal Småland as a capitalist, a

certain Ingvar Kamprad from Agunnaryd in southern Småland had just begun exporting chipboard furniture. Unlike the hundreds of thousands of
Scandinavian children and adults who loved Astrid Lindgren (and who were
gradually becoming dependent on Kamprad's furniture), the three literary
scholars were most displeased with Emil's reflection of developments in the
Scandinavian welfare state: "When Emil is 'better' than his father, he foreshadows a new age. With his authoritarian attitude and conservative small-
time farmer's stinginess, Emil's father represents patriarchal and economic
systems that have outlived their use. Emil's desire for expansion and his financial talents alter the picture. New, fresh winds from this rising agrarian-
capitalism hint at a new and even more treacherously oppressive society."

Astrid Lindgren was wise enough not to get drawn further into this
intense literary-political debate during the first half of the 1970s, when both
Danes and Swedes took more than a few ideological potshots at her work.
Some of those she brought on herself, partly with the provocative essay in
Barn och kultur and partly with the fantasy novel *The Brothers Lionheart*,
which was published in 1973 and in the eyes of many Wernström proselytes
read like something written by a witch on a broomstick. Some even claimed
that Astrid Lindgren was encouraging children and teenagers to commit
suicide rather than to rebel, or that she was promoting the notion of reincar-
nation and spreading esoteric ideas.

Astrid knew perfectly well that *The Brothers Lionheart* would challenge the prevailing spirit of the age. Six months before the book came out,
at Easter 1973, Rabén and Sjögren released some publicity material put together by Astrid Lindgren. It was intended mainly for booksellers, but it
also reached the press, as well as various foreign publishers who were going
to translate and publish the book. The author explained a little about her
forthcoming novel, hinting that it probably wouldn't be appropriate for
readers of all ages. It is difficult to imagine more effective bait, and over the
following months expectations ramped up throughout every link in the
book industry chain:

> I've called it a tale from the age of campfires and adventures, but
> perhaps that doesn't tell you very much. It's not a historical

book, in case anybody thought it was. Richard the Lionheart
plays no part in it. No, no. It's about two brothers who
quite prosaically have the last name Lion, and who quite
prosaically—at the beginning of the story—live in a wooden hut
somewhere in Poverty Sweden. Not Welfare Sweden. In a little
town where their mother makes a living as a seamstress. Yes,
it begins a little melodramatically! The two boys are ten and
thirteen. How they end up becoming the Brothers Lionheart at
Knights Farm in Cherry Valley in Nangijala, that I won't tell
you. I don't want to reveal too much. All I'll say is that the book
will be exciting, so exciting that you maybe shouldn't give it to a
child below the age of seven. Though, of course, I've tried it on
a hardboiled little four-year-old grandchild. And he fell asleep.
Possibly in self-defense. But his nine-year-old brother smiled
contentedly when things began to get sinister. I can say the
following about the book: first it's sad, then it gets wonderful for
a while, and then it gets sinister. And then—then comes the
ending! And that's the bit I'm going to write now.

The last part was no lie. The final chapters of *The Brothers Lionheart*
had been following Astrid like a shadow since the New Year, getting longer
and longer, from Dalagatan at the start of the year to Furusund and then to
Tällberg in Dalarna, where as usual she had spent the winter with some of
her grandchildren—making sure to bring her stenographic pads. After
Easter and the press release, progress continued at a sluggish pace. In her
correspondence with Astrid Lindgren, teenaged Sara Ljungcrantz witnessed the author battling with her material. Never before had an ending
been such a challenge. On May 4, 1973, Sara received the following message: "I'm missing two chapters from my book, two difficult chapters. Cross
your fingers for me!"
     The fourteen-year-old did, but still her older pen pal was having trou-
ble. She wasn't at all satisfied with what she was getting down onto her
writing pads. Ahead of her was a deadline—and a package holiday to
Crete with her children and grandchildren. By June 12 the deadline was

imminent, and Sara got another message, including an oath in English: "One chapter left, so help me God! But a tough one. And it must be finished by the 20th, because on the 21st I'm traveling to Crete."

First, however, the manuscript featuring the final chapter took a trip to Vimmerby, where Astrid's school class was having its fifty-year reunion. She spent the night at her childhood home, waking before the birds and immediately settling down to write, first in bed and later at Samuel August's desk. The pages accompanied her to Crete, too, although the rest of the book had already been copied out and delivered. In June, Elsa Olenius received a letter from Astrid, who had just read through the nearly finished manuscript and come away dissatisfied: "I delivered Lionheart yesterday, except for the 'sublime conclusion,' which I'll have to write in Crete, if that's possible. I thought the book was bad when I read it, and it upset me."

Even on the Greek island, Astrid was unable to finish the book, and on her return in early July, when she visited her sister Ingegerd and her husband Ingvar in Fagersta, she was still carrying the troublesome ending in her bag. Elsa was sent the latest news on progress: "In the little room where I sleep, I rewrote the ending of Lionheart during a few hours in the early morning. But it's still not properly finished even now. I've got to rewrite it one more time."

Not until July 31 were the finishing touches made, and Astrid could no longer tinker with the ending. In a letter to Sara, she expressed enormous relief. Now things simply had to take their course: "The book, as you know, has been sent for typesetting and will probably come out in November."

Freedom Cannot Die

With *The Brothers Lionheart,* Astrid Lindgren continued to forge her own apolitical path through children's literature, although the novel was hardly without "social consciousness" or "social criticism." The dynamic between popular resistance and oppressive power structures simply played out along metaphorical back alleys, which was presumably the reason why many Marxist critics read the book as the Devil reads the Bible, stubbornly insisting that there was nothing political about it. Looking more closely,

"I've been at Furusund more than normal, since it was necessary (and I wanted to) in order to write Lionheart," noted Astrid in her diary at Christmas 1973. "Almost nothing I've written has kicked up more fuss than this book. I've been interviewed into oblivion, and people have been writing and phoning and thinking and opining, it's quite astonishing. The reviews have been virtual panegyrics in most cases, although some people think the book is too sinister or the wickedness too much."

however, it's clear that there are numerous phrases in *The Brothers Lionheart* that match the revolutionary rhetoric of the 1970s, particularly in the descriptions of Thorn Rose Valley's uprising against the dictator, Tengil: "What he doesn't understand, Tengil, is that he can never cow people who are fighting for their freedom, and who stick together like we do."

Political undertones can also be found in her portrayal of the Che Guevara–like resistance leader Orvar, whom the brothers Jonathan and Karl "Rusky" Lionheart rescue from imprisonment in Katla's cave: "Orvar may die, but freedom never shall!" Equally political, of course, are the passages about the uprising itself. The warlike Orvar and pacifist Jonathan are in fundamental disagreement about the best strategy, and there are many words and phrases in their conversations that could easily have appeared in one of Sven Wernström's red-to-the-core young-adult novels: "The storm of freedom shall come, and it shall crack our oppressors like trees crack and fall. It shall enter with a roar, sweeping away all our servitude and making us free again at last!"

Instead of pointing out political parallels between her fantasy novel and reality in the year 1973, Astrid Lindgren talked in interviews about a conflict that has played out again and again over the course of human history, leaving its mark throughout the history of literature: the struggle between good and evil. As in *Mio, My Son,* she had chosen to view this ancient mythological clash through the imagination of a small boy.

On the one hand is evil incarnate—Tengil—and on the other is goodness, in two different versions: Orvar and Jonathan. The two leaders of the uprising both want evil destroyed, but profoundly disagree about how best to do so. Should terror be fought with evil or with goodness? The narrator, Rusky, the reader's eyes and ears on this journey through good and evil, sketches out the problem in perhaps the book's most important piece of dialogue:

> "But I can't kill anybody," said Jonathan. "You know that, Orvar!"
>
> "Not even if your life were at stake?" asked Orvar.
>
> "No, not even then," said Jonathan.
>
> "If everyone were like you," said Orvar, "evil would rule for all eternity!"
>
> But then I said that if everyone were like Jonathan, there wouldn't be any evil at all.

The words "if everyone were like Jonathan" are carried throughout the book like an invisible torch, as is another distinctive phrase that underscores the necessity for compassion, solidarity, and moral courage in a civilized society. This phrase is often quoted in attempts to explain what it was Astrid Lindgren wanted to do with her writing, apart from telling good stories: "There are things you *have* to do, or else you're not a human being but just a bit of filth."

If it was rare for a Scandinavian children's book author in the 1970s to write about oppression, terror, and treachery in such a fantastical, allegorical way, it was virtually unheard of for a modern children's book to depict death so naturally and unashamedly, venturing deep into childhood notions of what comes after life.

Telling children about death has always demanded a certain ethical and moral sensibility in a writer, argued Danish philosopher K. E. Løgstrup in his essay "Morality and Children's Books," printed in the 1969 scholarly anthology *Books for Children and the Young* (Børne-og ungdomsbøger). The book sat in Astrid Lindgren's study in Dalagatan and was probably read by her, given that it took a highly pragmatic approach to Scandinavian children's literature and also featured a ten-page analysis of *Mio, My Son.* The Danish philosopher argued that children's book writers always considered what effect the main character and the ending would have on the reader, to avoid "infecting the child with hopelessness," as he put it.

The risk of depressing the reader had never previously been a concern for Astrid Lindgren, but perhaps this was what made her hesitate and doubt herself as she struggled with the final chapters of *The Brothers Lionheart.* The small group of people who knew the novel's contents at that stage included some of the author's grandchildren, remembers Karin Nyman: "She read *Lionheart* to her grandchildren while it was still a work in progress, but I never thought of it as her seeing what they 'could cope with,' just to test whether the wording was fine. I saw her doubts and the long slog as a question of finding the right way to express this big subject."

For the first time in her career, Astrid Lindgren felt a kind of fear of the blank page. It wasn't about writer's block: this was a moral dilemma arising from the conclusion to the novel, in which a child chooses to leap to his death with his dying brother. Would it be clear enough that this leap was taking place "only" in Rusky's imagination, or would too many children assume it was real and be "infected with hopelessness"?

Astrid's feelings on this issue are clear from the many stenographic pads she went through in 1972–73. No. 50 in the archives at the National Library contains a draft chapter from *Lionheart* as well as sketches for a few longer letters; most remarkable, however, is the cardboard back of the pad, where Astrid Lindgren penciled a gravestone with both the Lionheart brothers' names and their dates of birth and death: Jonathan 1885–1898 and Karl 1888–1901. Above and below the gravestone is written: "A gravestone I came up with for Lionheart (which makes it clear that Karl outlives Jonathan by three years and uses that time to write the whole story)."

Whether the drawing on the back of the pad was meant as a sketch for a possible Ilon Wikland illustration at the back of the book, making it clear to readers that the whole story, including the dramatic ending, took place in Karl's imagination, is unknown. What the drawing does indicate, however, is that at some point before the book was finished Astrid Lindgren was in two minds about whether her readers would end up feeling comforted.

That her work on *The Brothers Lionheart* was hindered by more than just aesthetic issues is clear from a letter she sent to Gunnel Linde on July 1, 1973. The chairwoman of BRIS (Barnens Rätt i Samhället, Children's rights in society), she was eager for Lindgren to collaborate on a project and had written her a series of letters that went unanswered. When the author finally resurfaced, she explained the reason behind her unresponsiveness: "You should know I've been living like a hermit as long as I can remember, doing nothing but working—early this morning I finished off the book I've been fiddling with for more than a year. Still, I'll end up rewriting the last chapter several times before I let it go. I mention this so that you understand my silence. For all practical purposes I've been out of my mind all spring and up to now—now things will be different, I hope."

Children and Death

In the years following its publication, *The Brothers Lionheart* was met with both enthusiasm and criticism from political, pedagogical, and psychological quarters. This was a piece of literature that shifted the boundaries of what was permitted in a children's book, and repeatedly Astrid Lindgren was asked: should a story for children end so mysteriously, so uncannily? Each time she answered with a sureness and calm that revealed none of the uncertainty she had experienced during her unusually protracted writing process: "For a child it's a happy ending. The only thing children are really afraid of is loneliness. Being abandoned by the ones they love. The two brothers venture into another land together. They're together forever. And that's the kind of happiness children dream of."

Lindgren made this argument in December 1973 in *Politiken,* where the interview with the now sixty-six-year-old writer focused on the book's thematization of death and the way it related to the reader. Could Scandinavian children cope with the terrible truth about death? asked the Danish journalist. Astrid Lindgren answered: "Why not? Children are nowhere near as scared of death as adults. Many adults seem to have an intense horror of death, I discovered after *The Brothers Lionheart* came out. . . . For me there's nothing wrong about familiarizing children with death through an adventure. They don't yet have enough experience to get a sense of the realities. . . . Children aren't afraid of death yet. They're afraid of being left alone."

Yet the author's observation that *The Brothers Lionheart* was also a book about loneliness seems to have been largely ignored. The subject's most prominent treatment is in the final pages, as Rusky makes his decision: "No one has to stay behind alone, grieving and crying and being afraid." Astrid Lindgren did what she could to feed this compassionate message into the media storm when the book came out and the questions rained down. In the *Expressen* on December 2, 1973, she was quoted as follows: "Children are just as afraid of death as adults. Above all, what they're afraid of is being abandoned, and that's what I've tried to illuminate in the book. That's how Rusky feels. He can face any death so long as he's with Jonathan. It's really not a sad ending, it's not, it's actually a happy one. . . . I believe every single child has to have a good emotional bond with at least one adult to feel safe, or they won't cope."

Over and over, Astrid Lindgren was asked to account for her work, to explain and defend why she had written about death in a book for children.

Even in a self-professed age of rebellion, where dogmas were felled one after the next, certain taboos were unshakable. Yet Astrid Lindgren did her best, for instance by pointing out the thematic connections that already tied together several of her books, and by appealing to the ancient tradition of fairy-tales, which didn't shy away from death as a topic. On January 2, 1974, she commented to the *Vecko-Journalen:* "Yes, I'm sure there are similarities between *The Brothers Lionheart, Mio, My Son,* and *South Meadow.* They're all fairy-tales, after all, and both folk fairy-tales and modern fairy-tales are about the same themes, the struggle between good and evil, love, death, they're ancient motifs. An Andersen researcher in Norway has worked out that five-sixths of Hans Christian Andersen's fairy-tales are about death. More or less. And without wanting to compare myself to him, the same goes for my fairy-tales—more or less."

In the 1970s, it was mainly children who understood what Astrid Lindgren was trying to do with her book, and the one question many of them wanted to ask was what happened next to Rusky and Jonathan in Nangilima. The interest from her many dedicated and curious readers was so overwhelming and the piles of letters so impossible to get through that Astrid Lindgren decided to write a brief epilogue and circulate it in the media, reassuring everybody that Rusky and Jonathan were living contentedly on the other side.

Among those many letters were grateful messages from terminally ill children and their relatives, thanking her for everything *The Brothers Lionheart* had done to comfort them. Indeed, this was what Astrid hoped deep down the novel would be for many people: a comfort. As she explained to Egil Törnqvist in *Svensk Litteraturtidskrift* in 1975: "I believe in children's need for comfort. When I was a child I thought you went to Heaven when you died, and that idea was definitely not much fun. But if we could all go up there *together,* then . . . Anyway, it would be better than lying in the ground and not existing. But today's children don't have that comfort. They don't have that fairy-tale anymore. So I thought: maybe I could give them another fairy-tale to keep them warm while they wait for life's inevitable conclusion."

This had been her experience with Karl-Johan and Malin's little brother Nisse in 1972–73, when the eight-year-old boy brooded so much about death that his grandma sometimes wished she could comfort him a little. As she later explained in an article, "No, Be Quite Calm," which was printed in the anthology *The Meaning of Life* (Livets mening): "I read the story of *The Brothers Lionheart* to the boy who was so afraid, and when I got to the end he smiled slightly and said: 'Well, we don't know what happens, so it might well be like that.' He was comforted by the book."

The First Thing-Seeker

Another person in need of comfort was the author herself. So many close friends died in 1974 that by Christmas, when Astrid usually summed up the year, she began by sticking four small photographs into the pages of her diary: her housekeeper Miss Nordlund, her older brother Gunnar, literature professor Olle Holmberg, and radio host Per-Martin Hamberg. Then she began to write. "Well, 1974 has been a year of more deaths than ever before, and these four are the ones who've left the deepest void. I miss them, miss them, miss them. . . . Years that end in 4 are always significant for me in some way, and it was logical to expect it would be death that made it significant now. What else could I expect?"

It was a great personal loss for Astrid Lindgren. Olle Holmberg and Per-Martin Hamberg had been close, loyal, inspirational friends for decades, each significant for Astrid's artistic development in his different ways, but the biggest shock was when her housekeeper, Gerda Nordlund, died. One Sunday in February, twenty-two years to the day since she had entered Astrid's employment, "Nolle" dropped by Dalagatan to help with lunch. She turned down coffee and pie because she was going to the movies, shouted goodbye from the hallway, and was later knocked off her bike and died at the scene, a dangerous set of traffic lights near St. Eriksplan.

Yet it was Gunnar's death on May 27, after several years battling heart problems and breathing difficulties, that caused her the greatest sorrow. Before the funeral at Pentecost 1974, Astrid Lindgren wrote in her diary: "I'll never forget the night we sat him up so he could breathe more easily, how pitifully he clung to our arms, and the death sweat on his brow. No, I'm not able to write any more; I'm grieving for him. It's so terrible to be reminded of how close we were as children—Noisy Village's Lasse, the first thing-seeker, is dead. The first broken link in the sibling chain."

In addition to running the farm at Näs, Gunnar had been a political force in contemporary Sweden. For ten years he was a member of parliament with the Farmers' Union, which in 1957—the year after Gunnar Ericsson withdrew from party politics—changed its name to the Center Party. Afterward he dedicated himself to political satire, publishing an annual chronicle with the illustrator Ewert Karlsson about very real politicians transplanted into Viking times in Svitjod (an old Norse name for Sweden).

Norse languages were Gunnar Ericsson's great passion, and "the United States of Scandinavia"—connected via an Øresund bridge—was one of his big ideas. For several decades Gunnar was also an avid artist, exhibiting his pastels under the name "G. E. Näs" in various places, including Helsingfors and Vienna. But he was never happy as a farmer; his intellectual aspirations were too ambitious for that. The farm wasn't the aspect of her brother's multifaceted life that Astrid emphasized when she described Gunnar in a 1957 radio program:

> There's a fierce energy about the way he lives, and he's a very spontaneous man. Suddenly one day he began to read Finnish, suddenly one day he began to paint, suddenly one day he sat down and wrote about what "happened in Svitjod." . . . Gunnar's also musical. He can take a pencil and drum it on his skull so that it produces fully audible melodies. And if he holds his nose and sings, he sounds exactly like a Hawaiian guitar. I've often felt astonished that they had someone like him in parliament. But maybe he doesn't sound like a Hawaiian guitar there.

Gunnar was far from the only one of the Ericsson children with a flair for the political, but unlike Gunnar the three sisters were involved more with ideology than party politics. Public-mindedness and participation in

Brother and sister posed at the end of the 1950s for the radio program *Hörde ni* (Did you hear), where they were supposed to talk about each other. Astrid succeeded in illustrating what Gunnar had said when he left Swedish politics: "It felt as liberating as going home from the dentist."

grassroots democracy was something the four children had inherited, recalls Karin Nyman:

> Both Hanna and Samuel August took it for granted that they
> would help out and take responsibility for the community in
> Vimmerby—each of them held a position of trust—without feel-
> ing the least urge to agitate. Perhaps Hanna had role models for
> that in her own family. Her mother was involved in poor relief
> somehow. Ingegerd was never politically active, but as a journal-
> ist she dealt with issues concerning agriculture and domestic
> management. She accompanied Gunnar to his youth politi-
> cians' meetings in the 1930s for as long as she was living at
> home. Stina was a committed socialist like her husband, the au-
> thor Hans Hergin, and although she was capable of arguing for
> socialism she was never active, as far as I know.

And Astrid? After Gunnar's death in 1974 it almost seemed as though
she had decided to pick up the family torch as protector and spokesperson
of the people, a role that Kerstin Ekman characterized in a 2006 essay as akin
to the spirit of the Roman Plebeian Tribunes. In any case, less than eighteen
months after Gunnar's death, she began to get involved in social causes of
local as well as global relevance, which for the next twenty years encompassed everything from Swedish tax policy, Charter 77, nuclear power, child
pornography, and the closure of public libraries to racism, animal welfare,
the European Union, seal killing, and housing shortages for young people.

Without really wanting to, and with no particular objective, in the second half of the 1970s Astrid Lindgren acquired more political clout than any
other author in the history of Scandinavia. The downside to this became
apparent almost before she had begun. In June 1976, Astrid's good friend
Rita Törnqvist-Verschuur, a translator, received a deep sigh of a letter:

> I've become mother confessor to the entire population of
> Sweden. They call at every hour of the day and night, thinking
> I'm going to solve their problems with their divorce and their

troubles with their children and their affairs and their court cases and on and on and on. I've lived—and still live, at times— as if in a dark well. I've become deeply depressed by it, and it'll continue until the election on September 19 is over; I can't even manage to see my children, and everything to do with my books and my films feels like it no longer concerns me; I'm deeply anxious about where my country is headed, I'm worrying myself to death because I can't believe in our social democracy anymore, oh, I could talk about it forever. On top of that I've sunk even lower because of deaths, several deaths. Never have I experienced a spring like this. But in my heart I'm the same Astrid, and I hope you're the same Rita, for without my friends I can't live.

Pomperipossa and the Fat Cats

Nineteen seventy-six proved to be a turning point in Astrid Lindgren's life, and these changes are reflected in her collection of stenographic pads in the National Library in Stockholm. Running an eye down the index for the 660 pads is like lifting the lid off Astrid Lindgren's skull and peering inside, watching what was flowing through her brain each time a new book was created. From 1976 onward there is less and less fiction, other than the draft of *Ronia the Robber's Daughter.* Instead, the number and frequency of political texts increase: letters, talks, manifestos, op-ed pieces, and responses to other articles. They are mainly shorter pieces, with titles like "Sermon of Peace in Frankfurt," "Animal Husbandry," "War, Peace, and Nuclear Power," "Drug Abuse," "Environmental Destruction," "A Question for Olof Palme," and "Letter to Gorbachev." In type and scale they document the way in which Astrid Lindgren's social-political engagement overtook her career as a writer—and her life as a retiree—in the second half of the 1970s. At the age of sixty-eight, Astrid Lindgren wrote to Anne-Marie Fries on July 20, 1976, as the Swedish election was coming to a climax. Astrid had decided to help overturn the Social Democratic government, the party she had voted for since the early 1930s.

When I'm not brooding about the fundamental nature of existence and death and that sort of thing, it's only politics that's
whirling around in my head—it's lucky the election's on Sept.
19 and not later, or I'd be sent completely round the bend. I get
more and more upset the more I really see and understand what
the *sossarna* [the Social Democrats] are doing. We really do
have a fateful election in store for us.

Astrid Lindgren's showdown with the sossarna began on March 10,
1976, when the *Expressen* published a new Lindgren story quirkily titled
"Pomperipossa in Monismanien." According to the editor in chief, Bo
Strömstedt, husband to Margareta Strömstedt and thus one of Astrid's closest friends, the author called him up one day and announced: "You're talking to Astrid Lindgren, former Social Democrat. I've written a story about
Pomperipossa, who pays 102 percent in tax. Will you print it?" The cultured
editor did indeed want to print it—his antisocialist paper was Sweden's largest—thereby writing both political and literary history. As Strömstedt observed in a later article printed in the book *Not a Bit of Filth* (Ingen liten
lort): "She was thirty-eight when she debuted as a writer. She was sixty-nine
when she debuted as a political journalist. And she continued as such."

"Pomperipossa in Monismanien" was about the Social Democrats'
tax policies in Sweden in 1976. The main character, an independent, com-
mercially successful author, Pomperipossa, is instructed to pay a 102 percent tax rate by the government of Monismanien, and discovers that she
might as well give up being an author. In the future she'll have to live off
welfare and go begging in the streets for money to buy a crowbar, so she can
break into the national coffers and steal her money back. A tax rate of 102
percent—which Astrid Lindgren had in fact been asked to pay—was obviously an absurdity, the unfortunate result of a glitch in the recently rejigged
Swedish tax system that hit hardworking self-employed people particularly
hard. As the story points out, they weren't entitled to the same exemptions
as the rich and didn't have such direct access to creative accountants.
The whole mess arose from increasingly complicated tax legislation, and
the true villains of the tale were therefore not the wealthy and affluent but

the once socially responsible Social Democrats, who in Pomperipossa's youth had done away with poverty and transformed Sweden into a welfare state based on freedom and equality: "What's gotten into them? thought Pomperipossa in her dark nook. Are these really the wise men I so admired? The men I thought so much of? What are they trying to create—a society as wrong as possible? Oh, you pure, blossoming Social Democrats of my youth, what have they done with you? she thought (for now she was beginning to wax lyrical), how long shall your good name be abused to protect a high-handed, bureaucratic, unjust nanny state?"

This rather unusual op-ed had an impact Astrid Lindgren could scarcely have dreamt of when she called her friend at the *Expressen* six months before the election. It proved to be a milestone in Swedish history. After forty-four unbroken years in power, in September 1976 the Social Democrats had to submit to a nonsocialist coalition led by Thorbjörn Fälldin. It has since become part of Swedish political lore that Astrid Lindgren was one of the contributing factors to this systemic shift. After the election, when the author was presented with this claim by the media, she liked to respond with a story set in London during the Blitz, when a large building collapsed and the emergency services were looking for survivors. Suddenly they heard crazed laughter coming from the ruins, and found an old woman sitting in the remains of her bathroom. When they asked what was so funny, she replied, "Ha, ha, ha—I pulled the chain and the whole thing came down around my ears!"

At this point it's worth noting that Astrid Lindgren—ha, ha, ha—pulled the chain fourteen or fifteen times in the run-up to the election on September 19, each time hard and each time in the *Expressen,* where prime column space was at her disposal. Her purpose, like that of the newspaper, was to put the boot into Olof Palme's Social Democratic government, even though Astrid still felt herself to be a Social Democrat at heart.

Sträng's Blunders

It was finance minister Gunnar Sträng who ended up getting saddled with the Pomperipossa problem. Sträng had been a minister for twenty-one years and was considered the Grand Old Man of the administration, so naturally it fell to him to explain the 102 percent tax rate, which for ordinary citizens symbolized the explosive surge in taxation in Sweden during the 1960s and 1970s. He should simply have apologized and adjusted the legislation without further ado, but in advance of the vote, having not lost an election for thirty years, the experienced politician committed one tactical blunder after the next.

The same day as the story came out in the *Expressen,* he brushed off Pomperipossa/Lindgren with a chauvinistic remark about her limited talent for arithmetic and ignorance of issues of taxation. Sträng's rudeness proved the spark that made the political activist inside Astrid Lingdren flare up. Within twenty-four hours she had responded on the radio, and as always over the airwaves she was quick and crystal clear. With a deft flick of the wrist, she turned the minister's arrogance against him: "Gunnar Sträng has always been good at telling fairy-tales, but he's never learned much arithmetic. We ought to switch jobs, he and I."

Four days later—March 15, 1976—Astrid fired another salvo in what had already become a national debate. From her base camp at the *Expressen,* she sent an open letter to the finance minister: "Dear Gunnar Emanuel Sträng, Do you know what life is like for small tradespeople up and down the country right now?"

Her tone was sarcastic, ironic, derisive in places, but never malicious. A new and for many Swedes completely unknown side of the jovial, sweet-natured, cheery Astrid Lindgren was coming to light. The children's book author had shed her artist's cloak and found her voice as a political agitator, taking up the cudgels on behalf of the people—in the people's own language—against "the head honcho" (Gunnar Sträng) and his administration, who had to understand that they represented the nation: "This isn't about Pomperipossas earning millions, it's about countless small craftsmen and tobacconists and hairdressers and florists and farmers and lots of other independent workers you're taxing until the blood squeezes out from under their nails."

New, clever articles by Astrid Lindgren followed in the *Expressen* in March and April, including a response to an opinion piece by Social Democrat Nancy Eriksson, which painted Gunnar Sträng—who was one year

older than sixty-eight-year-old Astrid Lindgren (and sixty-eight-year-old
Nancy Eriksson)—as a little boy. Even the headline took on a feminist tone
that verged on the insolent: "Astrid, 68, answers Nancy, 68, and also, sort of,
little Gunnar." Yet Sträng was reaping what he'd sown. Farther down Astrid's
response to Nancy Eriksson, she mentioned perhaps his biggest blunder of
the spring: comparing her to the populist politician Mogens Glistrup. Glistrup had set up the Progress Party, a protest party based around its leader's
anarchistic, antisocial ideas about tax, which would later earn him a lengthy
spell in prison. What was Sträng thinking? Much could be said about Astrid
Lindgren, but she was neither antisocial nor suspected of tax evasion.

Among the many Swedes who waded into the Pomperipossa discussion, there were naturally some who supported the finance minister and
defended his insinuations about Glistrup. For a children's book author
with astronomic sales figures and a dizzyingly high income to fling herself
so passionately into a debate about tax legislation, she must have some sort
of financial ulterior motive. This was precisely the argument Astrid tried to
combat in her response to Nancy Eriksson and Gunnar Sträng on April 8 in
the *Expressen:* "I might even succeed in convincing you [Nancy] that I'm
not having this Pomperipossa debate for my own sake. I've got something to
tell you: I'm afraid of money, I don't want money, I don't want lots of things
and possessions, I don't want the power money can give, because it cor-
rupts almost as much as political power. But I don't think anybody, whoever
that might be, should have to go out and steal so they can scrape together
the money to pay their tax bill."

For the majority of the Swedish populace, the sound of Pomperi-
possa/Lindgren's voice was hugely liberating, and the beginnings of a genuinely popular movement directed against more than just the Social
Democrats' tax policies seemed to be in the offing. Letters poured into the
editorial offices of the *Expressen* and through the mail slot at Dalagatan.
Astrid Lindgren thanked her readers for all their positive messages in another article, in which she also took the opportunity to take to task a male
journalist who had asked whether there were any women writing to Mrs.
Lindgren about tax policy: "Have I heard from any women? Ha! If only he
knew how many smart, clear-sighted, indignant, funny, and fierce women

I've encountered, both in letters and on the phone. When it comes to the women of Monismanien, the words of the folklorist hold true: 'Women are tough and strong as donkeys, and bake good bread with many currants, but if they're baited they'll immediately go on the attack.' Precisely! So duck, boys at the Chancellery! The women are cocking their pistols. The attack will come in September! Trust Pomperipossa."

And in the Chancellery, where the prime minister's office was located, there was profound unease about this development in the duel between the finance minister and the author. Couldn't Sträng handle her? As Henrik Berggren explains in his biography of Olof Palme, the prime minister had originally wanted the election campaign to be about employment, industrial democracy, and family policy, before Astrid Lindgren suddenly sprang out of nowhere and threw a wrench in the works. It didn't help that a number of countries overseas, usually so admiring of Sweden and its welfare model, got wind of the story about the children's book author—a grandmother— waging war against a government that had been in power for half a century. Global publications like *Time, Newsweek,* and *Reader's Digest* published articles with headlines like "Sweden's Surrealistic Socialism" and "Uto-pia's Dark Side." Among the foreign horror stories was that of Ingmar Berg-man, who in January 1976 was arrested by plainclothes police officers in the middle of rehearsals for *The Dance of Death,* accused of fiddling his taxes. Bergman was cleared by spring, but as a result he decided to leave his homeland in April 1976.

"The People's Home"—the Social Democrats' Edenic concept—was coming under heavy fire from both inside and outside Sweden. Interna-tional Workers' Day was approaching, and again Gunnar Sträng misjudged popular sentiment regarding the Pomperipossa affair. On May 1 he used his speeches at Helsingborg and Malmö to trivialize Lindgren's and Bergman's significance for the election: "Those who believe that the currently topical names Astrid Lindgren and Ingmar Bergman can be used as weapons against Social Democracy in the election are mistaken. These 'circum-stances' have no significance for the campaign."

How wrong he was! Yet on one point in his Mayday comments about the Pomperipossa business, Sträng was right: "We have a vociferous opposition." Caricaturists were having a field day. The most popular motif was to put a slender Astrid Lindgren, clad as Pippi Longstocking, her braids sticking out anarchically, juggling a stubborn, round-as-a-ball finance minister. Sträng didn't get much chance to regain his balance: Four times between May 11 and June 2, Astrid Lindgren published fresh articles in the *Expressen,* including new polemics and deft answers to readers' letters, in which her fundamental message was repeated again and again: "The Social Democrats have let me down, and everybody else who dreamt of living in a just and fair People's Home." Around the same time, the magazine *Veckans Affärer* published a major interview with Astrid Lindgren, in which she responded to questions about her motivations and reasons for waging this campaign in the *Expressen:*

> *Why are you—or, indeed, have you been—a Social Democrat?*
> I'll be a democrat for as long as I live. But, as I see it, those currently in power are no longer defending democracy, and might as well be called the Social Bureaucratic Party.
> *Can you be a Social Democrat without socialism being your goal?*
> Socialism carried to its logical conclusion requires a dictatorship, and I'm not fond of dictatorships.
> *Do you feel you're being punished?*
> No, I don't feel I'm being punished. It's just infuriating when Sträng compares me to Glistrup. If I'm Glistrup, then Sträng's the archangel Gabriel, a strident shi—no, what am I saying . . . a shining white creature of light and rare purity. And I don't think he is! Although he does have many good sides.

Democracy for Dummies

Summer came, and it was time for Astrid to take a break in the archipelago, gathering her strength after a turbulent spring in the big city. In August, however, she picked up where she had left off: with an open letter, "To a Social Democrat," which hit the front page of the *Expressen* on August 31,

1976. Three weeks before the date of the election. It was a long and emotional appeal to all the professed Social Democrats who planned to vote for the party again, stirring them to mutiny with the words: "Democracy means taking turns in power." The letter was signed by "Astrid Lindgren, former Social Democrat—now just a democrat." It took up a whole spread in the tabloid, the leftover space on the two pages adorned with a portrait of Pippi Longstocking in Ingrid Vang Nyman's classic depiction. Astrid Lindgren's art had now become unequivocally political, and in column after column she castigated the Social Democrats' moral decay and hunger for power. Every speechwriter in parliament must have envied the writer her linguistic skill. This was democratic criticism for dummies: "If it's true that politics is the art of stopping people having a say in issues that concern them, then nobody has mastered the art better than the Swedish Social Democrats and their administration. They decide everything for us, where and how we live, what we eat, how our children should be raised, what we think, everything!"

What had happened to freedom, that core value of Social Democracy? asked Astrid Lindgren. If Social Democrat brothers and sisters across the country didn't change their minds and vote Palme's government out of the Chancellery on September 19, Sweden would be ruled by a single-party power unrivaled in any European country west of the Iron Curtain.

These were strong words in a public debate that was already influencing voters, and it has since been said that Olof Palme blanched when he read the open letter in the *Expressen,* while the Social Democrats' party secretary, Sten Andersson, simply shook his head in resignation.

"Pomperipossa has struck another blow in the middle of the election campaign's final push," echoed the media around September 1. The tone of the election had taken on a sharper edge, as always when a campaign comes down to the wire, and there was plenty of harsh criticism directed at Astrid Lindgren. Was she acting under orders from Strömstedt, the editor in chief, and the political strategists at the *Expressen?* The *Örebro-Kuriren* was one of several papers to view the author's motives and credibility with suspicion: "Why is Astrid Lindgren writing this letter now? She has previously said she doesn't want to participate further in the tax debate." And in many other newspapers up and down the country, the lapsed Social Democrat attracted critical headlines like "Author of Fairy-Tales Despises Voters" (*Västerbottens Folkblad*), while fellow author—and Social Democrat—Max Lundgren wrote a feature for the newspapers *Arbetet* and *Aftonbladet* entitled "You're Childish, Astrid!" in which he questioned Lindgren's judgment: "You've turned into a reactionary, Astrid! All that's left of your childish charm is the childishness. . . . Your words, Astrid, reflect terribly on you, not as a writer but as someone who believes they know the truth about us here in Sweden. Think how much you've underestimated people!"

Instead of responding to her colleague, Astrid Lindgren posed another question, three days before the election: Had anybody glimpsed any women involved in the Social Democrats' campaign, which would soon be over and had centered mainly on nuclear power, to which the Social Democrats were favorably disposed? Once again, she hit the venerable old party where it hurt:

> Where are the Social Democratic women in this election campaign, that's what I'd like to know. I think they've been conspicuously silent. Perhaps they share their sisters' concerns about the threat of nuclear power? Are they as painfully aware as other women that they're now facing something unlike any other danger they've ever feared in their lives? Somewhere inside their femininity, where motherhood is—in the heart, the brain, or the womb or wherever it may be—Social Democratic women are probably sensing an emphatic no! We don't want to unleash forces that could damage our children, irrevocably and for all time.

The election on September 19, 1976, wasn't a huge defeat for the Social Democrats, but the loss of votes was significant enough that they had to cede power to other, nonsocialist parties. Gunnar Sträng's career as finance minister was over, although he remained in parliament until 1985. Olof Palme returned as prime minister in 1982, around the same time Ingmar Bergman came home to Sweden. And Astrid Lindgren? She never came closer to party politics than in 1976, when many Swedes acquired new respect for Pippi and Emil's mother, although others saw her as politically naïve, even as something of a traitor. As a *Västerbottens Folkblad* editorialist wrote a few weeks before the election: "Astrid Lindgren has changed course and come out as a fully fledged reactionary, with a mentality that belongs in the darkest right-wing circles."

On the day of the election itself, Astrid Lindgren retreated to Switzerland. The *Aftonbladet* announced its belief that the wealthy author was using the country as a tax haven. This was rapidly contradicted on the front page of the *Expressen,* and the *Aftonbladet* later apologized, also on the front page. So, what did Pomperipossa think about the election results? She expressed satisfaction—without a trace of gloating—in a telephone conversation with a journalist from the *Expressen,* and on September 23 she published a sympathetic farewell to the outgoing finance minister: "I'm deeply sorry for Gunnar Sträng. He's an old man with a long political career behind him. I wish he could have finished it with his flag flying high."

There was no hint of sympathy in Astrid's remarks about a few of the *Aftonbladet*'s journalists, however, who had tried to dig up dirt on the author during the campaign. The final word from Pomperipossa was a lengthy opinion piece entitled "If the Truth Is Going to Out" on October 17 in the *Expressen,* where she tried to knock it into various journalistic heads that her quarrel with the Social Democrats wasn't about her own fortune and finances. Nor was it about animosity toward the workers' movement. And anybody who thought she was wandering around in the triumphant conviction that she had single-handedly toppled the government could think again: "The result of the election has nothing whatsoever to do with me. I just came out and said what people were feeling and thinking, so it should have been possible to respond objectively to it. The *Aftonbladet* would have helped the Social Democrats much more by doing so, instead of launching a kind of Watergate-inspired inquiry into my affairs."

But what, deep down, had made Astrid Lindgren assume the role of plebeian tribune, despite coming under attack? Why, having declared many times that she wasn't interested in being a celebrity and would rather keep to herself, had the author suddenly gone out on a limb and left herself so exposed? What had induced a world-famous children's book author to wade into a heated election campaign at a moment in her life when she finally had the chance to devote herself to "sweet solitude"?

She gave Margareta Strömstedt the answer ten years later in the documentary film *Astrid Anna Emilia*, in which the nearly eighty-year-old Astrid Lindgren was asked what she might have done if she hadn't become a writer. Her response was as follows: "I would have been an active little antagonist in the workers' movement when it was young . . . a people's champion."

It was this more populist form of parliamentarianism, based on firm principles and idealism, that Astrid Lindgren participated in from the mid-1970s onward. It couldn't be otherwise, or she would be just "a bit of filth." After three decades battling evil in the world of the imagination, she now turned her hand to fighting for good in the real one.

I Have Been Dancing in My Solitude

O N E   W A R M   J U L Y evening in 1980, when the moon hung low above the neighboring island of Yxlan and the big liners and ferries to Åland, Åbo, and Helsingfors passed the old custom house on Furusund on their way into the Baltic, Astrid Lindgren walked out onto her jetty with a small tin. She took something out of it, weighing it in her hand before flinging it far out over the water:

> Farewell, you stupid gallstone!
> You've hurt me long enough.
> It's time to say goodbye now,
> Frankly, it's been rough.
> If only you'd behaved yourself
> Not acted like a beast,
> Then maybe I'd have let you stay—
> We could have lived in peace.
> Now you're at the hospital,
> Swirling down some drain.
> I bet that you're regretting now
> Causing all that pain.
> You treated me so badly,
> Though I was always kind!
> Farewell, you stupid gallstone!
> You're being left behind!

Astrid had written this poem on a scrap of paper the day before her operation at Sabbatsberg Hospital, and while the rest of Sweden was sitting down to herring, schnapps, and new potatoes with dill, celebrating midsummer, she was having something removed from her body, an object that had developed into what the seventy-two-year-old author believed must be Scandinavia's largest gallstone. It had been tormenting her since the New Year, as had various articles about nuclear power she needed to finish. They were supposed to be done before the important referendum in March—one year after the accident on Three Mile Island near Harrisburg, Pennsylvania, which all opponents of nuclear power, including Astrid Lindgren, had warned about.

The gallstone also disrupted work on *Ronia the Robber's Daughter,* which had come to her as a blurry vision in 1979, like so many previous books. Would she ever finish it? After *The Brothers Lionheart* and the Pomperipossa debate, Astrid Lindgren doubted it, given how much else she had to occupy her time. In a letter to Rita Törnqvist-Verschuur on June 20, 1977, she wrote: "What I'll write next I don't know. I don't even know if there'll be another book; one fine day the gunpowder will run out, that's what I'm afraid of."

After her extraparliamentary battle with Palme's government in 1976, she had been approached by an overwhelming number of organizations, committees, and popular movements trying to get the author on board with their political causes. In an age when everything was politicized, Pippi and Emil's mother had become a highly sought-after brand.

But what did her other children have to say about this development, which didn't exactly make for a smooth and peaceful retirement? Weren't they worried about the constant pressure? Not really, recalls Karin Nyman: "I didn't feel I needed to be worried. Astrid was so strong. The only sign that she thought it was all getting too much was when she moaned, 'Why is everybody flinging themselves at me?' And when it came to all the inquiries about whether she would support this or that, I'd just tell her, quite insensitively, 'But you can just say no.' And she would answer, 'You don't know how long it takes to say no.' Everything she did was done with such great commitment and drive that it never occurred to me to try and prevent something so unavoidable. I was more upset by all the enmity and rejection she was shown during the Pomperipossa era—I wasn't used to that, of course."

Her role as people's champion didn't get any easier when, in October 1978, Astrid Lindgren was awarded the Peace Prize of the German Book Trade. She gave an acceptance speech whose clear message—"Niemals Gewalt!" (Never violence!)—resonated powerfully during a period of diplomacy and disarmament. The speech's humanistic content and the way Astrid Lindgren delivered it speak to how determined she was to stand up and make a political difference wherever possible and appropriate.

The prestigious prize, which had been given to Albert Schweitzer, Martin Buber, and Hermann Hesse, among others, was due to be awarded at St. Paul's Church in Frankfurt as part of a grand ceremony, but when the organizers read her speech in advance, they returned it with the message that she should simply accept the prize and make her thanks "kurz und gut" (short and sweet). Astrid Lindgren immediately replied that if she wasn't allowed to give the speech in full, she would call in sick, and someone from the Swedish embassy could attend instead to give a "kurz und gut" thanks. This made the organizers in Frankfurt back down. Despite their concerns—in the front row sat various members of the political nobility, including Minister President Holger Börner—Astrid Lindgren was allowed to give her Bertrand Russell–inspired speech. She argued that the fate of the world was decided in nurseries, and that all talk of disarmament was a waste of time if society didn't begin to tackle the "domestic tyrants" within families:

> Literary depictions of cruel childhoods are teeming with these domestic tyrants, who frighten their children into obedience and submission and more or less ruin their lives. Luckily they're not the only kind. Thankfully there have always been parents who bring up their children with love rather than violence. But it's probably only in our century that parents have more generally begun to regard children as equals, allowing them the right to let their personalities develop freely in a familial democracy without oppression and without violence. So how can we not

despair to hear these sudden calls for a return to the old, authoritarian system?

The speech caused a sensation, and in subsequent years Astrid Lindgren's name took on an almost Mother Teresa–esque aura abroad. Pleas for
help and support streamed in from across the world, but even earlier in the
year—in June 1978—Astrid had complained in a letter to Anne-Marie Fries:

> Otherwise I spend all my time fending people off. People wanting
> me to call the government and stop them deporting a mentally
> handicapped, sick, thirteen-year-old Turk. People who want me
> to make sure old people who are only a little confused don't get
> forcibly committed to a psychiatric hospital. People who want me
> to renounce Jesus and support Heimholungswerk Jesu Christi [a
> religious movement now known as Universal Life]. Soon I'm go-
> ing to be talking like that little Vimmerby boy when Margareta
> Strömstedt asked him his opinion on Pippi Longstocking: "All
> sorts of idiots are coming over here and asking *me!*"

The Flat Rock

More than ever, Furusund had become Astrid Lindgren's refuge. A place
where she could always find peace and quiet, where she wouldn't be dis-
turbed by the mail addressed to Dalagatan, by the ringing telephone and
knocks on the door. Out here among the rocky islands, whose inhabitants
respected the author's wish to be alone, she was always able to spiritually
recuperate and enjoy the care and sustenance of nature. It never failed her.
As she said in the *Svenska Dagbladet* in August 1989: "If I want to be comforted, I go out into nature. It's the greatest comfort life has to offer." And to
the journalist's rather cheeky question "What sort of playmates do you have
on Furusund?" she answered honestly, "Playmates! I don't want any playmates. Out here I keep myself to myself. I don't have time to socialize."

On Furusund, like Ronia the robber's daughter, Astrid gorged herself
on spring and summer like a wild bee on honey. It was the closest she could

get to her happy childhood in Småland, where the area around Näs—despite written protests to the local authority in 1974 from Vimmerby's Selma Lagerlöf—had been transformed from ancient, open farmland to a modern, asphalted, residential district. But on Furusund, at the tip of the Stockholm archipelago, beside the narrow channel of water leading back to the capital, life continued in its customary, unbroken way. There she had direct, unfettered access to water, woods, and a starry sky. As Astrid Lindgren wrote in a letter to Anne-Marie Fries in fall 1965, when, for the first time in twenty-one years, she wasn't publishing a new book in time for Christmas and was instead enjoying being away from the constant pressure: "I've been alone in Furusund, and it's been so beautiful it could make you swoon, with still blue water and blue skies and red and yellow trees and starry evenings and sunsets so mournful and autumnally beautiful it's nearly unbearable. But I've been dancing in my solitude for sheer delight at being totally alone. Solitude is a good thing, at least in small doses."

Stenhällen (The flat rock) was the name of Astrid Lindgren's red wooden house, a hundred yards from Furusund's old custom house and pilot station, and from the jetty where the ferries from Stockholm moored continually from midsummer to August. A house, a flat rock, and a little garden, on an island among thirty thousand other islands a good hour's sail or drive from the capital, in a part of the Stockholm archipelago called Roslagen, about which Swedish balladeer Evert Taube wrote and sang.

Sture's parents had bought Stenhällen in 1940 as their permanent residence, after having lived in other houses on the island, and they borrowed half the purchase price of ten thousand kronor from Hanna and Samuel August. By that point Furusund was no longer the fashionable spa and health resort it had been at the turn of the century, when royalty, prosperous Stockholmers, and prominent artists like Carl Larsson and Anders Zorn spent time on the island. In the 1930s it was largely run down, and disrepair had left its mark on the remaining hotels and villas, which had romantic-sounding names like Romanov, Bellevue, Bellini, and Isola Bella. Strindberg had once spent a few summers there, too, after his Parisian "Inferno crisis" in the 1890s. He rediscovered the pleasure of writing, but his marriage to Harriet Bosse remained unhappy.

In the latter half of the 1930s, however, when Astrid and Sture vacationed on Furusund with Lasse and Karin, the Lindgrens were a contented family. They kept up this tradition even in the final years of the war, after Sture's father died, when Furusund was overrun with people from the Baltic states who were fleeing the Russians in anything that would float. When Sture's mother died, Stenhällen was inherited by her son, and gradually it came to be used only by Astrid and Karin—and Lasse, of course, when he came to visit with his wife, Inger, and little Mats.

With children, sons- and daughters-in-law, and several small grandchildren descending on Stenhällen and the small annex in the corner of the plot, it was initially difficult for Astrid to get enough peace to write during the summer. "Being up to my ears in children and grandchildren," as she ironically but affectionately called being a grandmother, wasn't something she wanted to avoid, exactly, but having them around all day long was destructive to the literary ideas she tried to get down on stenographic pads in the mornings. Thus, in 1960, Astrid bought a nearby plot of waterside land, where there was a smaller holiday home. She called it Sunnanäng (South meadow), and in 1964 she acquired the 150-year-old Stentorp (Stone cottage) on the neighboring plot, providing Lasse and his new wife, Marianne, and Karin and Carl Olof with a permanent summer cottage each. Every year throughout the 1960s and 1970s—from midsummer to the beginning of August—Furusund became a lively gathering place for old and young members of the Lindgren-Nyman clan.

Yet Astrid Lindgren preferred Furusund once Lasse's and Karin's families had returned to the city, or when she was there alone, outside tourist season. She didn't have to say anything and almost didn't have to hear anything—except the seagulls' cries, the rustling of sycamore leaves, the splashing of waves, the creaking of the boat down by the jetty, the rain against the windowpanes on the veranda, the smack of sailing ropes in the wind, and the gravel crunching beneath the wheels of the mail van bringing news from the outside world, from which she had happily retreated for a while.

In a symbolic sense, Furusund was to Astrid Lindgren what Walden Pond had been for Henry David Thoreau in the 1840s, when he set out on

The whole "brood of snakes" as Astrid Lindgren darkly but humorously called her lively family, with its many children, gathered on the jetty at Furusund in the early 1970s. Top, from left: Karl-Johan, Marianne, Lasse, Carl Olof, and Karin. Middle: Annika and Malin. Bottom: Anders, Olle, Astrid, and Nisse.

a spiritual journey of discovery, intending to conduct a personal social experiment. For two years, two months, and two days, the author lived in the woods around Concord, near Boston. He built a cabin out of materials from the forest and tried to live as simply and independently as possible, far away from the materialistic urban culture he'd fled. Thoreau later described this difficult balancing act in his essayistic memoir *Walden; or, Life in the Woods.*

An autobiographical mixture of philosophy and poetry, it was mentioned several times by Astrid Lindgren as one of the books she read over and over again, and which she kept on the bookshelf above her bed in Stockholm until the day she died. More than almost any other book, she felt, *Walden* had a soothing effect on the reader, especially those trapped in cities and yearning for nature. On December 13, 1947, for instance, Astrid was home alone in Dalagatan, reading and drawing inspiration from Thoreau's meditations on being an independent and solitary living being: "I love to be alone. I never found the companion that was so companionable as solitude. We are for the most part more lonely when we go abroad among men than when we stay in our chambers. A man thinking or working is always alone, let him be where he will."

Sture was on a business trip, Lasse out with some friends, Karin at the movies, and Astrid, who had just turned forty a couple of weeks earlier, was enjoying the company of a veteran loner and his reflections on simple living and the interconnectedness of nature and humankind. As she wrote in her diary on that memorable day:

> I'm sitting here alone this evening. . . . I've read Frans G. Bengtsson's introductory biography of Thoreau in my newly acquired *Walden; or, Life in the Woods*. I cried at Thoreau's words about himself: "My greatest skill has been to want but little. For joy I could embrace the earth. I shall delight to be buried in it. And then to think of those among men who will know that I love them, though I tell them not." . . . Sometimes I get an urge like that. To become a philosopher, renounce all the trivialities of life and "want but little." Live a bit of the forest life, possibly, at Walden. I *might* just manage it, if I get the chance.

Summer of Love

Ronia the Robber's Daughter, first published in the fall of 1981, is about two children who, like Henry David Thoreau, turn their backs on the materialistic order of the world. Each has grown up as the only child in a separate half of the same castle, each living among a patriarchal gang of robbers where life revolves around stealing from others and waging war with the rival gang. Eventually the two children decide to leave home, in a youthful, antiauthoritarian protest against their fathers' norms, embracing the boundless freedom of the woods instead. They plan to build a new home and live in harmony with nature, "in day as well as night, under sun, moon and stars, and during the silent passing of the seasons."

Eleven-year-old Ronia and Birk are described at the beginning of the novel as loners, à la Thoreau. They have no need for the company of others, and from a young age they have learned to roam through the woods, where they feel no more lonely than the sunrise, the blueberry bushes, the rainbow, the North Star, or the squirrels, elk, foxes, and hare. As the novel's narrator observes of Ronia: "She lived her solitary forest life. Yes, she was solitary, but she never missed anybody. Who was there to miss? Her days were full of life and happiness."

Things change, however, when Ronia meets Birk, and after overcoming various social barriers they "become affectionately attached," as Astrid Lindgren put it in an interview before publication in 1981. This attachment centers around a psychological affinity and connectedness to nature, something that's emphasized in a near-wordless scene after the children have survived both a forest witch and a waterfall. They lie hidden underneath the dense green branches of a big tree: " 'My sister,' said Birk. Ronia didn't hear him, but she read his lips. And although neither of them could hear a word, they talked. About things that had to be said before it was too late. About how nice it was to love someone so much you didn't even need to fear things that were terrifying. That was what they talked about, although neither of them heard a single word."

Another emotional force in the novel, equally powerful as the one that unites Ronia and Birk, is their devotion to nature. "The wild woods are dear to them," the narrator declares of Ronia and Birk, who live in triumphant harmony with all the living creatures around them. A "summer's ecstasy" was Astrid Lindgren's term for their intense day-to-day life in the woods: " 'We have only this summer, you and I,' said Birk. . . . Summer doesn't last forever. He knew that, and Ronia knew it too. Yet they began to live as though it did."

It was exactly this concentrated, vegetative calm that Astrid Lindgren sought and found on Furusund. A life purposefully inactive, simple, and quiet, in glaring contrast to her stressful urban existence in Dalagatan, with its daily meetings and countless tasks. Out among the islands, Astrid did nothing, she felt, except give herself over to nature and her books and steno-graphic pads. Here "life played with her," as she explained in a letter to Anne-Marie in July 1980, after the operation on her gallstone: "The glori-ous thing about being a convalescent is that you can do absolutely *nothing* without feeling guilty. Now I'm going to hurry down to the mailbox with this letter—oh yes, I can cycle—and afterward I'll ride home again and do *nothing*. Life is glorious."

Nowhere in her work is the symbiosis between humanity and nature, so essential to Astrid Lindgren, more accurately described than in *Ronia the Robber's Daughter*. The two children haven't yet left the castle for good, but after being cooped up all winter they're both eager to escape into na-ture. As spring puts its soothing arms around them, they feel six months' cold and darkness trickle out of every pore:

> For ages they sat there, silent, being in the spring. They heard the blackbird sing and the cuckoo call, filling the whole forest. Newborn fox cubs tumbled around outside their holes, a stone's throw away. Squirrels scurried around in the treetops, and they saw hares come bounding over the moss and disappear into the underbrush. An adder, soon due to give birth, lay peacefully in the sun nearby. They didn't disturb her, and she didn't disturb them.

All her life, Astrid believed in a connectedness to nature that was rooted in the intuition and immediacy of children. As Melker Melkerson wonders during a contemplative moment on Seacrow Island: "Why can't we hold on to the ability to see earth and grass and pattering rain and starry skies as blessings all our lives?" Melker's question is prompted by his youngest son, Pelle, a child of nature who experiences life as a series of miracles, and is always busy examining nature down to the tiniest detail.

While Melker struggles to find the child of nature within himself, Astrid Lindgren was an example of the possibility even for an adult to "be one with nature, to be immersed in it and feel its power wash over you," as she said in an interview in the newspaper *Göteborgs-Posten* in May 1983. "It's a love I've never lost," she added. "It's a love you keep for as long as you live." In her book about her parents from 1975, and in the illustrated volume *My Småland* (Mit Småland) from 1987, Astrid described the huge significance nature had for her as a catalyst for childhood memories: "If somebody asks me what I remember from my childhood, my first thought isn't people, actually. It's *nature*, which encircled my days and filled them so intensely that as an adult it's hard to grasp. . . . Stones and trees were as dear to us as living creatures, and nature was what surrounded and sustained our games and dreams."

Astrid Lindgren wasn't much older than Ronia when she first expressed this closeness in writing. In 1921, the thirteen-year-old schoolgirl wrote a school paper titled "En promenad från Vimmerby till Krön" (A walk from Vimmerby to Krön), which depicted a young girl's delight in nature and her Ronia-like intimacy with the magic, beauty, and stillness of the woods:

> I don't really know how it happened, but I found myself standing on the edge of the woods one winter's morning, looking at the earnest trees, heavy with snow, which gazed questioningly down at me as if to say: "What do you want here, little human child?" "I think it was longing for you and all the other wonderful things about nature that drove me out here, before anybody else in the house had awoken, and before the sun had risen," I answered softly. I stood there for a while, sunk in thought. "Everything is so beautiful," I thought. . . . By the road a little farther away stood a tall spruce. Several stumps around it revealed that they had been chopping down the young trees previously encircling the larger one. I leaned up against the trunk and stroked the tree's rough bark, asking: "Poor old Father Spruce, who's taken your children?" Old Father Spruce shook his head

mournfully in reply. . . . I enjoyed it indescribably, filling my
lungs with fresh air. It was completely silent inside the temple
hall. The silence was only broken now and then by a startled
bird, and the occasional bell tolling in the distance. I felt so solemn and grave.

The Swedish Animal Factory

Humanity's relationship with nature was such a key issue for Astrid Lindgren that it became the focus of her last major political efforts: fighting for
animal welfare in Sweden and protecting the country's open spaces. Like
the Pomperipossa debates, these efforts attracted huge attention from the
media, those in power, and the Swedish people at large. They would last
more than ten years, from her initial articles in 1985 to her final, impas-
sioned call to arms in the *Expressen* in fall 1996: "Hello? Does anybody remember an interview in the *Expressen* on October 27, 1985? No, we didn't
think you would. But it was around that time we were promised by our then
prime minister Olof Palme that we'd get new legislation regarding animal
welfare, so that the poor hens didn't have to live their whole lives indoors,
trapped inside cramped cages."

Her animal welfare campaign in the 1980s and her conservation campaign in the 1990s made Astrid Lindgren a major force in the green movement in Sweden, which had mobilized as a result of the nuclear power
debates in the 1970s and the referendum about nuclear power in 1980. She
had participated in those debates at the time, arguing that the nuclear power
issue was something that concerned all humanity. As she put it unequivocally in the magazine *Året Runt* in December 1979: "It's not just a bunch of
hysterical women who are against nuclear power, as some people try to
make themselves and others believe!"

Out of the protests against nuclear power grew a powerful environmental movement in Sweden. De Gröna—The Greens—were formed in
1981, the same year *Ronia the Robber's Daughter* came out, with a lush green
jacket, and Ulf Lundell wrote the first lines to his patriotic, romantic song
"Öppna landskap" (Open landscapes).

The animal welfare debate, which Astrid Lindgren sparked in 1985 with veterinarian Kristina Forslund, who became her faithful collaborator and source of expertise, did eventually result in new legislation—the "Lex Lindgren," which drew international attention when it took effect in 1988. Astrid Lindgren had so much political clout in modern Sweden that prime minister Ingvar Carlsson turned up to the author's grand eightieth-birthday bash at the Göta Lejon movie theater in November 1987. In the middle of the stage, Carlsson embraced the garlanded Lindgren and announced that the government was going to secure decent living conditions for Rölla the cow, Lovisa the hen, and Augusta the sow. It was the best gift Astrid Lindgren could have received, and her celebrants were moved. But when the final phrasing of the new legislation was unveiled, Lindgren resolutely disavowed it. She wrote, in the *Expressen* on March 23, 1988: "Lex Lindgren—who came up with the idea to call the new piece of legislation that? Am I supposed to be flattered by having this law—meaningless in its current form—named after me? And who has frightened the government into this hollowed-out interpretation of a noble promise: All animals shall have the right to a way of life that's natural for them?"

The tone was straightforward and challenging. Astrid knew whom she was dealing with. In 1985–88 she had written open letters in the *Expressen* to the minister for agriculture, Mats Hellström, and the prime minister, Carlsson, who had assumed leadership of the Social Democrats after Palme's assassination in February 1986. The nation's new leader had recently developed an interest in organic farming, having eaten a soft-boiled egg that wasn't laid by a battery hen. In an open letter that played on her well-loved Karlsson character, Astrid dubbed him "Best Carlsson!" and in a longer opinion piece on October 27, 1985, in the *Expressen*—again lending space to one of Lindgren's critical campaigns—she introduced him to Lovisa the hen and Augusta the sow with a line adapted from *Karlsson-on-the-Roof*: "The prime minister? Well, he's a handsome, thoroughly clever, and suitably fat man in his prime."

As in the Pomperipossa affair in 1976, it was a stroke of rhetorical genius to give the debate a fairy-tale tilt, which Astrid accomplished primarily through the text's orality and familiar, jaunty tone. Writing a contemporary political discussion in an ancient literary genre that nearly all human beings have imbibed with their mother's milk was a brilliant move, because it awoke people's curiosity and, more important, prompted their active involvement.

Livestock, which in previous agricultural discussions had been termed "production units," were suddenly given names—Rölla, Lovisa, Augusta—and this cozy humanization of them prompted a sizable chunk of the meat-eating Swedish population to take an interest in the debate about animal welfare. Their eyes were opened to something that had never previously been articulated in Sweden: "Our animals are living creatures, which can feel suffering and fear and pain just like people. . . . Do we have the right to prioritize ourselves above animals' need for a good life, just so we can have cheap food?"

The carefully judged political activism in these elegant articles was based on Kristina Forslund's veterinary knowledge, and thus Astrid was scrupulously accurate about feeding, living space, antibiotics, and slaughtering. At the same time, her accounts were framed in a way that made you feel like Astrid Lindgren was actually sitting at your breakfast table, reading aloud from the newspaper: "Hello there, all you piglets and calves and chickens in the Swedish animal factory!"

Astrid Lindgren's alternative form of political speechmaking rested on the fundamental notion that a democracy is disempowered when the populace no longer understands or listens to those in government. As she had pointed out during the Pomperipossa debate in a 1976 interview in *Husmodern,* in which she'd sounded a call to arms: "Politics is much too important to be left to politicians."

Lasse's Death

Astrid Lindgren and the political establishment had no direct confrontations in 1986, although the debate about agricultural policy continued to simmer in newspapers and on television and radio. As Astrid Lindgren and Kristina Forslund observed in *My Cow Wants to Have Fun* (Min ko vill ha roligt, 1990), which collected their articles from the 1980s, "In 1986, so much happened that shook us all." They cited the murder of Olof Palme and the nuclear disaster at Chernobyl, but not the fact that Astrid's own world had ground to a halt in July, when Lasse died of cancer, five months before his sixtieth birthday. In an interview with the *Svenska Dagbladet* several years later—in August 1989—she was asked, "What has been the biggest blow of your life?" She answered: "It was when my little Lasse died. That was without doubt the most terrible blow. I still cry about it sometimes. I think of him when he was little. For that matter, I think about him when he was older, too."

Lasse had once been her life's greatest joy. Even after he became an engineer and a father in the 1950s, she still occasionally called him "My little Lasse Lucidor," referring to the orphaned Swedish psalmist and songwriter Lars Johansson (1638–74), who was known during his short, solitary, stormy life as "Lasse Lucidor, the Unhappy."

Lasse was also the major, decisive problem in Astrid Lindgren's life. That was how she put it in her diary in 1972. A child born into foreign surroundings, whom she'd had to give up, whom she had missed so desperately, tormented by indescribable pangs of guilt, yet for whom she had done so much, hoping that the boy's life would be as harmonious and happy as it was during his first three years at Håbets Allé and the next eighteen months at Näs. Only after all that had the nearly five-year-old Lasse been reunited with his real mother. It had been difficult for them both, and it never got easier. "My little slowpoke" Astrid called him in June 1946 in a letter to Hanna.

It was painful, but she was forced to acknowledge that the first five or ten years of a person's life were crucial in determining how the rest of it would turn out. In part, it was this recognition that enabled her to write with such authenticity and power in her fiction and in her articles, speeches, and columns about upbringing and the parent-child relationship. As she phrased it in her ambitious essay "More Love!" in 1952, a message echoed twenty-five years later in her Peace Prize acceptance speech in West Germany: "No treatment in the world can replace the love he didn't get before he was ten."

Neither of those texts was explicitly about Lars Lindgren, but they were both about children who had bad starts in life and ended up alone and unhappy because they didn't feel safe and free enough in early childhood. "Those are the two things," wrote Astrid in 1952, "that the human plant cannot do without if it's going to flourish."

Lasse's significance for Astrid Lindgren's work, in which unhappy, lonely, parentless boys abound, has often been noted. We have to go to the National Library, however, to discover that Astrid Lindgren realized it too. In pad 343, we find a note to Margareta Strömstedt in which she put words in her biographer's mouth, though she didn't want to be quoted directly. Some parts were crossed out:

> There are critics who have objected to Astrid Lindgren's sensi-
> tivity ~~and sentimentality~~ when she tells stories about children in
> trouble. It's true that there are flashes of unrestrained emotions
> in her books, emotions that can be read as sentimental, but
> those who perceive this negatively and believe it to be a cover
> for something false, something suspect, haven't learned enough
> about Astrid Lindgren's deep and unfailing commitment to vul-
> nerable children. This commitment is no doubt connected to
> her experiences in Copenhagen before Christmas 1926, when
> Astrid ~~gave birth to~~ had her child and was obliged to give ~~him~~ it
> up, and it was reinforced over the difficult years that followed,
> when young Astrid began to fight to be able to take care of ~~her~~
> ~~child~~ her Lasse.

Lasse died on July 22, 1986, leaving a wife and three children. It took Astrid the rest of the year to get through the initial, paralyzing grief, but by January 1987 she was settling once more into the role of environmental activist. And it proved a formidable comeback.

Her piece in the *Expressen* on January 14 was about a dream she'd had, in which God had come down to Earth to conduct an inspection of Sweden. He wanted to see how animals were being treated, he said, and in the dream Astrid Lindgren was the guide he had chosen to show him around. The Lord's reaction had been unmistakable: "What kind of pea-brains have I given dominion over all Earth's creatures?" Minister for

Agriculture Mats Hellström also put in an appearance during the heavenly tour of inspection, not as a "pea-brain" but as a prince, one who possessed the philosopher's stone: agricultural legislation that set appropriate goals for the future protection of Swedish livestock.

More than ever, the Social Democrats' leadership was keenly aware that the party must not commit the same tactical errors as Gunnar Sträng had during the Pomperipossa debate. So when Astrid Lindgren wrote an open letter to Ingvar Carlsson on September 20, 1987, published—thanks to the *Expressen*'s and the author's exquisite sense of timing—to coincide with the Social Democrats' annual convention, the prime minister made a surprising response. The tone of the beloved author's letter left him no choice: "Dear Ingvar Carlsson! Sorry for disturbing you in the middle of the party convention. I know, of course, that you've got a lot on your mind, both at home and among all the bigwigs and presidents in the outside world. Yet I come to you in the modest hope that you'll devote a little time and consideration to the pitiable situation of creatures in this country. After all, in the final analysis it's you and your government who are responsible for the way Swedish farm animals are kept."

Amid the stream of speeches and ovations at the Social Democratic convention, Carlsson vanished without trace for a whole hour. He'd asked his private chauffeur to drop him off at Astrid Lindgren's apartment in Dalagatan, where Margareta Strömstedt was visiting. In the 1999 edition of her biography, she relates that the writer greeted the prime minister and "cheerfully gave him a dressing down, wagging her finger and promising reprisals if he didn't do something about it. Afterward she patted him on the cheek like the little boy she considered him to be. His bodyguards stood and watched."

Astrid the Environmental Party

The elderly Astrid Lindgren's gentle yet firm handling of this powerful politician—a skill she had also exercised during the Pomperipossa debate—hints at the gender perspective that lay like volcanic subsoil beneath all the political causes she got involved in during the final twenty-five years of her

life. When campaigning for animal welfare, Astrid Lindgren made no secret
of the fact that the people fighting for better living conditions for Swedish
livestock were two women, facing an array of male ministers, politicians,
and senior figures within the agricultural industry. Nor did she think this
was a coincidence. The majority of those men shared Mats Hellström's
view, though he didn't dare articulate it until twenty years later, in the book
Not a Bit of Filth: "Should a writer of fairy-tales be allowed to dictate
modern-day food production as a birthday present from Ingvar Carlsson?"

Of course, two men could equally have decided to fight for more humane treatment of hens, pigs, and cows in Swedish farming, but as Astrid
Lindgren observed in January 1986 in an open letter to Anders Dahlgren,
former Swedish minister for agriculture, the popular animal welfare debates
were dominated by women, as were the anti–nuclear power movement and
the peace movement. In the letter she repeated the feminist mantra she had
used during the Pomperipossa debate, threatening Dahlgren and his masculine supporters (with a twinkle in her eye):

> Women in particular, I think—judging by the letters I've re-
> ceived—are coming out in force, wanting to see results. And
> women make up more than half the population of this country.
> Dear oh dear oh dear—woe betide us if they decide to get seri-
> ously angry! It's not primarily political issues but ethical ones
> that need to be resolved if we don't want to lose our standing as
> a cultured nation. I think it would be good to see some tangible
> results over the coming years, ideally before the next election.
> Can't you talk to the prime minister and the minister for agricul-
> ture and other sensible people, maybe quoting that old folklor-
> ist on Swedish women: "Women are tough and strong and bake
> good bread with currants in it, but if they're baited they'll im-
> mediately go on the attack"?

You can almost see Lovis and Undis—the wives of the two robber
chieftains in *Ronia the Robber's Daughter*—before you, each standing in her
woodland castle, each surrounded by a gang of men. Tough, strong women

who bake excellent bread, cultivate their kitchen gardens, take care of their extended families, and show respect for nature. Both women know that men make the majority of decisions, but they also know that there are things in life their husbands have no control over or insight into, things they only partly understand. Ethical questions, for instance. In that sense, the men in *Ronia the Robber's Daughter* are "pea-brains." As a despairing Ronia tries to explain to Birk, just as Lovis and Undis tried to explain to their husbands: "Life is something you have to take good care of, don't you see that?"

In a pioneeringly feminist country like Sweden, it's remarkable that Astrid Lindgren's name has never been linked with the controversial term "ecofeminism," because in many ways her advocacy for environmental issues in the 1980s and 1990s suggests the connection. Astrid Lindgren would never have accepted such an absolute term, however, which refers to the much-criticized notion that there's a connection between the patriarchy's oppression of women and its unwillingness to protect nature and the environment. In her *Introduction to Ecofeminism* (Introduktion till ekofeminism), Lotta Hedström, former spokesperson for the Greens, writes that the Småland writer Elin Wägner "must be considered the first Swedish ecofeminist," although she draws no connection between her and the environmental movement in 1980s and 1990s Sweden, in which Astrid Lindgren was an especially active participant.

Like Elin Wägner before her, Astrid Lindgren didn't consider women better than men, and she never called herself a feminist. Yet she wasn't shy about speaking up for women's rights and gender equality when provoked, or when confronted with male prejudice or shows of force. Astrid Lindgren considered herself part of a generation that had continued women's historic struggle to attain the same rights, opportunities, and responsibilities as men, without resorting to demonstrations or barricades. In this respect she resembled most of the women she associated with over the years: Elsa Olenius, Anne-Marie Fries, Eva von Zweigbergk, Greta Bolin, Louise Hartung, Stina, Ingegerd, and others.

It seems paradoxical that Astrid Lindgren never became a prominent member of the feminist movement, especially when you consider that she was the brains behind modern feminism's undying role model: Pippi

Longstocking. As the artist Siri Derkert once yelled across the table at Astrid during a ceremonial royal dinner: "Pippi's the most distinguished feminist of our age!"

Yet it was only as an elderly woman in the 1990s that Astrid let go of some of her reservations about feminism and began sounding more combative, particularly with foreign journalists. A case in point: an interviewer from the Danish newspaper *Kristeligt Dagblad* visited Dalagatan in April 1992 and asked how Astrid felt about the movement. She answered: "I would be very eager to fight for women. Because in reality there's still only one gender—male. Recently I saw a well-known American on TV, visiting somewhere in Europe, with a whole army of pinstriped gentlemen on his heels. Not so much as a skirt in sight. Not even among the servants was there a member of the female sex. And there are so many talented women. But when it really comes down to it, it's still only men who count."

Many of Astrid Lindgren's power struggles with men indicate that she was acutely aware of gender politics. The way she forced Reinhold Blomberg into a corner in 1943 is a particularly clear example, when the aging, prosperous editor revealed his tightfisted side and tried to weasel out of paying child support for Lasse. Lassemamma's letters were hard-nosed in tone, based on dry legal facts and with the constant threat of dragging Reinhold back into the courtroom, where he had already faced another furious woman in 1926–27. Putting further pressure on Lassepappa, she asked Stina to visit Blomberg in person and make it clear to him that this was serious—and that Stina's sister wasn't to be toyed with. In case Reinhold had forgotten that.

Another issue that demanded a feminist approach arose in fall 1957, in the form of a national debate about women priests. Were they conceivable—or permissible—in church? Senior figures in the church had strong opinions on the matter, and so did Astrid Lindgren. She outlined them in a letter to Louise Hartung dated October 18, 1957:

> In my diocese, Linköping, not a single vote was cast in favor of women priests. Before the synod I was asked by a parish magazine called *Linköpings Stiftsblad* whether I would write something about the town for their Christmas issue. And since I'm a

kind and obliging person, I said yes. But then I saw in the newspaper, in the *Dagens Nyheter*'s report on the synod, that the Linköping diocese was the *only* one where there wasn't a single vote in favor, and so I got angry and wrote to the *Linköpings Stiftblad,* "Let women be silent in the assemblies, believe the diocese's priests, like the apostle Paul. If newspapers had existed two thousand years ago, Paul would probably have said: let women also be silent in parish magazines. So that's what I've decided to do. I will no longer be working with the parish magazine. I'm sure Paul up in Heaven will be satisfied with that."

Twenty years later, Astrid Lindgren helped topple Olof Palme's man-heavy government at the 1976 election, just as in 1988—with the help of another woman—she pushed Lex Lindgren through, although the law in its final incarnation wasn't quite what Astrid Lindgren and Kristina Forslund had hoped. The story drew fervent attention abroad. After astonishing news reports in the mid-1970s about world-famous Swedes being hounded out of their own country due to colossal tax bills, the new law helped "Sweden, the People's Home," regain its reputation as the globe's most idyllic society, a place where even animals led happy lives.

Yet Astrid wasn't finished with the fight for a more environmentally friendly Sweden. On the contrary: around 1990 she was drawn into another campaign for greater environmental awareness, emphasizing better food quality and—most important—the preservation of the open landscape in which she had grown up, and to which she owed so much. Collaborating with the politician Marit Paulsen and the biologist Stefan Edman, in June 1991 Astrid Lindgren published an article that caused a stir, one that should be read in the light of Sweden's application for membership of the European Union (which Astrid voted against in 1994). It argued the following: "Our environment and our biologically species-rich cultural landscape need the kind of agriculture that produces food *with* nature, not against it."

In subsequent years, several similar articles appeared in the agricultural newspaper *Land,* where Astrid's younger sister Ingegerd had once been employed as a journalist. Aided by Volvo CEO Pehr G. Gyllenhammar and several other campaigners, Astrid was trying to drum up support for the newspaper's petition for land conservation and area payments for environmentally responsible farmers. Like a true extraparliamentarian, she called upon Swedish farmers to organize a noisy protest march: "One thing is important, more important than anything else. For farmers to give their opinion on this issue, and not just through their organizations; no, every single farmer struggling on his farm should raise his voice. Speak up, cry out, tell people what things are like, tell people what you think is good and what you think is bad, for yourself and your animals and Swedish farming in general! ... P.S.: I'm game for a Swedish farmers' march. To push something through!"

The last major political fight of Astrid Lindgren's life brought her back full circle. Back to life on the farm at Näs, where she and her family had lived in close contact with all kinds of people and animals, earth and crops, fields, meadows, and woods. Back to her happy Noisy Village–esque childhood. Those among her adversaries who claimed that Astrid Lindgren's political visions were pure nostalgia, dreams unanchored in reality, seemed to be proved more and more correct as she aged. Whether in the animal welfare debate or the conservation campaign, the farmer's daughter couldn't hide how much she missed the "age of the horse," which had been irretrievably outstripped by the "age of the machine." She longed to return to an earlier stage in her own and her country's development. As early as 1982, in a text published in the magazine *Allers,* "My Piece of Sweden," she recalled with cheerful naïveté the paths and idyllic fields of her childhood, which came under threat in the 1990s from both local urban planning and large-scale European politics:

> Narrow paths run through grassy fields enclosed by hedges,
> trodden from the outset by cows on their way to and from the
> pen where they're milked. Cows and sheep have always walked
> here, keeping the grass suitably short. Children have always run
> about, picking wild strawberries among the ancient gray stones.
> Birdsong has always echoed here. Finches and chickadees have
> twittered, blackbirds have celebrated the bright early summer's

evenings, and cuckoos have called to their hearts' content on early summer mornings. . . . A Småland field, an angel's field, with children and animals and flowers and grass and trees and birdsong. Now soon to be gone.

Part Cyborg

When the magazine *Välkommen* inquired in 1976 how sixty-eight-year-old Astrid Lindgren was finding old age, she answered that she hadn't reached that stage yet: "So long as I'm still working as usual, so long as I'm completely healthy, so long as I can sprint a hundred meters without getting terribly out of breath, I refuse to feel old. It's not like I'm going round shouting for joy and thinking, 'Oh, how young I am,' but I don't think of it as old age. Of course, when I suddenly can't remember names or what I was supposed to be fetching from the kitchen, I realize it's a sign of getting older, which I have to learn to live with."

After the deaths of Elsa Olenius and her sister-in-law Gullan in 1984, and especially after Lasse lost his battle with cancer in 1986, the aging Astrid Lindgren entered a difficult phase. Her eyesight began to fail: she had trouble focusing on specific points and could no longer read, even with glasses. In a letter to Rita Törnqvist-Verschuur on January 10, 1986, Astrid introduced herself as a "cyborg with magnifying-glass spectacles and a hearing aid, but at least I've still got my teeth." And when *Vi* came to Dalagatan for the author's eightieth birthday in November 1987, she called herself half-blind and half-deaf, pointing out the two phones that rang at the same time, making the living room sound like a rural landscape full of bell-wearing animals.

From there it was only a hair's breadth to being declared as good as dead. In Germany in November 1991, going on a badly translated interview in the *Expressen,* the *Bild* and *Hamburger Abendblatt* announced the aging writer's tragic blindness and isolation from the outside world: "Ihr Haar ist wirr und die Augen starren in die Leere" (Her hair is disheveled and her eyes stare emptily into space). When Astrid Lindgren got wind of this grievous news she asked her private secretary, Kerstin Kvint, to reach for the

typewriter—Astrid could no longer see well enough to type—and dictated a
few letters. The first was dispatched on December 2, 1991:

> Herr Redacteur, ich glaube, es war Mark Twain, der gesagt hat:
> "Das Gerücht von meinem Tod ist erheblich übertrieben" [Dear
> Editor, I believe it was Mark Twain who said: "Reports of my
> death are greatly exaggerated"]. . . . After having read your grip-
> ping article of November 30 in the *Hamburger Abendblatt*, I'd
> like to say that reports of my "blindness" are also greatly exag-
> gerated. All I told the *Expressen* (the paper you've clearly got this
> from) was that I can't read anymore (and actually I can, if I use a
> strong magnifying glass). Reading your article, one is seized
> with sympathy for the exhausted, half-blind author, who barely
> has the strength to dictate a letter. Neither my secretary (whom
> you didn't contact, by the way) nor I recognize anything in your
> description. Just for fun, I totted up the letters I've dictated over
> the last few days in only a few hours—and it came to 18.

The two German newspapers had described how the elderly Astrid
Lindgren sat all day at the window, gazing down into Vasa Park, at the children she once had depicted so vividly. Astrid objected to being relegated to
the role of spectator: over the course of that year she had been on trips to
Russia, Finland, Poland, Austria, Germany, and Holland, and she was soon
off to Poland again. Afterward, however, she would be sure to sit in the window, take a quick breather and watch life pass her by in Dalagatan and Vasa
Park.

Kerstin Kvint could attest to Astrid Lindgren's flourishing capacity
for work throughout the 1980s and well into the 1990s. Having previously
worked with Astrid at Rabén and Sjögren, she now visited Dalagatan twice
a week to sort out the mail, pay bills, fetch packages, conduct telephone
conversations, and write all the letters Astrid dictated: "She maintained a
fantastic pace all the way into her eighties, actually. Then she got age-related
macular degeneration, which created problems for her eyes. Yet despite
that, she always had a precise idea of how our meetings should go, and

dictated lots of letters at a furious pace. Others were the kind I could sort out, with her approval. I might suggest an answer to a letter, and she would say, 'Yes, write it!' Or she would say, 'You're much kinder than I would have been.'"

In the 1990s, however, Astrid Lindgren's life grew increasingly more difficult, bearing out something her elderly mother had once told her: "The last quarter is the worst." One by one her old friends passed away, and in December 1991 she lost her beloved former schoolmate Anne-Marie Fries, who died after a painful period of illness. On January 5, 1992, Astrid made a note in her diary, which by now had been reduced to brief summaries and retrospective appraisals around the New Year. As ever, she took a view on world history, as well as on life for the Ericsson-Lindgren-Nyman clan and her circle of close friends: "Anne-Marie died on Dec. 7 after a long and tragic stay at the hospital. I visited her at Blackeberg Hospital once a week for several years. But our 77-year friendship came to an end on December 7 at ten o'clock in the morning. I had wished that death would free her from all that sadness, but when it actually happened it felt unbearable. It's wrong to say that our friendship stopped after 77 years. Our friendship endures even though one of us is dead."

Anne-Marie Fries was buried on her parents' plot at Vimmerby Churchyard, which the old best friends from Prästgårdsallén—and former cocompanions on the walking tour to Ellen Key's house in 1925—had agreed they would haunt together after they were both dead. As ever, Astrid would be the clever and brave one, Anne-Marie the strong one. And just as in childhood, they would fight with all the boys, but never with each other.

Did the loss of Anne-Marie make Astrid fear her own death? The *Dagens Nyheter* put the question to her in an interview printed on April 10, 1992. "No, it really didn't. I have nothing against dying. But not tomorrow. There are things I've got to do first." Stina and Ingegerd said the same thing, and throughout the 1990s the bond between the Ericsson sisters remained strong. This bond was rooted in their childhood, which Astrid had immortalized in three *Noisy Village* books as well as the two Mardie books that came out sixteen years apart (1960 and 1976). Astrid was represented by older sister Mardie, Stina by younger sister Elisabeth, and Ingegerd by the

baby of the family, Kajsa, who is born at Christmas and welcomed by her
big sisters as a "blessed gift" the next morning.

The bond between the sisters continued to develop after Astrid,
Stina, and Ingegerd left home, got married and had children. Then came
the war, and Astrid suggested setting up a "letter circle" in order to maintain a conversation and sense of family cohesion, despite the terrible
events unfolding in the wider world. On September 19, 1939, shortly after
Germany invaded Poland, Astrid wrote to Stina and Ingegerd to propose
her chain-letter idea:

> Ideally the letters would be a reasonably continuous stream.
> And I think we should keep them and put them in a little ar-
> chive at home at Näs—not because I think the letters will be
> literary pearls (well, mine will be, of course), but for fun. When
> we're old it might be rather amusing to read about our earlier
> silliness. And if any of our offspring survive the "Untergang des
> Abendlandes," they can read a bit about what the world was like
> in the days when Hitler was furnishing his German "leben-
> sraum." Like reading about Napoleon.

At the beginning of the war they promised to keep the letter circle going, and as elderly women they called each other every day until Ingegerd's
death in 1997. Astrid would talk to one sister in the morning and the other
in the afternoon, and each time they began the conversation with a shared
incantation: "Death Death Death . . ." All three had gone another twenty-
four hours without bumping into the man with the scythe. Another day
could be added to their already long lives.

Astrid's grandniece Karin Alvtegen witnessed the close, lively bond
between the sisters from the driver's seat of her car when she ferried
the sisters from Stockholm to Vimmerby and back again in November 1996,
the year before Ingegerd's death. It proved an exceptionally merry trip. The
ladies may have been a little stiff in body and limb, recalled Alvtegen in one
of the Astrid Lindgren Society's newsletters from 2006, but their spirits
were undimmed.

The three sisters in the 1930s, and in the 1990s. Still going strong and still close, they were connected no longer by a stream of letters but by daily telephone conversations in which Hanna and Samuel August's daughters reassured each other that they were still alive. Ingegerd died in 1997, Astrid in January 2002, and Stina in December that same year.

"Over the course of the weekend I realized that better female role models could scarcely be found. And it struck me that not once while I was growing up did I ever hear any of them give an opinion on feminism or the lack of equal rights for women. It was as if the thought had never occurred to them that all people shouldn't be treated as equals. What they did was simply to make room for themselves, as though it were the most natural thing in the world, and then they were treated accordingly. Instead of dividing the world up into 'feminine' and 'masculine' at any price, they chose to think 'humanly.' "

Life and Play

"It goes so dizzyingly fast, and then it's over," said Astrid Lindgren, when she was asked to explain in April 1992 what human life was. The person asking was the journalist and critic Åke Lundqvist, who was doing an interview for a series of articles about death in the *Dagens Nyheter*. To emphasize and illustrate her words, Astrid had made a swift motion with her hand and blown a puff of air, as though extinguishing a candle. Human life was just as fleeting.

One book of the Old Testament that Astrid Lindgren often returned to was Ecclesiastes, which takes a profoundly realistic view of the way in which the world is structured, and how it is perceived by human beings. Famous and much quoted, not least by world-weary authors, are the first lines, which in the New American Standard Bible run as follows: "The words of the Preacher, the son of David, king in Jerusalem. 'Vanity of vanities,' says the Preacher, 'Vanity of vanities! All is vanity.' " In the most-thumbed of the six Bibles that stood on the bookshelf above Astrid Lindgren's bed—a Swedish translation from 1917—the word used is "fåfänglighet," vanity, in the sense of something without content or purpose.

This was how Astrid Lindgren understood and used the word, using it in several letters to Louise Hartung, including in one dated December 4, 1956: "Now, my little Louise, I want to tell you that for me, deep down, the words of Ecclesiastes hold true: "All is vanity and striving after wind." And in an undated letter from 1961, she concluded with the words: "Louise, one shouldn't write letters when one is downhearted and sad, but I'm doing it anyway, because I want you to write and comfort me. Think of something good to say about why we're alive, if you can come up with anything. I think everything is vanity and striving after wind, but maybe that's because the sun never shines in this dark country."

All is vanity and striving after wind. These exact words expressed the middle-aged Astrid Lindgren's fundamental, existential perception of life: something fleeting, transient, unstable, and occasionally meaningless; a big, heavy, static emptiness that echoed throughout the whole of existence. Yet Lindgren rarely dwelt on the thought for long, and her complex philosophy of life hinged on this very tension—as a girl, in middle age, and as an elderly woman, when she no longer felt as sure of her relationship with God as she once had. Over the years she frequently acknowledged the Christian legacy of her childhood home, usually with a sense of distance and humor. In an interview in the *Expressen* on December 6, 1970, for instance, she explained that as a child she had believed God was an old man in the sky to whom you prayed. To the journalist's follow-up question—"Do you still believe in God?"—she replied: "No, frankly I don't. But if my father were alive I'd never dare say that, because it would make him very sad. Perhaps it's shameful of me to disavow God, since I still thank him so often and pray to him when I'm in despair."

In the Åke Lundqvist interview, Lindgren remarked that toward the end of her life she had acquired a more inquisitive relationship with God: "I doubt my own doubt. Frequently." Even though life is striving after wind, she explained, that doesn't mean it's nothing but emptiness and meaninglessness. Why not? Because nature has an order, declared Astrid, a method, which indicates that human existence has meaning. The journalist wasn't about to get an unambiguous confession out of her, however; the old relativist refused to oblige: "How do flowers know they're supposed to bloom in spring? How do birds know they're supposed to sing? Scientists believe they can explain the whole of creation and the whole of human history. But I, I ask: how can everything be so methodical and regular? And how can it be that people are so preoccupied with religious thoughts? What is it that makes people that way? So I doubt my own doubt. Frequently."

Toward the darker, graver end of Astrid Lindgren's philosophy of life, we find her realization of its brevity and ephemerality, paired with a sense of humankind's inevitable loneliness. This was a psychological-philosophical viewpoint she never abandoned. She expressed it many times throughout her life, as a young woman in letters to Anne-Marie Fries and as an older woman to the teenaged Sara Ljungcrantz, to whom Astrid once remarked: "Every single one of us is trapped in our loneliness. All people are lonely." In middle age, in September 1961, she wrote to Louise Hartung in a similar vein: "When all is said and done, every single person is a lone little creature with no hope of leaning on another one." Astrid Lindgren communicated this pessimistic perspective on the fundamental condition of humanity even in some of her children's books, and rarely did she do so with more clarity than at the end of *We on Seacrow Island,* when the grown-up narrator steps forward and sounds, for a brief moment, almost like the Preacher in Ecclesiastes: "In dreams sometimes you rush around, searching. There's someone you've got to find. And you're in such a tremendous hurry. That's true of life. You run around in fear, searching more and more anxiously, but you never find who you're looking for. All is in vain."

And yet it wasn't. Or, as Astrid Lindgren wrote in letters to Anne-Marie, Elsa, Louise, Sara, and others: "Life is not so rotten as it seems." These words were the necessary counterweight to melancholy, sadness, and "the common sorrow," as she called it. For Astrid, sorrow was bound up with a sense of loneliness, and as a mature, older person she had a virtually chronic need to live out this feeling.

The coherence and wholeness of Astrid Lindgren's perspective on life hinged on the fact that amid all the nuisances, the disappointments, and the frustrations at striving after wind, there was also time for happiness, time for pleasure, time for poetry, time for love, and time for play. And who better to embody this capacity for presence in the now than children—and the child within adults? As Anders explains at the beginning of *Bill Bergson and the White Rose Rescue:* "Life was short, and what mattered was playing while you still could."

This day, one life.

Life can be over in a single day, and a single day can feel like a lifetime. In its essence, Astrid Lindgren's philosophy was about getting the most and best you could out of your brief time on earth. But how? In 1967 the women's magazine *Femina* inquired how Astrid Lindgren could still seem so "ageless," as the journalist put it, at the age of sixty. She replied:

> I just live. . . . I always think the now is so exciting and rich in content that I don't really have time to brood about what will happen next. I take each day's knocks as they come. I think you should treat every day as if it's the only one you've got. "This day, one life." But now and again I feel there's still so much I want, and I realize I won't manage all of it. . . . I think, really, that life is a swiftly fleeting absurdity, and afterward comes the great silence. But the short span you're here on earth you have to fill with things.

Birthday and Philanthropy

In 1997, fourteen days after her ninetieth birthday, Astrid Lindgren wrote a thank-you note to an old friend and colleague from the mail censorship office during the war: Lennart Kjellberg, a professor of Slavic languages. Rather than talk about the almost surreal birthday celebration and the fourteen sacks of mail hauled down from the post office at the corner of Dalagatan and Odengatan, Astrid wanted to discuss the old days at the office. Yet that, too, felt unreal. "Everything is so long ago now," she concluded.

There had been an avalanche of interview requests from newspapers, TV stations, and radio channels across the world to mark the occasion. Two veteran reporters from Sveriges Radio were offered an audience, and it was a qualified success, as Karin Nyman recalls. There were several misunderstandings during the interview, and when Astrid was asked whether she'd had any particular linguistic-pedagogical purpose with her children's books, her curt response was: "No, I couldn't give a crap about that." Those proved to be the national heroine's last words on Sveriges Radio.

The grotesquely inordinate volume of letters she received on her birthday seemed almost to frighten Astrid Lindgren, who had always found birthdays a chore, though she would take part in the celebrations—within limits. Letters poured in from all corners of the world, and as in previous years, remembers Karin Nyman, Astrid was genuinely astonished by her fame and the unstinting adulation she received. In 1997, for instance, she was named Swede of the Year Abroad: "As I sat and read the day's letters aloud, which were all about the crucial significance her books had had for people, my mother looked at me and said, 'But don't you think that's odd?' 'Yeah,' I said, because I did think so, and then I picked up the next letter. When she found out she had been named Swede of the Year Abroad, she laughed for two days at the absurdity of it, given how 'ancient, half-deaf, and completely nutty' she thought she was."

On top of these many letters of praise, Astrid Lindgren received numerous begging letters and requests for financial help from private individuals and organizations in Sweden and abroad during the final twenty-five years of her life. The elderly Astrid Lindgren tried to stay matter-of-fact about them, but it wasn't easy. She had so much empathy and sympathy for other people, like her character Mardie, who spontaneously gives her expensive golden heart to poverty-stricken Mia on Christmas Eve, since Mia's only Christmas present is a ham donated to the family by the local charity: "It's sad, thinks Mardie, and also strange, that Father Christmas comes to some families while others only get a visit from the poor-relief people. The ham is lovely, of course, but surely Mia could have gotten something else too, a proper Christmas present. Is there anything she could give Mia, Mardie wonders?"

Astrid Lindgren's philanthropy was on such a large scale that she wasn't aware of the full scope, and neither Kerstin Kvint—Astrid Lindgren's private secretary—nor Karin Nyman is willing to hazard a guess as to how many millions of kronor she gave away to charitable causes or people in need over the years. After her death, Lena Törnqvist, her bibliographer, systematized the papers left to the author's archive at the National Library, which included hundreds of thank-you letters regarding donations and financial aid. She believes the total sum is somewhere in the ballpark of ten million Swedish kronor, adjusted for inflation—more than a million dollars.

Lena Törnqvist can attest to the fact that Astrid Lindgren not only answered many letters and calls for help but also reacted spontaneously to the events, wars, natural disasters, and famines she saw on TV or heard about on the radio. Money would instantly be sent to the Red Cross or Save the Children, and a series of thank-you letters in the archive document the large sums she donated. In the 1970s these sums would often come to ten thousand kronor or more. "A huge amount of money in those days, which always prompted a personal letter of thanks from the chairman himself," remarks Lena Törnqvist.

Many other idealistic organizations received regular support from Astrid Lindgren: BRIS (Children's rights in society); Stockholms Stadsmission (help for the homeless and addicts), SOS Children's Villages, Amnesty International, the Salvation Army, the World Wildlife Fund, Greenpeace, Svenska Afghanistankommittén (the Swedish committee for Afghanistan), and a range of similar institutions.

Refugee children had always been close to Astrid's heart, and in 1996–97 she got involved in an asylum case relating to two Kurdish families with ten children, who after sixteen months staying in a church in Swedish Lapland had been roughly evicted and sent "home" to Turkey. The elder sister in one of the families, seventeen-year-old Rojda Sincari, had previously written to Astrid Lindgren and asked for help. The girl said that she had read Astrid Lindgren's books in Kurdish, and that her teachers in Åsele called her Ronia. Astrid's response to the Swedish authorities' treatment of the two families was to financially guarantee Rojda's and her cousin Jinda's education, which meant that the girls could return to Scandinavia in 1997. Today Rojda is a dentist and doctor living in Sweden. As Kerstin Kvint explains: "That donation alone came to around half a million. It was probably the biggest single sum Astrid gave to a private individual she didn't already know, but Astrid had a genuine, unfeigned goodness in her. She really wanted to help vulnerable people."

For this reason she also gave money to handicapped children who needed rehabilitation, bought a horse for a girl from a socially disadvantaged background, and paid the hospital bills for an eastern European girl receiving treatment in Sweden because she couldn't get suitable medical care in her home country. Back home in Vimmerby, Astrid contributed 250,000 kronor to help save a beautiful eighteenth-century building in the town center, which was on the verge of being torn down and replaced with a shopping mall. Then there were all the individual people she helped over the years with large or small amounts of cash. As early as the 1950s, poor families she heard about through friends and acquaintances would often receive a financial helping hand, while other people in varying degrees of distress could find help in Dalagatan if they spoke earnestly enough, and if they didn't just write but actually called and cried on the phone line. As Karin Nyman explains: "She gave to individuals, of course, if they asked for money, but rather haphazardly and without a system. A young man came and asked to borrow 80,000 kronor to buy an apartment for himself and his girlfriend. He got it without much justification and never paid it back, of course. A single mother in Dalarna needed 50,000 to keep a roof over her children's heads. Astrid's method of dealing with these various pleas was neither especially considered nor wise. But I know the way she looked at it was this: here's someone who badly needs money, turning to someone who clearly has a lot. But obviously not everybody who came and asked got some."

What was the deeper purpose underlying Astrid Lindgren's philanthropy? She rarely wanted any publicity for it, unless it served to spur those in power into action, as was the case with the two deported Kurdish families. Was it a form of indulgence, or symptomatic of the desperate instinct to care for others that Astrid herself called "abnormal"? Hardly. The true answer lies in a handwritten philosophical meditation among the author's papers at the National Library, which was subsequently printed in the book *The Meaning of Life:*

> "Life really is strange," said the young daughter.
> "Yes," said her mother, "and it *should* be strange."
> "Why?" asked the daughter. "What is the meaning of life? Really?"

Her mother thought it over.

"I don't know. Honestly! But Marcus Aurelius, if you know who that was, put it like this: Don't live as though you had a thousand years ahead of you! Death hangs over your head. For as long as you live, for as long as you can—be good!'"

Ah, Well

Astrid Lindgren eventually came to be as old as the grandfather in Noisy Village, who has the paper read aloud to him on his birthday and promises the children that war will never come to North Farm, Middle Farm, and South Farm. God will protect Noisy Village. Then he sighs, "ah, well," which means he's thinking of the days when he was young. Astrid did the same when she was past ninety, yet in her final years she never thought about what happened after Lasse's death: those memories had abruptly disappeared.

In May 1998 Astrid had a stroke, which meant that she always had to have a nurse nearby, and during her last three years she seemed to be living in a time before Lasse's death. You couldn't talk to her about anything that had happened after that, explains Karin Nyman. Yet there were no major changes to her personality; certainly her sense of humor seemed unimpaired. During one of Karin's visits to Karolinska Hospital, where her mother was recuperating after her stroke, she asked whether Astrid wanted her to switch the radio on before she left. The answer was a brief, clear "no." Karin was surprised:

> "Surely you're not just going to sit here getting a bit bored?"
> "No, I'm going to lie here getting completely bored."

Outside, the sun rose and fell. A new millennium announced its hectic arrival, but in Dalagatan 46 things took their usual tranquil course. Only nurses, family, and close friends had access to Astrid Lindgren. Apart from Karin, her family, and Lasse's family, visitors included her sister Stina; Margareta Strömstedt and her sister Lisa; her former colleague and successor at

Astrid Lindgren knew that her urn would one day rest in Vimmerby Cemetery beside her mother and father and two of her siblings. Anne-Marie Fries was a little more than 150 feet away, and at twice that distance was Reinhold Blomberg, one of the men with whom Astrid Lindgren had once had a relationship but whom she'd never loved. As she said in an interview with Stina Dabrowski in 1993: "My great loves have always been children. . . . I'm more a mother than anything else, so I've got more joy from my children."

Rabén and Sjögren, Marianne Eriksson; and her friend from the park, Alli Viridén. And Kerstin Kvint, of course, who still went through the mail twice a week, and had now become stenographer to one of literary history's most assiduous stenographers: "For a while after the hemorrhage she was very sad and reticent and couldn't really get interested in the letters, but I read them to her just as I used to, and answered them myself. Our work continued like that up until Christmas 2001. Then there was a period when she seemed happier and spryer, and could laugh and say long sentences."

Her final years were spent in the rooms overlooking Vasa Park, where Astrid had lived and written so intensely with her husband and children, family, and friends. She had entertained a stream of guests, from authors, child psychologists, and feminists to national and international politicians. Often, however, she had simply danced to the gramophone, alone and happy. Now it was mostly the radio she listened to, and most of all she loved the second movement of Mozart's divinely beautiful Violin Concerto No. 3 in G major, which she had called "my funeral adagio" in a letter to Anne-Marie Fries in the summer of 1978.

After the stroke in 1998, Astrid occasionally declared that she'd had enough of living. "I want to die!" she told Karin. On better days, however, she would ask her daughter or Kerstin Kvint to read to her. She requested Swedish classics like Pär Lagerkvist or Verner von Heidenstam, or some of Astrid's own texts, including the poem "Om jag vore gud" (If I were God) and selected chapters from *Pippi Longstocking*. This wasn't because she wanted to enjoy her world-famous narrative voice, but rather so that she could relive the sense of freedom and fullness, of eternity, that had accompanied the creation of every single book. Of euphoric solitude, in which she had never been alone. As Astrid put it in a letter to Louise Hartung in November 1958: "I'm probably only completely happy when I write. I don't mean during a particular period of writing, but in the moments when I'm in the act of writing itself."

She died on January 28, 2002, at ten o'clock in the morning, at home in her bed in Vasastan. By her side were two nurses, a doctor, and Karin. For the rest of the day, Stockholmers of all ages flocked to Dalagatan 46 to lay down a flower or light a candle. That evening there was a special television broadcast, and the next day all the newspapers in Scandinavia and Germany printed comprehensive obituaries; larger publications in Sweden also devoted special sections to her. The funeral, worthy of a queen or statesman, took place on March 8, International Women's Day. Everyone was in attendance: feminists, with children and grandchildren; the Swedish prime minister; several generations of the royal family; and a hundred thousand ordinary Swedes, who lined the streets as the coffin was carried to Storkyrkan, the ancient church in Stockholm's old town.

What a day, what a life.

Astrid Lindgren: Selected Titles

Confidences of Britt-Mari (1944)
Kerstin and I (1945)
Pippi Longstocking (1945)
Pippi Longstocking Goes Aboard (1946)
Bill Bergson, Master Detective (1946)
The Children of Noisy Village (1947)
Pippi in the South Seas (1948)
Happy Times in Noisy Village (1949)
Nils Karlsson the Elf and Other Adventures (1949)
Kajsa Kavat and Other Children (1950)
Kati in America (1950)
Bill Bergson Lives Dangerously (1951)
Nothing but Fun in Noisy Village (1952)
Kati in Italy (1952)
Bill Bergson and the White Rose Rescue (1953)
Mio, My Son (1954)
Kati in Paris (1954)
Karlsson-on-the-Roof (1955)
Rasmus and the Vagabond (1956)
Rasmus, Pontus, and Toker (1957)
South Meadow (1959)
Mardie (1960)
Lotta on Troublemaker Street (1961)
Karlsson Flies Again (1962)
Emil in the Soup Tureen (1963)
We on Seacrow Island (1964)
Emil's Pranks (1966)
The World's Best Karlsson (1968)
Emil and His Clever Pig (1970)
The Brothers Lionheart (1973)

Samuel August from Sevedstorp and Hanna from Hult (1975)
Mardie to the Rescue (1976)
Ronia the Robber's Daughter (1981)
Original Pippi (2007)

Sources

Adolfsson, Eva, Ulf Eriksson, and Birgitta Holm. "Anpassning, flykt, uppror: Barnboken och verkligheten." *Ord och Bild,* no. 5 (1971).

Ahlbäck, Pia Maria. "Väderkontraktet: Plats, miljörättvisa och eskatologi i Astrid Lindgrens Vi på Saltkråkan." *Barnboken: Tidskrift för Barnlitteraturforskning* 2, no. 33 (2010).

Alvtegen, Karin. "Min gammelfaster Astrid." *Astrid Lindgren sällskapets medlemsblad,* no. 15 (2006).

Andersen, Jens. *Andersen. En biografi* (2003).

———. "Det begynder altid i et køkken." *Berlingske,* December 26, 2006.

———. "Jeg danser helst ensom til grammofonen." *Berlingske,* November 2, 2012.

Andersson, Maria. "Borta bra, men hemma bäst? Elsa Beskows och Astrid Lindgrens idyller." In *Barnlitteraturanalyser,* ed. Maria Andersson and Elina Druker (2009).

Barlby, Finn, ed. *Børnebogen i klassekampen. Artikler om marxistisk litteratur for børn* (1975).

Bendt, Ingela. *Ett hem för själen. Ellen Keys Strand* (2000).

Bengtsson, Lars. *Bildbibliografi över Astrid Lindgrens skrifter 1921–2010* (2012).

Berger, Margareta. *Pennskaft. Kvinnliga journalister under 300 år* (1977).

Berggren, Henrik. *Olof Palme. Aristokraten, som blev socialist* (2010).

Bettelheim, Bruno. *The Uses of Enchantment* (1976).

Birkeland, Tone, Gunvor Risa, and Karin Beate Vold. *Norsk barnlitteraturhistorie* (2005).

Blomberg, Reinhold. *Minnen ur släkterna Blomberg-Skarin* (1931).

Bodner Granberg, Ingegerd, and Enge Swartz, eds. *Tourister. Klassiska författare på resa* (2006).

Boëthius, Ulf. "Skazen i Astrid Lindgrens Emil i Lönneberga." In *Läs mig—sluka mig!* ed. Kristin Hallberg (2003).

Bohlund, Kjell, et al. *Rabén, Sjögren och alla vi andra. Femtio års förlagshistoria* (1972).

Bolin, Greta, and Eva von Zweigbergk. *Barn och böcker* (1945).

Bugge, David. "At inficere med håbløshed: K. E. Løgstrup og børnelitteraturen." *Slagmark,* no. 42 (2005).

Buttenschøn, Ellen. *Smålandsk fortæller* (1977).

Christensen, Leise. "Prædikerens Bog." *Bibliana*, no. 2 (2011).

Christofferson, Birger, and Thomas von Vegesack, eds. *Perspektiv på 30-talet* (1961).

Dabrowski, Stina. *Stina Dabrowski möter sju kvinnor* (1993).

Edström, Vivi. *Barnbokens form* (1982).

———. *Vildtoring och lägereld* (1992).

———. *Sagans makt* (1997).

———. *Kvällsdoppet i Katthult* (2004).

———. *Det svänger om Astrid* (2007).

Egerlid, Helena, and Jens Fellke. *I samtidens tjänst. Kungliga Automobil Klubben 1903–2013* (2013).

Ehriander, Helene. "Astrid Lindgren—förlagsredaktör på Rabén och Sjögren." *Personhistorisk Tidskrift*, no. 2 (2010).

Ehriander, Helene, and Birgen Hedén, eds. *Bild och text i Astrid Lindgrens värld* (1999).

Ehriander, Helene, and Maria Nilson, eds. *Starkast i världen! Att arbeta med Astrid Lindgrens författarskap i skolan* (2011).

Ekman, Kerstin. "I berömmelsens lavin." In Harding, *De Nio—litterär kalender*.

Ericsson, Gunnar, Astrid Lindgren, Stina Hergin, and Ingegerd Lindström. *Fyra syskon berättar* (1992).

Eriksson, Göran, ed. *Röster om Astrid Lindgren* (1995).

Estaunié, Édouard. *Solitudes* (1922).

Fellke, Jens, ed. *Rebellen från Vimmerby. Om Astrid Lindgren och hemstaden* (2002).

———. "För pappans skull." *Dagens Nyheter,* December 5, 2007.

Forsell, Jacob, ed. *Astrids bilder* (2007).

Fransson, Birgitta. *Barnboksvärlder. Samtal med författare* (2000).

Gaare, Jørgen, and Øystein Sjaastad. *Pippi og Sokrates* (2000).

Gardeström, Elin. *Journalistutbildningens tillkomst i Sverige* (2006).

Grönblad, Ester. *Furusund. Ett skärgårdscentrum* (1970).

Gröning, Lotta. *Kvinnans plats—min bok om Alva Myrdal* (2006).

Hallberg, Kristin. "Pedagogik som poetik. Den moderna småbarnslitteraturens berättande." *Centrum för barnlitteraturforskning*, no. 26 (1996).

Hansson, Kjell Åke. *Hela världens Astrid Lindgren. En utställning på Astrid Lindgrens Näs i Vimmerby* (2007).

Harding, Gunnar, ed. *De Nio—litterär kalender* (2006).

Hedström, Lotta. *Introduktion till ekofeminism* (2007).

Hellsing, Lennart. *Tankar om barnlitteraturen* (1963).

Hellsing, Susanna, Birgitta Westin, and Suzanne Öhman-Sundén, eds. *Allrakäraste Astrid. En vänbok till Astrid Lindgren* (2002).

Hergin, Stina. *Det var en gång en gård* (2001).

Hirdman, Yvonne, Urban Lundberg, and Jenny Björkman. *Sveriges historia 1920–1965* (2012).

Holm, Claus. "Lad ensomheden være i fred." *Information,* August 25, 2008.

Holm, Ingvar, ed. *Vänkritik. 22 samtal om dikt tillägnade Olle Holmberg* (1959).

Israel, Joachim, and Mirjam Valentin-Israel. *Det finns inga elaka barn!* (1946).

Johansson, Anna-Karin. *Astrid Lindgren i Stockholm* (2012).

Jørgensen, John Chr. *Da kvinder blev journalister* (2012).

Kåreland, Lena. *Modernismen i barnkammaren. Barnlitteraturens 40-tal* (1999).

———. "Pippi som dadaist." In *Svenska på prov. Arton artiklar om språk, litteratur, didaktik och prov. En vänskrift till Birgitta Garme,* ed. Catharina Nyström and Maria Ohlsson (1999).

———. *En sång för att leva bättre. Om Lennart Hellsings författarskap* (2002).

———. *Barnboken i samhället* (2009).

Karlsson, Maria, and Sharon Rider, eds. *Den moderna ensamheten* (2006).

Karlsson, Petter, and Johan Erséus. *Från snickerboa till Villa Villekulla. Astrid Lindgrens filmvärld* (2004).

Key, Ellen. *Barnets århundrade* (1996).

Knudsen, Karin Esmann. "Vi må håbe du aldrig dør—døden i dansk børnelitteratur." In *Memento mori—døden i Danmark i tværfagligt lys,* ed. Michael Hviid Jacobsen and Mette Haakonsen (2008).

Knutson, Ulrika. *Kvinnor på gränsen till genombrott. Grupporträtt av Tidevarvets kvinnor* (2004).

Kümmerling-Meibauer, Bettina, and Astrid Surmatz, eds. *Beyond Pippi Longstocking: Intermedial and International Aspects of Astrid Lindgren's Works* (2011).

Kvint, Kerstin. *Astrid i vida världen* (1997).

———. *Astrid världen över* (2002).

———. *Bakom Astrid* (2010).

Lindgren, Astrid. *Hujedamej och andra visor av Astrid Lindgren* (1993).

———. *Det gränslösaste äventyret* (2007).

———. *Livets mening* (2012).

———. *Jultomtens underbara bildradio* (2013).

Lindgren, Astrid, and Kristina Forslund. *Min ko vill ha roligt* (1990).

Liversage, Toni, and Søren Vinterberg, eds. *Børn Litteratur Samfundskritik* (1975).

Løgstrup, K. E. "Moral og børnebøger." In *Børne-og ungdomsbøger,* ed. Sven Møller Kristensen and Preben Ramløv (1969).

Løkke, Anne. "Præmierede plejemødre. Den københavnske filantropi og uægte børn i 1800-tallet." *Den jyske Historiker,* no. 67 (1994).

Lundqvist, Ulla. *Århundradets barn. Fenomenet Pippi Långstrump och dess förutsättningar* (1979).

——. *Kulla-Gulla i slukaråldern* (2000).

——. *Alltid Astrid. Minnen från böcker, brev och samtal* (2012).

Marstrander, Jan. *Det ensomme menneske i Knut Hamsuns diktning* (1959).

Metcalf, Eva-Maria. *Astrid Lindgren* (1995).

Mitchell, Lucy Sprague. *Här och nu* (1939).

Møhl, Bo, and May Schack. *Når børn læser—litteraturoplevelse og fantasi* (1980).

Ney, Birgitta, ed. *Kraftfelt. Forskning om kön och journalistik* (1998).

Nikolajeva, Maria. "Bakom rösten. Den implicita författaren i jagberättelser." *Barnboken. Tidskrift för barnlitteraturforskning,* no. 2 (2008).

Nørgaard, Ellen. "En vision om barnets århundrede." *VERA,* no. 11 (2000).

Ödman, Charlotta. *Snälla, vilda barn. Om barnen i Astrid Lindgrens böcker* (2007).

Ohlander, Ann-Sofie. "Farliga kvinnor och barn. Historien och det utomäktenskapliga." In *Kvinnohistoria: Om kvinnors villkor från antiken till våra dagar* (1992).

Ørvig, Mary, ed. *En bok om Astrid Lindgren* (1977).

Ørvig, Mary, Marianne Eriksson, and Birgitta Sjöquist, eds. *Duvdrottningen. En bok til Astrid Lindgren* (1987).

Östberg, Kjell, and Jenny Andersson. *Sveriges historia 1965–2012* (2013).

Rabén, Hans. *Rabén och Sjögren 1942–1967. En tjugofemårskrönika* (1967).

Riwkin, Anna, and Ulf Bergstrøm. *Möten i mörker och ljus* (1991).

Rosenbeck, Bente. *Kvindekøn. Den moderne kvindeligheds historie 1880–1980* (1987).

Runström, Gunvor. "Den yppersta gäddan i sumpen." *Astrid Lindgren sällskapets medlemsblad,* no. 34 (2011).

Russell, Bertrand. *On Education, Especially in Early Childhood* (1926).

Schwardt, Sara, Astrid Lindgren, and Lena Törnqvist, eds. *Jeg lægger dine breve under madrassen* (2014).

Sjöberg, Johannes, and Margareta Strömstedt, eds. *Astrids röst.* CD and book (2007).

Sköld, Johanna. *Fosterbarnsindustri eller människokärlek* (2006).

Søland, Birgitte. *Becoming Modern* (2000).

Sønsthagen, Kari, and Torben Weinreich. *Værker i børnelitteraturen* (2010).

Strömstedt, Margareta. *Astrid Lindgren. En levnadsteckning* (1977/1999).

——. "Du och jag Alfred—om kärlekens kärna, om manligt och kvinnligt hos Astrid Lindgren." In Eriksson, *Röster om Astrid Lindgren.*

——. *Jag skulle så gärna vilja förföra dig—men jag orkar inte* (2013).

Surmatz, Astrid. *Pippi Långstrump als Paradigma* (2005).

———. "International politics in Astrid Lindgren's works." *Barnboken,* nos. 1–2 (2007).

Svanberg, Birgitte. "På barnets side." In *Nordisk Kvindelitteraturhistorie,* at nordicwomensliterature.net.

Svensen, Åsfrid. "Synspunkter på fantastisk diktning." In *Den fantastiske barnelitteraturen* (1982).

Svensson, Sonja. "Den där Emil—en hjälte i sin tid." In Harding, *De Nio—litterär kalender.*

Thielst, Peter. *Nietzsches filosofi* (2013).

Thoreau, Henry David. *Walden; or, Life in the Woods* (1854; 2007).

Törnqvist, Egil. "Astrid Lindgrens halvsaga. Berättartekniken i Bröderna Lejonhjärta." *Svensk Litteraturtidskrift,* no. 2 (1975).

Törnqvist, Lena. "Astrid Lindgren i original och översätning. Bibliografi." In Ørvig, Mary, *En bok om Astrid Lindgren.*

———. "Astrid Lindgren i original och översätning. Bibliografi, 1976–1986." In Ørvig, Eriksson, and Sjöquist, *Duvdrottningen.*

———. *Astrid från Vimmerby* (1998).

———. "Från vindslåda till världsminne." *BIBLIS* 33 (2006).

———. "140 hyllmeter, 75 000 brev och 100 000 klipp." *BIBLIS* 58 (2012).

Törnqvist, Lena, and Suzanne Öhman-Sundén, eds. *Ingen liten lort. Astrid Lindgren som opinionsbildare* (2007).

Törnqvist-Verschuur, Rita. *Den Astrid jag minns* (2011).

Turkle, Sherry. *Alone Together* (2011).

Vinterberg, Søren. "Astrid og Lasse lille på Haabets Allé." *Politiken,* December 26, 2006.

Wågerman, Ingemar. *Svenskt postcensur under andra världskriget* (1995).

Wahlström, Eva. *Fria flickor före Pippi. Ester Blenda Nordström och Karin Michaëlis: Astrid Lindgrens föregångare* (2011).

Watson, John B. *Psychological Care of Infant and Child* (1928).

Westin, Boel. *Tove Jansson. Ord, bild, liv* (2007).

Zweigbergk, Eva von. *Barnboken i Sverige 1750–1950* (1965).

Websites

www.astridlindgren.se.
www.haabetsalle.com.
www.stenografi.nu.
nordicwomensliterature.net.

Other Sources

Astrid Lindgren Archive, National Library, Stockholm.
Private letters, diaries, and images, Karin Nyman/Saltkråkan AB.
Astrid Lindgren's collection of letters at Kulturkvarteret Astrid Lindgrens Näs, Vimmerby.
Private letters and images, Lisbet Stevens Senderovitz.
Sevede Häradsrätts Record Books, 1926–27, Regional State Archives, Vadstena.
Gyldendal's Archive.
Samrealskolan, Vimmerby Archives, Regional State Archives, Vadstena.
Jens Sigsgaard's Papers, The Royal Library, Copenhagen.
The Astrid Lindgren Society Newsletter, 2004–14.

Conversations and Interviews

Kerstin Kvint, Karin Nyman, Lisbet Stevens Senderovitz, Margareta Strömstedt, Lena Törnqvist.

Index

Page numbers in *italics* refer to illustrations.